In this important study David Arm lytical metaphysics that synthesizes but also develops his thinking over the last twenty years. Armstrong's analysis, which acknowledges the 'logical atomism' of Russell and Wittgenstein, makes facts (or states of affairs, as the author calls them) the fundamental constituents of the world, examining properties, relations, numbers, classes, possibility and necessity, dispositions, causes and laws. All these, it is argued, find their place and can be understood inside a scheme of states of affairs. This is a comprehensive and rigorously this-worldly account of the most general features of reality, argued from a distinctive philosophical perspective, and it will appeal to a wide readership in analytical philosophy.

CAMBRIDGE STUDIES IN PHILOSOPHY

A world of states of affairs

CAMBRIDGE STUDIES IN PHILOSOPHY

RECENT TITLES

WILLIAM G. LYCAN *Judgement and justification*
GERALD DWORKIN *The theory and practice of autonomy*
MICHAEL TYE *The metaphysics of mind*
DAVID O. BRINK *Moral realism and the foundations of ethics*
W. D. HART *Engines of the soul*
PAUL K. MOSER *Knowledge and evidence*
D. M. ARMSTRONG *A combinatorial theory of possibility*
JOHN BISHOP *Natural agency*
CHRISTOPHER J. MALONEY *The mundane matter of the mental language*
MARK RICHARD *Propositional attitudes*
GERALD E. GAUS *Value and justification*
MARK HELLER *The ontology of physical objects*
JOHN BIGELOW AND ROBERT PARGETTER *Science and necessity*
FRANCIS SNARE *Morals, motivation and convention*
CHRISTOPHER S. HILL *Sensations*
JOHN HEIL *The nature of true minds*
CARL GINET *On action*
CONRAD JOHNSON *Moral legislation*
DAVID OWENS *Causes and coincidences*
ANDREW NEWMAN *The physical basis of predication*
MICHAEL JUBIEN *Ontology, modality and the fallacy of reference*
WARREN QUINN *Morality and action*
JOHN W. CARROLL *Laws of nature*
M. J. CRESSWELL *Language in the world*
JOSHUA HOFFMAN & GARY S. ROSENKRANTZ *Substance among other categories*
PAUL HELM *Belief policies*
NOAH LEMOS *Intrinsic value*
LYNNE RUDDER BAKER *Explaining attitudes*
HENRY S. RICHARDSON *Practical reasoning about final ends*
ROBERT A. WILSON *Cartesian psychology and physical minds*
BARRY MAUND *Colours*
MICHAEL DEVITT *Coming to our senses*
SYDNEY SHOEMAKER *The first-person perspective and other essays*
MICHAEL STOCKER *Valuing emotions*
ARDA DENKEL *Object and property*
E. J. LOWE *Subjects of experience*
NORTON NELKIN *Consciousness and the origins of thought*
PIERRE JACOB *What minds can do*

A world of states of affairs

D. M. Armstrong

Emeritus Professor of Philosophy, University of Sydney

Published by the Press Syndicate of the University of Cambridge
The Pitt Building, Trumpington Street, Cambridge CB2 1RP
40 West 20th Street, New York, NY 10011–4211, USA
10 Stamford Road, Oakleigh, Melbourne 3166, Australia

First published 1997

Printed in Great Britain at the University Press, Cambridge

A catalogue record for this book is available from the British Library

Library of Congress cataloguing in publication data

Armstrong, D. M. (David Malet), 1926–
A world of states of affairs / D. M. Armstrong.
p. cm. – (Cambridge studies in philosophy)
Includes bibliographical references and index.
ISBN 0 521 58064 1 (hardback) – ISBN 0 521 58948 7 (paperback)
1. Metaphysics. I. Title. II. Series.
B5704.A753W67 1996 111–dc20 96–8598 CIP

ISBN 0 521 58064 1 hardback
ISBN 0 521 58948 7 paperback

SE

FOR JENNY

The nature of the enterprise

'grubbing about in the roots of being'

Donald Williams

The hypothesis

'The universe consists of objects having various qualities and standing in various relations.'

Whitehead and Russell

A warning

'it is the mark of an educated man to look for certainty in each class of things just so far as the nature of the subject admits'

Taken from Aristotle, but with 'certainty' substituted for his 'precision'

Contents

Preface

During the past twenty years or so, I have been working on ontological questions. What are universals, laws of nature, dispositions and powers, possibilities and necessities, classes, numbers? The present essay tries to bring all these topics together in a unified metaphysical scheme, an ontology. As a result, there is a certain amount of recapitulation of earlier writing. But putting the pieces together turned out to be quite difficult. A good deal of further work was necessary. Many mistakes, as I now think of them, had to be corrected. So what follows is not a mere sum of past thinking.

It has proved very hard to decide upon an order of exposition. Exposition must be serial, but I have continually felt hampered by this. It has often seemed that I could not discuss A without first having discussed B, but that to reverse the order would produce an equal and opposite problem. As a result, I do not know whether the chapters are in the best order. In particular, some readers may find it convenient to read the central chapter 8 at the beginning, or perhaps immediately after chapter 1, and then go back. Again, chapter 5, on Powers, is put in early because it is part of the theory of properties, and properties are discussed in chapters 3 and 4. But the topic of Powers is very closely linked with the discussion of Cause, and of Law, discussed in chapters 14 to 16. Chapters 5 plus 14 to 16 are a natural package.

A briefer presentation of much of the material to be found in chapters 14 to 15 will be found in my article 'Singular Causation and Laws of Nature', in *The Cosmos of Science*, edited by John Earman, published by the University of Pittsburgh Press. That article, however, was written in 1993, antedating the present chapters.

I am no lover of footnotes, and have not used any in the book. Some readers will feel that certain passages should have been relegated in this way. I apologize to them in advance.

There is no certainty in philosophy. No philosopher can *know* that his or her arguments are true. This makes it important, I think, that philosophers should be prepared to explore, and bring into their discussions, positions for which they have sympathy but which differ from the views that they actually take. 'Fall-back' positions are particularly important to specify, that is, positions which one would adopt if forced out of one's actual position. (An example from my own views on the mind: if forced out of a physicalist view of the mental, I would retreat to a Dualistic rather than an Eliminativist view.) I have therefore included a certain amount of this sort of discussion. Some readers may wish to go lightly over this material.

Philosophy, or at any rate analytic philosophy, has changed greatly during the time that I have been a student of the subject. For the most part, it has been changed for the better. One of the changes for the better has been the way philosophers have increasingly found it possible to co-operate with each other. Of course, they argue and criticize each other just as much as they ever did. But often today they find colleagues who they can agree with quite closely about the general approach in some area. Sometimes they even 'get the same result', for all the world as if they were scientists! It seems that our unruly discipline is becoming a little more of a *discipline*.

At any rate, while writing this book I have solicited and received comment and criticism of drafts from a great many people. They have given me invaluable help. I list them, with apologies to anybody inadvertently omitted: Peter Anstey, John Bacon, John Bigelow, Michael Bradley, Keith Campbell, John Carroll, Evan Fales, Peter Forrest, Jim Franklin, Reinhardt Grossmann, Herb Hochberg, Frank Jackson, David Lewis, Bill Lycan, Michael McDermott, Storrs McCall, Daniel Nolan, John O'Leary-Hawthorne, Charlie Martin, George Molnar, James Moulder, Michael Murray, Michael Pendlebury, Gideon Rosen, Glen Ross, Scott Shalkowski, Brian Skyrms, Jack Smart, Chris Swoyer, Bill Tarrant, Michael Tooley, Peter van Inwagen, Kevin Wilkinson and Peter Woodruff. Sydney Shoemaker was one of the readers for Cambridge University Press, but besides sending valuable detailed comments he asked that I be given his name.

A very preliminary draft of the material was presented to a graduate class, attended by a number of faculty, at the University of California at Irvine in the Fall Term of 1992. The exercise was repeated for a faculty seminar at Franklin and Marshall College in the Fall Semester of 1993. I thank all who participated in these seminars. During May, 1994, I was a

Visiting Fellow in the Philosophy Program of the Research School of the Social Sciences, at the Australian National University. During that time a greatly advanced draft of the book was produced. I thank Professor Frank Jackson and others who made me so welcome and discussed issues with me. Some of the material was presented in seminars at the University of Graz in October–November 1995. Many thanks are due to Rudolf Haller and Johannes Marek. During this time I also gave three seminars on the book in the lively Philosophy department at the University of Maribor in Slovenia. I thank, in particular, Bojan Borstner and Nenad Miscevic.

Bill Tarrant and Peter Anstey were, in turn, invaluable research assistants. Their work was financed by a grant by the Australian Research Council (Small Grants Scheme) for which I am very grateful. Keith Campbell as Challis Professor of Philosophy at Sydney University, together with Anthea Bankoff and Veronica Leahy as Administrative Assistants in the Department of Traditional and Modern Philosophy, provided invaluable support. Special thanks go to Anthea. My wife Jenny put up with it all, and has even encouraged the enterprise. I dedicate the book to her.

Sydney

1

Introduction

1.1 AN OVERVIEW

The hypothesis of this work is that the world, all that there is, is a world of states of affairs. Others, Wittgenstein in particular, have said that the world is a world of facts and not a world of things. These theses are substantially the same, though differently expressed.

The general structure of states of affairs will be argued to be this. A state of affairs exists if and only if a particular (at a later point to be dubbed a *thin* particular) has a property or, instead, a relation holds between two or more particulars. Each state of affairs, and each constituent of each state of affairs, meaning by their constituents the particulars, properties, relations and, in the case of higher-order states of affairs, lower-order states of affairs, is a contingent existent. The properties and the relations are universals, not particulars. The relations are all external relations.

It is useful to admit *molecular* states of affairs. These, however, are mere conjunctions (never negations or disjunctions) of the original states of affairs. Molecular states of affairs constitute no ontological addition to their conjuncts. But in one special case, to be mentioned in a moment, they become very important.

For first-order states of affairs, that is, states of affairs that do not have states of affairs as constituents, the Tractarian thesis of Independence is somewhat speculatively, but nevertheless hopefully, advanced. No such state of affairs entails or excludes the existence of any other wholly distinct state of affairs. Given Independence, a rather simple and straightforward Combinatorial theory of what possibilities there are, can be put forward. If Independence fails, things get more complicated.

The present theory is not biased towards Atomism nor is it biased against Atomism. An *epistemic* possibility that requires to be noted is the possibility that every (first-order) state of affairs is molecular, that is, analysable into a conjunction of states of affairs. (A simple if to a degree controversial example: *a*'s being F may be equivalent to *a*'s being G & *a*'s being

H, with F=G & H. The pattern may be repeated for G and H, and so for ever.) Every first-order state of affairs may be a nest of first-order states of affairs: states of affairs all the way down. To allow for this epistemic possibility, a Combinatorial theory of what possibilities there are requires further elaboration.

It is the hypothesis of the *Tractatus*, one which re-appears in the work of Brian Skyrms (1981), that all facts are first-order facts. There are no facts about facts. In the present work, however, it is argued that (non-supervenient) states of affairs having states of affairs as constituents are required in two rather different sorts of case. First, as Russell urged (1972 [1918] pp. 93–4), there are facts or states of affairs of totality: for instance, the state of affairs that a certain collection of first-order states of affairs are *all* the first-order states of affairs. Second, there are the laws of nature, construed in the present work as states of affairs contingently linking universals, or, putting it differently, contingent connections between state-of-affairs types. Both sorts of higher-order states of affairs violate Independence (in a fairly unpuzzling way, it will be argued) because they exclude what would otherwise be certain possibilities at the first-order level. The discussion of laws of nature will be preceded by preliminary discussions of, first, powers and dispositions, and, secondly, singular or token causation. But in the end it is laws of nature that will be appealed to in order to explain powers and causation, rather than, as in some other theories, the other way around.

These contingent states of affairs, first-order and higher-order, including their constituents, constitute the sole *truthmakers* for all contingent truths. The notion of a truthmaker is central to the argument of this work, but it cannot be fully elucidated until the central chapter 8. For the present let us just say that it is whatever in the world makes a truth true. The hyphen that is often used in this term 'truthmaker' (to which I was introduced by C. B. Martin) has been dropped for simplicity's sake. But there are necessary truths, for instance the truths of mathematics, of set theory, of logic, or truths that certain internal relations hold. What sorts of truthmaker, if any, do necessary truths have? It will be argued here, in the general spirit of the *Tractatus*, that necessary truths have no further truthmakers over and above the contingent states of affairs. Very often, their truthmakers are the mere *constituents* of states of affairs: particulars and universals. (Mere constituents are truthmakers for a small class of contingent truths also.) Thus, between any two universals an internal relation of difference obtains. The truthmaker for this rather trivial necessary truth is nothing more than the two universals themselves. Necessary truths have truthmakers of a reduced sort, and this is taken to imply that they have a correspondingly reduced informativeness. Accounts of the nature of numbers (they are internal relations), of classes (they are certain sorts of states of affairs or possible states of affairs), complete this metaphysic.

Our task now is to expand, to explain and to defend these brief sentences. Flesh must be put on these bare bones. The order of exposition will not necessarily follow the order of the summary just presented. I have already considered at length elsewhere, most of the topics covered, and will be relatively brief at certain points, referring the reader who wants more detail to earlier work. This does not mean, I hope, that earlier writing will be presupposed. The book is intended as a self-contained story.

The chief novelty from my own point of view will lie in bringing the topics together in a systematic framework. But philosophy is very difficult. Mistakes and, still more depressing, failure to follow through promising insights in a convincing manner, abound in our subject. The hope is that here, besides a more synoptic view, there is improvement in detail on what I have written previously about a number of matters. At any rate, there is change!

1.2 HISTORICAL REMARKS

It is useful to say something about the background from which this essay emerges. The debt to Russell's Logical Atomism and Wittgenstein's *Tractatus* is obvious. (Robert Fahrnkopf has convinced me that Wittgenstein's 'objects' included both particulars and universals. Given this, the priority of Russell's work becomes evident. See Fahrnkopf, 1988.)

I was, however, still more profoundly influenced by the doctrine put forward by my teacher in Sydney, the Scots philosopher John Anderson, that reality, while independent of the mind that knows it, has a 'propositional' structure. The resemblances and differences holding between Wittgenstein and Anderson are usefully explored by Douglas Gasking in an article 'Anderson and the *Tractatus Logico-Philosophicus*' (1949). Anderson did not accept the distinction between necessary and contingent truths. He would also have thought that my general orientation, and in particular the way that my doctrine of universals is worked out, is excessively 'scientistic'. But the propositional view of reality which he championed is the facts or states of affairs view of reality. Some more recent contributions to this way of thinking about the structure of the world, contributions to what will here be called a *Factualist* metaphysics or ontology, will be acknowledged as the exposition unfolds.

But why is it that a Factualist position has been so slow to emerge in two-and-a-half thousand years of Western philosophy? Scholarship may yet show that Factualist as opposed to Thingist ways of thinking about the world (if I may be permitted the latter expression) were never entirely absent. But why has it taken so long for Factualist ontologies to be advocated explicitly?

One thing that is fairly clear is that an explicit and ungrudging acceptance of the category or sub-category of *relation* is a relatively recent phenomenon. This was carefully documented by Julius Weinberg in his 1965 book. In a monograph *An Essay on Facts* (1987, ch. 2) Kenneth Olson shows again how both ancient and medieval philosophers constantly tried to assimilate relations between objects (fathering, say) to relational properties (being a father, and being a child) of the related objects. This, of course, hinders the recognition of polyadic as opposed to monadic facts or states of affairs. Yet the situation is still puzzling. After all, these same thinkers did have, indeed held very firmly to, the substance/attribute distinction. And, as will be argued in what follows, making the substance/attribute distinction can rather naturally turn into the recognition of *monadic* states of affairs.

My suggestion about what happened is that the muddle about relations eventually led the tradition to a turning point. There was a choice. It could go on to recognize both the substance/attribute distinction *and* a knitting together of a plurality of substances by relations, a double doctrine that should then have led on to a states of affairs ontology. Or else it could turn against even the substance/attribute analysis. The latter choice, the wrong choice, was made. Because of the confusion about relations, the linking of a plurality of substances by relations in polyadic states of affairs could not be countenanced. So the substance/attribute analysis could not be transformed into the recognition of monadic states of affairs. Untransformed, and standing on its own, substance/attribute came under attack. *One* conception of substance was retained: the conception of that which is capable of independent existence. No metaphysic can reject substance in *that* sense. But the substances thus admitted were apples and suchlike. Any suggestion of a further distinction between substance and attribute *within* the apple was scorned as metaphysical rubbish.

Especial scorn was, and still is, reserved for the substance side of the substance/attribute distinction. But if that sort of substance is at risk, substratum as it is often pejoratively called, then obviously attributes, that is properties, are at risk also. The fall of one must at least imperil the other. Moderates might try to retain attributes by substantializing them in the acceptable sense of the word 'substance'. Such moderates made the attributes into 'junior substances' (to adapt Ayer's inspired phrase for sense-data) and then tried to bundle up these juniors to yield ordinary things. Extremists such as the later Wittgenstein and Quine scorned this device and tried to get along without any objective properties and relations at all. *Hinc illae lacrimae*, which being translated is: it had to end in tears.

1.3 TWO FURTHER DOCTRINES

The main object of this work is to defend a version of Factualism, that is, to defend an ontology of facts, or states of affairs as they will be called here. But two constraints will be put upon Factualism as expounded here. It should be compatible with what will be called Naturalism and also with Physicalism. In this section something is said about these two doctrines.

1.31 Naturalism

This term, which often has an epistemic flavour, is here appropriated for an ontological doctrine. It is the contention that the world, the totality of entities, is nothing more than the spacetime system. (An epistemological stance comes rather naturally with Naturalism thus defined. It is the contention that, except for the primitive verities of ordinary experience, it is natural science that gives us whatever detailed knowledge we have of the world.) The positive part of the thesis, that the spacetime system exists, is perhaps not very controversial, although some thinkers, including Idealist philosophers, do question it. The negative thesis, that the spacetime system is *all* that there is, is more controversial. Many religious persons wish to postulate a god that transcends spacetime. Many philosophers, not necessarily religious ones, maintain that there are entities, such things as numbers and universals, which exist and transcend spacetime.

It seems clear that one can be a Factualist without being a Naturalist. For instance, a Factualist might accept the existence of a transcendent deity. It is perfectly clear that one can be a Naturalist without being a Factualist. Many philosophers are. But if one wishes to uphold *both* theses, as in this work, then one must hold an identity thesis. One must hold that the spacetime system *is*, is identical with, a certain set or aggregate (the distinction between the two does not seem very important here) of states of affairs, a set or aggregate that is the totality of states of affairs.

One might work out the details of the identification in various ways. Here is one that at least has the merit of being simple, and so will serve as an illustration. The spacetime world is a structured (that is, related) set of spacetime points. These points are the fundamental particulars. That the points have certain properties and are related to each other in certain ways constitutes the fundamental states of affairs. This is illustration alone. This work neither affirms nor denies this sparse account of the spacetime world.

Notice that the thesis of Naturalism, as it is understood here, is not committed to the view that space and time, or even spacetime points, are ontologically fundamental. The nature of space and time is to be discovered *a posteriori*. It is a matter for science. And who is to say, given the present situation in quantum physics and cosmology, that space and time will not turn out to be analysable in terms of entities more fundamental?

1.32 Physicalism

The third thesis to be upheld in this work is the thesis of Physicalism. It asserts that the only particulars that the spacetime system contains are physical entities governed by nothing more than the laws of physics. The thesis is to be understood as a thesis about a *completed* physics. As a result, it has a certain in-built vagueness and imprecision. It may also be useful to distinguish between a *weak* and a *strong* Physicalism. Weak Physicalism is simply a doctrine about the spacetime world: that this contains only physical entities governed by nothing more than the laws of physics. It could even be accepted by a believer in a transcendent deity. Strong Physicalism is the view that everything there is, is governed by the laws of physics. Weak Physicalism plus Naturalism yields Strong Physicalism.

If we assume Naturalism, and also wish to combine Physicalism with the Factualist theory already adumbrated in Section 1, the main thesis of this work, then Physicalism can be presented as the thesis that (1) all fundamental universals, whether properties or relations, are those studied by physics, and all other first-order universals are structures involving nothing but these fundamental universals; (2) all fundamental laws are connections holding between these fundamental universals and other laws are no more than the fundamental laws operating under specific boundary conditions.

1.4 EPISTEMIC CREDIT RATINGS FOR THESE THREE THESES

How plausible are these three theses? Or, if this question is too difficult, how should we rank the three theses in terms of creditworthiness? The right answer, it is suggested in this section, is (1) Naturalism; (2) Physicalism; (3) Factualism.

Naturalism is the least controversial of the three theses. Its positive component, the existence of the spacetime system, is a fairly secure anchoring point for our investigation. Obviously, we do not have here some indubitable Cartesian datum. The existence of the system may be intelligibly denied, and *is* denied by some philosophers and others. But its existence would generally be granted, and will be taken for granted here. As already noted, the (somewhat more controversial) negative thesis subdivides into two denials. First there is the denial that there is any transcendent deity or other spiritual force standing outside the spacetime system. Second there is the denial of the additional entities postulated by the philosophers.

It appears to many of us that the spacetime world does not need, and so in all likelihood does not have, any external spiritual ground of its existence. The overwhelming impression of external design and purpose given by living things, which used to be a rather strong argument for a designer, seems to be satisfactorily explained by Darwin's theory of natural selection when combined with contemporary genetic theory. However, that does not finish the Argument from Design. It appears to be the case that the very existence of stars and planets, and so the physical possibility of an evolutionary process, depends upon very delicate settings of values in fundamental physical equations, settings which it seems 'could very well have been otherwise'. See, for instance, the evidence marshalled by John Leslie (1989). This appears to make a case for external, and non-physical, forces directing the spacetime world.

At the same time, there is not wanting informed cosmological speculation that what we at present call spacetime is really just a *local* portion of all-embracing spacetime and that there are other localities, now isolated from us, where it is likely that different settings of critical values obtain. (See for instance, Guth and Steinhardt, 1989, and Andrei Linde, 1994.) If so, then the apparently remarkable fact that our locality permitted the emergence of life could be explained *away*. It would be no surprise that we found ourselves in a 'kind' locality. We would not have existed in any other!

Nevertheless, in the spirit of attending closely to any weak points that appear in one's position, the Naturalist needs to devote quite careful attention to the new form the Argument from Design has taken.

In contemporary philosophy, as opposed to scientific speculation, even in philosophy that is empiricist *and* scientifically oriented, entities that are thought to be additional to the spacetime system are often postulated. Following Quine, the additional entities are often spoken of as 'abstract'. They include, among other candidates, possible worlds, universals and classes. It will be part of the task of this work to argue that either such entities can be dispensed with or, as is preferable in general, that an account can be given of them *within* the spacetime system, with that system taken to be a system of states of affairs. It seems in any case that the postulation of these entities lying outside the spacetime system, a postulation made by philosophers only, is a dubious postulation. (A point to be expanded upon shortly.) So, in the epistemic order, the thesis of Naturalism is a reasonably plausible one.

We pass to Physicalism, though for the moment we abstract from the particular Factualist gloss that interprets it as a thesis about what sorts of properties and relations there are and how these universals are nomically related. Physicalism is a high-level, somewhat speculative and open-ended, scientific hypothesis. In particular it is a reductive hypothesis. Among philosophers, the case for Physicalism has been articulated at length, in my view persuasively, by J. J. C. Smart (see his 1963 in particular). Mention should also be made of an article 'The Thales Problem' by Gerald Feinberg (1966). There it is argued that the behaviour of ordinary physical objects, all the physical phenomena that could be observed by one like Thales, are pretty well explained, and explained comprehensively, within our current physics. That part of physics is substantially complete and unlikely to need revision. Falsification of Physicalism must come, if it does come, from elsewhere. So the thesis of Physicalism can, to a degree, draw on the authority of science itself. (For a very attractive defence of Physicalism by a contemporary physicist, see Steven Weinberg's *Dreams of a Final Theory*, 1993.) So the credit of Physicalism seems to stand quite high. But since it is a specific thesis about nature, that credit can hardly stand as high as Naturalism, or at any rate as high as the positive thesis of Naturalism that spacetime exists.

We come now to the Factualist thesis that the world is a world of states of affairs. It is fundamental to the methodology of the present inquiry that Factualism is put forward here as a hypothesis only, and a philosopher's hypothesis at that. Not all the beliefs of mathematicians about mathematical matters of fact, nor all the beliefs of natural scientists about scientific matters of fact, are true, and even where they are true they are not always *known* to be true. But, agreeing with mathematical and scientific commonsense, it is here maintained against sceptics that in these fields much is known and that, in the past four centuries or so, there has been a huge increase of knowledge, indeed a steady increase in the rate of increase of knowledge, a phenomenon that is rather astounding. Not so for philosophy! It was not so long ago that the late Donald Williams could wittily and penetratingly declare that the philosophical agreements between him and the editor of his collected papers represented 'a rather impressive consensus in the present state of our subject' (1966, p. v).

The fact that philosophers disagree in such a thoroughgoing way, disagreeing even after a lifetime's difficult, painstaking and certainly intelligent reflection, can be explained plausibly only on the assumption that every one of them lacks *knowledge* in the sphere of philosophy. It seems to me, perhaps optimistically, that the situation has improved a little since Williams wrote his words. Something a little bit more like *results* seem to be emerging in philosophy, or at any rate in philosophy conducted with an analytical/scientific orientation. But philosophical arguments and conclusions must still be given a low epistemic credit-rating. The reason for this is that, while rightly aspiring to be a rational discipline, philosophy lacks the compelling (although not infallible) tribunal of observation that serves as the *ultima ratio* for natural science, and the still more compelling (although still not infallible) tribunal of calculation and proof that disciplines mathematics and logic.

The uncertainty that attaches to philosophical arguments and conclusions is compounded by the fact that, especially in metaphysics, every question proves on examination to be subtly intertwined with every other. The strategy of divide and conquer that has served natural science and mathematics so well is far harder (though not quite impossible) to apply in philosophy. Metaphysicians, in particular, find over time that they must present a position as an assemblage of more or less interlocking doctrines that cover the whole ontological field. That multiplies the chances of error.

That is not to say that there cannot also be fruitful *uncouplings* in philosophy, a point recently made by Keith Campbell (1991). A package is needed but, *a priori*, there are different (and often overlooked) ways of assembling the package. That is why, at various points in this essay, choice-points will be indicated and some attempt will be made to assess the advantages and disadvantages of the different ways of proceeding available to those who have arrived at these points.

Nevertheless, it is the difficulty of the enterprise that needs to be stressed, and with it the difficulty of having any rational assurance that what one is saying is true. (Mere assurance is common enough among philosophers, and may even be a psychological necessity in order to keep going.) The theme of this work is that states of affairs are ontologically basic. It would be absurd to think that a philosophy of states of affairs is epistemically basic.

So although this book is written to defend Factualism, that thesis cannot be accorded as high an epistemic credit-rating as the nevertheless somewhat speculative, science-based, thesis of Physicalism. Still less does it have the credit-rating of the fairly attractive (though perfectly disputable) thesis of Naturalism.

2

Some preliminary doctrines

This chapter will put forward a number of theses which, though of great importance for the course of the subsequent argument, are in great degree independent of the metaphysic of states of affairs.

2.1 SUPERVENIENCE

2.11 Definition of supervenience

We shall say that entity Q supervenes upon entity P if and only if it is impossible that P should exist and Q not exist, where P is possible. *Impossibility* here is the strongest or absolute impossibility, the sense in which (most philosophers would say) it is impossible that 7+5 should equal 11. *Possibility* is the weakest possibility, the possibility, for instance, that the Earth and its inhabitants do not exist.

A number of contemporary philosophers give definitions of supervenience in terms of properties, though usually taking a relaxed view of what a property is. For our purposes here, it is convenient not to restrict the scope of our definition in any way. Hence the use of the term 'entity'. There are other contemporaries who think that talk of supervenience has led to mere muddying of the waters. It may perhaps help to point out that supervenience in my sense amounts to entity P *entailing* the existence of entity Q, but with the entailment restricted to the cases where P is possible.

It is also convenient, because comfortable to the human intellect which handles extensions more easily than intensions, to define supervenience in terms of possible worlds. No ontological commitment to such worlds is intended. We shall say that Q supervenes upon P if and only if there are P-worlds and all P-worlds are Q-worlds. (A P-world is a world that contains the entity P. If P is a universal, then the world contains at least one instantiation of P.)

An important case for us that falls under these definitions, and which will also serve here to illustrate them, is that of *internal relations*. 'Internal relation' itself is an ambiguous term. But in this work it will be said that a relation is internal to its terms if and only if it is impossible that the terms should exist and the relation not exist, where the joint existence of the terms is possible. Or again, the joint existence of the terms being possible, they entail the existence of the relation. Or, finally, there are worlds in which all the terms exist, and in all those worlds the relation holds.

These definitions of supervenience leave it open that P also supervenes upon Q. An example of symmetrical supervenience is furnished by mereology, the simple calculus of *whole and part*, and mereological notions will prove to be of great importance in the course of our argument. The mereological whole supervenes upon its parts, but equally the parts supervene upon the whole. In a world where all the parts exist, then there is just one whole which they compose, the same whole in all worlds. In a world where the whole exists, then all the parts exist, the same parts in all worlds.

2.12 The ontological free lunch

It will be used as a premiss in this work that whatever supervenes or, as we can also say, is entailed or necessitated, in this way, is not something ontologically additional to the subvenient, or necessitating, entity or entities. What supervenes is no addition of being. Thus, internal relations are not ontologically additional to their terms. Mereological wholes are not ontologically additional to all their parts, nor are the parts ontologically additional to the whole that they compose. This has the consequence that mereological wholes are *identical* with all their parts taken together. Symmetrical supervenience yields identity.

It is not clear how the thesis that what supervenes is no addition of being is to be proved. But that it is a plausible thesis may be seen by considering that when we contemplate hypotheses of isolated monads, or different possible worlds, we find no difficulty in allowing that they are related by internal relations, in particular by resemblance or by difference of nature. This suggests that the supervenient entities, the internal relations in this case, add nothing to the monads or to the worlds. The terminology of 'nothing over and above' seems appropriate to the supervenient. One may call this view, that the supervenient is not something additional to what it supervenes upon, the doctrine of the ontological free lunch. Like other free lunches, this one gives and takes away at the same time. You get the supervenient for free, but you do not really get an extra entity.

If the supervenient is not something ontologically additional, then this gives a charter to, by exacting a very low price for, an almost entirely permissive mereology. Do the number 42 and the Murrumbidgee river form a mereological whole? Some philosophers doubt it (see Simons, 1987, pp. 108–12). Few doubt that there is a *class* which has just these two members. But do they form a mereological whole or *aggregate*? The whole, if it exists, is certainly a strange and also an uninteresting object. But if it supervenes upon its parts, and if as a consequence of supervening it is not something more than its parts, then there seems no objection to recognizing the whole. So in this essay permissive mereology, unrestricted mereological composition, is embraced.

A note of caution. The doctrine of the ontologically free lunch rids us of superfluous entities, because the supervenient is ontologically nothing more than its base. But some ontological doctrines appear to lead to superveniences that *are* more than their bases. If one still wishes to hold that the supervenient is no addition of being, then one has either to explain away these appearances as mere appearances, or else reject these doctrines just because they lead to superveniences that are additional to their bases. The latter course, a bold one perhaps, but I trust not foolhardy, is the one that I generally find myself advocating.

2.2 TRUTHMAKERS

The truthmaker is whatever it is *in the world* that makes a truth true. Gustav Bergmann and his followers have used the phrase 'ontological ground' and have had the same thing in mind. The idea is an old one. We may instance Aristotle in the *Categories* where he says:

> The fact of the being of a man carries with it the truth of the proposition that he is, . . .

following this up by saying:

> . . . the fact of the man's being does seem somehow to be the cause of the truth of the proposition, for the truth or falsity of the proposition depends on the fact of the man's being or not being.
>
> (*Categories*, 14b,14–22, trans. E.M. Edghill,1941. Peter Anstey drew my attention to this reference.)

In the *Discourse on Metaphysics* (sec. VIII) Leibniz says that:

> . . . all true predication has some foundation in the nature of things . . .
> (trans. Peter G. Lucas and Leslie Grint, 1953.)

and seems to express the same thought. Anybody who is attracted to the Correspondence theory of truth should be drawn to the truthmaker. Correspondence demands a correspondent, and a correspondent for a truth is a truthmaker.

The need that truths have for truthmakers is a central theme of this essay, and will serve as the main premiss in the argument for states of affairs. There will have to be much discussion of truthmakers and the truthmaking relation. (See ch. 8 in particular.) What is said here is still preliminary. One thing that it is important to say immediately, though, is that the relation is not one–one. For instance, the truth that there exists at least one human being has as truthmakers every human being that has existed or will exist.

2.3 IDENTITY

2.31 Strict and loose identity

In earlier writing about universals (1978a in particular) I set great store by the fact that we speak of different things having the *same* property. I thought that this was some reason, though obviously not a conclusive reason, for thinking that universals exist. This, however, seems to be a mistake. The word 'same' does not always mean what logicians and philosophers mean by the identity sign '='. The latter is certainly the logically fundamental meaning, but it is not the only one. Besides this strict sense there is a looser sense, now to be introduced.

One philosopher who appreciated that 'same' has a strict and a loose meaning is Bishop Joseph Butler. In his remarks on personal identity added to his work *The Analogy of Religion* (1736) he says that the identity over time of material things that change is a mere 'loose and popular' identity. He, I assume, thought of matter as made up of unchanging Newtonian atoms that are strictly identical over time. Yet although the Newtonian atoms of a tree or a human body or a mountain are constantly changing, we still speak of the tree or the body or mountain as the same tree or body or mountain over time. He thinks (rightly or wrongly) that this cannot be strict identity and so calls it 'loose and popular' identity. I shall abbreviate Butler's phrase, and speak of *loose* identity.

We are not here concerned with Butler's theory of the nature of material objects, nor with whether he has good reasons for thinking that this sort of identity really is loose only. But I think that he is right to think that there are two senses of the word 'same', one strict, classical, identity, and the other a looser sense of the word. It would be nice to have some reasonably uncontroversial example of loose identity. I have, unfortunately, been unable to identify such a case. It seems that what a philosopher identifies as strict or as loose identity depends on that philosopher's ontology. But I think that a very brief discussion of the problem of universals, and then of the identity of particulars over time, will show that almost all metaphysicians have need of the distinction.

It has already been mentioned that we regularly speak of different objects having the *same* property, being of the *same* kind, and so on. Can this be strict identity? Only realists about universals can say yes. Nominalists, and this includes most Empiricists, must say no. They argue, for instance, that the very same thing cannot be located in two places at once, and so that there cannot be universals. The argument is not contemptible, even if, as I think, it is not sound. But the argument implies that the sameness of type that our ordinary speech constantly attributes to different particulars is no more than a loose sense of sameness.

Even realists about universals are likely to require a loose sense of the word 'same'. For it is a very extreme Realist position that wherever, in ordinary language, it can be said with truth that two things have the same property, there the two things instantiate the very same universal. For most realists, there can be sameness of type in the absence of identity of the universals involved. Such samenesses will be loose.

Turn now to the identity of particulars over time. Consider the identity of persons over time. This person that now stands before me is the very same person as the one before me yesterday. Good ordinary language, and true because it really is Jim on both occasions. But is there strict identity here, or is the identity of the same person at different times a loose identity holding between different temporal parts of a temporally extended thing? Both views have their vigorous supporters and, as is generally appreciated, the issue is not to be settled by consulting ordinary language. The question whether 'very same' is here being used in the strict or the loose sense is a deep and difficult one.

Even those who hold that persons are strictly identical over time are likely to require a loose sense of the phrase 'very same'. For it is an extreme and unattractive position that wherever it can be said with truth that we are dealing with numerically the same particular at different times, there the particular is strictly the same particular at the different times. Are nations or famous football teams strictly identical at the different times of their existence? Most philosophers, I suppose, would think this identity loose and popular only.

In possible world theory, the dispute between identity across worlds and 'mere counterparts' in other worlds also appears to be a dispute concerning the force of 'very same'. 'Counterparts' are the very same thing in the loose sense only.

Metaphysicians pick and choose between strict and loose identity in their analyses of different problems. This work, for instance, will argue for strict identity in the case of (carefully selected) properties and relations, loose identity for particulars over time, and loose identity, in many cases though not in all, for the same thing 'in different possible worlds'.

We are assuming, then, that there is a distinction in our language and our thought between strict and loose senses of 'same' and 'very same'. We go on to ask what rules govern the loose sense. Butler gives no account of his loose and popular identity. To give such an account we turn to Peter Geach. Instead of 'loose' identity, Geach speaks of 'relative' identity. Relative identity for him is identity relative to some sortal. Two things can be the same F, but not the same G. (See his 1968 [1962].) Geach further takes the very radical view that *all* identity is relative identity. There seems to be no reason to accept this. What, for our purposes, we may interpret Geach as doing is calling our attention to *loose* identity. What is more, we can extract from his discussion a plausible rule governing this secondary or loose sense, although it does not seem that we require his restriction to sortals. Where we are prepared to say that different things are the same, they are always (different) members of the identical ('the same' in the strict sense) equivalence class, where the equivalence relation for this class (a symmetrical, transitive and reflexive relation) is somehow salient in the situation where the loose identity is asserted. (I am here greatly indebted to Peter Anstey, who, as an undergraduate at Sydney University, pointed out to me that Butler's loose and popular identities appear to be a matter of equivalence classes.)

It needs further to be added that ordinary discourse, in its rough and ready way, will often content itself with a decent approximation to an equivalence class and an equivalence relation. Near enough is good enough. And it may take difficult philosophical analysis to winkle out what is the equivalence relation, or approximation to one, that we are unselfconsciously using. Furthermore, different metaphysical positions may yield different accounts of the equivalence relation involved in certain sorts of situations. For instance, a believer in temporal parts for all physical objects will give a different account of loose identity over time, say of a tree, than will one like Butler who believes in atoms that are strictly identical over time.

The distinction that I claim exists between strict and loose identity does not, of itself, settle any particular metaphysical issue. But, as already indicated, I hope that it will prove useful in *understanding what is at issue* in various important disputes.

After making this distinction between strict and loose identity, I discovered that what I had argued for had been anticipated much more thoroughly than I had realized. First, Glen Ross pointed out to me, there is the contribution of Hans Reichenbach (1956, p. 38). Reichenbach is concerned with identity through time, and holds to a doctrine of temporal parts. Between different temporal parts of the one thing, the relation of *genidentity* holds. This relation, Reichenbach says, is symmetrical, transitive and reflexive. It is thus an equivalence relation. It is true, though, that he does not come up with the idea that this loose sense of identity may be found in other fields besides that of identity through time.

But William Lycan has pointed out to me that the more general result is to be found, not merely in a somewhat submerged form as in Geach, nor in one particular sort of case as in Reichenbach, but in its generality in the work of Hector-Neri Castañeda. See, for instance, 'Thinking and the structure of the world' in his 1989.

2.32 Partial identity

We are not yet finished with identity. Besides the distinction between strict and loose identity we also require the notion of a strict *but partial* identity. The notion was introduced in Armstrong 1978b, probably influenced by F. H. Bradley. In his dispute with William James about the nature of resemblance, Bradley defends the idea that resemblance is partial identity (1893a & b). John Bacon has pointed out that the notion of partial identity is also to be found in Guido Küng, 1967, another possible source for me. Michael Pendlebury has drawn my attention to the *Critique of Pure Reason*, where, at A7/B10, Kant says that where predicate B is contained in the subject concept A, the connection is 'thought through identity'. This appears to be countenancing partial identity. Finally, partial identity has recently been endorsed by David Lewis, who offers considerations designed to show that the notion is helpful in solving Geach's paradox of the 1001 cats. ('Many, but almost one', in Bacon, Campbell and Reinhardt, 1993. The cat Tibbles is a cat, but so are the thousand cats which are Tibbles minus a different one of a thousand of Tibbles' hairs. So although the cat is alone on the mat, it seems to have a thousand companions.)

The general thought is that the philosophical tradition has been hypnotized by such cases as the identity of the morning star and the evening star, on the one hand, and the non-identity of the morning star and the red planet, on the other. These cases tempt us to overlook such a case as that of Australia and its state of New South Wales and also that of two adjoining terrace or town houses that have a wall in common. These are partial identities. One is whole/part, the other is overlap. Mereology, which deals with these notions, may be thought of as an extended logic of identity, extended to deal with such cases of partial identity.

Some philosophers reject the notion of partial identity. These cases, they argue, are no more than cases of non-identity. All that is involved, they say, is the having of a (completely) identical part. There is no partial identity, only non-partial identity of parts.

The dispute is rather a frustrating one, because it seems to be one where 'all the facts lie open before us' and the question is no more than which way of talking we should adopt. It does seem, however, that to admit partial identity is metaphysically illuminating. Are not the parts of a thing part of the *being* of that thing? After all, if you take *all* the parts of a thing, then you take the thing. And as you come nearer and nearer to taking all the parts of a thing, so you are nearer to taking the thing.

A concept that is worth considering here is Hume's notion of a distinct existence. Hume held, plausibly enough, that in the case of distinct existences there is no contradiction in the one existing without the other. But for this principle to apply, the existences must be *wholly* distinct existences. For distinct things that stand to each other as part to whole, or which overlap, the principle fails. I live in a terrace (town) house. If the *whole* of the two houses on either side are removed, I am in a bad way. I have not got a (whole) house any longer because I have no side walls. All this suggests, without of course proving, that partial identity is a clarifying notion.

For the rest, it is to be hoped that the value of allowing the notion of partial identity will emerge at various points in our subsequent discussion.

3

Properties I

3.1 PRELIMINARY

We now take up the main line of the argument. The world is a world of states of affairs. The phrase 'state of affairs' will be used in the same way that Wittgenstein in the *Tractatus* used the term 'fact'. Indeed, his famous proposition 1.1: 'The world is the totality of facts, not of things' may serve as charter of the present enterprise. Wittgenstein's terminology has been followed by Brian Skyrms in his brief but penetrating paper 'Tractarian nominalism' (1981, reprinted in Armstrong 1989b). For Wittgenstein, states of affairs are no more than possible facts. It seems, however, that the word 'fact' is too much a term of ordinary speech. In particular, contemporary use ties it too closely to the notions of statement and proposition. It is natural for philosophers to think of facts as the 'tautological accusatives' of true statements and true propositions. Facts in this sense are what true statements state and true propositions propose. More simply, they are *truths*.

Given this, and given a semantic condition of identity for statements, propositions and truths, then to each different true statement, proposition and truth there corresponds its own peculiar fact. This is quite unsatisfactory for present purposes. The phrase 'state of affairs' seems better. In addition, it sounds less colloquial and more like a term of art, which is what is required.

We require at this point a distinction between *atomic* and *molecular* states of affairs. Because disjunctive and negative states of affairs will be rejected, molecular states of affairs are all of them mere *conjunctions* of atomic states of affairs. It is the atomic states of affairs that concern us at present. We may further distinguish between atomic states of affairs *strictly so-called*, and atomic states of affairs in a *loose* sense. The former are not susceptible of ontological analysis, even in principle, because their constituents are all simple. The trouble about them, though, is that, *pace* the Wittgenstein of the *Tractatus*, we do not know whether there really are any atomic states of affairs of this strict sort.

But it is atomic states of affairs in the loose sense that we are at present concerned with. They may be susceptible of ontological analysis, turning out to be ontologically equivalent to conjunctions of simpler, if not simple, states of affairs. To repeat the example given in 1.1: *a*'s being F may be equivalent to the conjunction of *a*'s being G & *a*'s being H, with F=G & H. Here G and H are universals, and I am assuming that if G and H are instantiated by the same particular, then G & H is a universal (a conjunctive universal), and so F is a universal.

We can give a very simple definition of atomic states of affairs in the loose sense of the phrase. An atomic state of affairs exists if and only if a particular has a property, or a relation holds between two or more particulars. These properties and relations are, of course, universals. We will call the particulars, properties and relations the *constituents* of the states of affairs. They are objectively real entities. We will not, incidentally, require existentially quantified states of affairs, though there are, of course, existentially quantified *truths*. Truths and their correspondents, the states of affairs, do not stand in one–one correspondence.

Although upholding the ontological reality of (our) states of affairs involves admitting the ontological reality of particulars, properties and relations, not every philosopher thinks that the reverse entailment holds. Even where the constituent entities are admitted, it is nevertheless regularly denied that they are brought together in states of affairs. It may be conceded that this electron, a particular, exists, and that it has a certain mass, the mass being an objective, that is a mind-independent, property of the electron. (Though the objective property is a more controversial entity among philosophers than the particular.) But it may still be, and frequently is, denied that there is an entity: *the-electron's-having-this-mass*. So there is a good deal of work to be done to make it plausible that there are such things as our states of affairs. Let us, however, begin by concentrating on the objective reality of their constituents, starting with properties. The constituents will be matter enough for some chapters (3–7).

3.2 NOMINALISM

3.21 Extreme and Moderate Nominalism

It is not proposed to argue at length for objective properties (and relations), because this has been done elsewhere (Armstrong, 1978a & b, and 1989a). Those who deny the existence of properties and/or relations as items in the ontological inventory must face the problem of what marks off classes of particulars whose members are more or less alike from classes whose members are indefinitely unalike. The utter promiscuity with which numerically different particulars can be grouped together in one class ensures that the heterogeneous classes will vastly outnumber the more or less homogeneous ones. The class of particulars to which the predicate 'grue' applies (in Goodman's definition: all things examined before *t* just in case they are green but to other things just in case they are blue) is, intuitively, a class through which a great fault-line runs with respect to the resemblance of its members. But, of course, it is a model of unity compared with the indefinite multitude of truly heterogeneous classes.

By 'Nominalism' in this work will be meant the ontological doctrine that there are no universals: there are only particulars. ('Universal' here has its classical meaning. Classes and numbers, for instance, are not automatically to be classified as universals. Universals are entities that are identical, strictly identical, in different instantiations, and so are the foundations *in re* for all genuine resemblances between particulars.) The term 'Nominalism' is not entirely appropriate, and might with advantage have been reserved for a particular variety of Nominalism: *Predicate* Nominalism. But, as not infrequently happens, the genus has got its name from one of its species, and the usage has been entrenched for centuries. So we will stick with it.

There are a number of varieties of Nominalism, but a useful broad division of Nominalisms is into the extreme and the moderate varieties. An *extreme* Nominalist denies that there are universals, and furthermore denies the existence of objective properties and relations. The *moderate* Nominalist agrees that there are no universals, but does hold that there are properties and relations. They are particulars. There is a truly horrifying number of terms for properties and relations conceived of as particulars. Each happy discoverer, it seems, names them anew. Here we will follow Donald Williams (1966, ch. 7) and speak of them as 'tropes'.

3.22 *Extreme and Moderate Realism*

While we are at it, it will be convenient to distinguish between extremists and moderates among the upholders of universals. An *extreme* or Platonic realist about universals holds that they are transcendent, standing apart from particulars. (It seems reasonable to call a doctrine that postulates transcendent entities that are not particulars an extreme view, ontologically speaking.) A *moderate* or Aristotelian realist holds that universals exist only in particulars, with the word 'in' subject to interpretation. The realism of this work is Aristotelian.

I confess to a lack of sympathy for both extreme Nominalism and extreme realism. In my view, the last battle between Nominalism and realism (the Grand Final) should be fought between trope theories (of various sub-types) and Aristotelian realists (also of various sub-types).

3.23 *Tropes*

(This sub-section may be omitted, as irrelevant to the main line of the argument.) As just foreshadowed, we will not concern ourselves further with the extreme Nominalisms. Criticism of them is to be found in Armstrong 1978a and 1989a. But the view that properties and relations exist yet are particulars, is an important alternative which in many ways respects the spirit of the present enterprise. It deserves some discussion.

A realist about universals can solve ontological problems about sorting and classification in a particularly robust manner. The basis for saying that two or more particulars are the same in some respect can be (though it does not have to be in every case) that they instantiate the very same universal. No such solution is available to the trope theorist. Instead, appeal is generally made, and best made, to the relation of resemblance. The important resemblances here are not those between ordinary particulars, but rather those that hold between the tropes themselves. Of particular importance is the relation of *exact* resemblance between tropes. Where the upholder of universals finds strict identity of universal, there the trope theorist finds exact resemblance of numerically different tropes.

But does not one piece of linguistic evidence favour the universals theory? We regularly say that two different particulars have the *very same* property. It is here, though, that our discussion in 2.31 of the *loose* sense of the word 'same' is relevant. The trope theory can quite fairly claim that the two particulars have the very same property in the loose sense only. ('Very same' does not necessarily mean *strictly* the same.) It was argued in 2.31 that the proper conditions for an assertion of loose identity are that the entities *called* the same should be different members of the one equivalence class, where the equivalence relation involved is salient in the situation. The condition is satisfied for exactly resembling tropes, because exact resemblance is an equivalence relation. Classes of exactly resembling tropes can therefore go substitute for instantiations of the same universal.

(See Armstrong, 1989a, ch. 6, for more detail.)

Here are two reasons for preferring universals to tropes. The first of these is the axioms that govern resemblance. The trope theory must take resemblance as a primitive notion. There can be no question of analysing it away in terms of respects of resemblance, as a universals theory will analyse it. Resemblance between tropes, in particular, must be a primitive notion, although one that admits of degree. There will be, in theory at least, a lowest degree (0) where there is no resemblance at all, and a highest degree (1), that of exact resemblance. The relation of resemblance is reflexive and symmetrical but is not transitive. It is, however, reflexive, symmetrical and transitive for the particular case of *exact* resemblance. That particular case is a substitution-instance of a more general principle: if *a* resembles *b* to degree D, and if *c* exactly resembles *b*, then *a* resembles *c* to degree D. We may dub all these principles the *Axioms of Resemblance*. They appear to be necessary truths.

Once they are stated, these principles are obvious enough. But since a trope theory must take resemblance to be a primitive, there seems to be no prospect of explaining them by deducing them from anything else. (Except for the *symmetry* of the relation, which may reasonably be explained by the hypothesis that what we have ontologically, as truthmaker, is just the one relation. See ch. 9.) But for the other axioms we can ask what their truthmaker is. They seem to be 'brute' necessities (presumably involving necessary states of affairs), and as such to be avoided unless outweighed by other disadvantages in the realist position. The situation may be contrasted with the orthodox analysis of resemblance in terms of common, that is strictly identical, properties. On this view, complete lack of resemblance is complete lack of common properties, exact resemblance is having all properties in common, and inexact resemblance is having some but not all properties in common or at least some partial identity of some properties. The Axioms of Resemblance are then transparent.

What we have here is, of course, no formal refutation of the Tropes+Resemblance theory. But it is surely quite a disadvantage of that position, when compared with the Universals theory, that it has to abjure the presenting of the Axioms of Resemblance as simple truisms based on the properties of strict identity. In philosophy, as in science, the theory that explains by appealing to the least number of principles is to be preferred, other things being equal.

A second reason for preferring universals to tropes is that the former permit what I take to be a very much more plausible theory of the nature of laws of nature. It is very hard for a trope theory to get away from a Regularity theory of laws, but this account of laws is deeply unsatisfactory (see 15.1). If as a trope theorist one argues for a 'strong' theory of laws, one is likely to be defeated by what van Fraassen (1989) calls the 'Inference problem', the problem of explicating the inference from the law to the regularity it is supposed to entail. (See 15.2.) With universals, the possibility arises of construing laws as relationships between universals. In this conception of laws, the having of certain properties by a particular or particulars (which is the obtaining of a certain sort of state of affairs, the obtaining of a state-of-affairs type) *brings about*, or has a certain probability of bringing about, a further state of affairs of a certain sort, the bringing about occurring in virtue of the antecedent properties. This is a very natural way to conceive of the operation of laws, and brings with it advantages, including some progress with the Problem of Induction.

It is true that the trope theorist can put forward a quite plausible general principle of 'like causes like'. Exactly resembling tropes will play exactly the same nomic or causal role. But the problem is to find a suitable truthmaker for this alleged truth, without falling back on mere regularities of the behaviour of particulars.

It remains true, also, that the choice between universals and tropes rests upon relatively delicate and/or controversial matters. A trope theorist, even if moved by the arguments just presented, may argue that there are still worse disadvantages for the universals theory. As a result, while cleaving to universals, we will not lose sight of trope theory in this essay. It is an important alternative view that deserves development.

One point about the trope theory may be dealt with immediately. It is customary to construct ordinary particulars out of *bundles* of tropes. This is the view taken by G. F. Stout (1921), D. C. Williams (1953), Keith Campbell (1990) and others. But it is possible, and I think much preferable, to combine a trope theory with a substance/attribute position. This seems to have been the position of Locke. We know that Locke accepted substance. It seems that we can take his continual talk of *qualities* with ontological seriousness. Michael Bradley has drawn my attention to a quotation from the *Essay*:

> In the notice, that our Senses take of the constant Vicissitude of Things, we cannot but observe, that several particular, both Qualities, and Substances begin to exist;
> (bk. 2, ch. 26, sec. 1)

Furthermore, Locke is an avowed Nominalist, allowing nothing but *similitudes in things* as the ontological correlate of, the truthmaker for, our classing and sorting. So, although he never to my knowledge says so, his qualities should be particulars. Again, there is no need to hold the substance/attribute view in the sceptical and unlovely form upheld by Locke himself. A Lockean, but non-sceptical, form of the trope view is argued for by C. B. Martin (1980). For comment see Armstrong (1991a).

An important advantage that this position has over a bundle of tropes account is that it gets us away from the idea that properties are like things. Properties exist, they are entities, but they are not things. Rather they are *ways* that things are. This point will be developed further in 3.6.

3.3 *A POSTERIORI* REALISM

This section deals with a matter that I have often laboured elsewhere and will not labour here. But it is both so important in itself, and so central to the present enterprise, that it requires the dignity of a separate section. Although universals are here upheld, they are not upheld, as many have upheld them, in order to give semantic values to general words and phrases. Universals are here postulated, in the main, in order to explain the resemblances and differences that we find among particulars, beginning with our perception of particulars in our environment. This perceptual acquaintance with the natures of particulars is extended, deepened, and in many ways corrected by the whole great enterprise of natural science (though under the ultimate epistemic control of perception). It is to natural science, then, that we should look for knowledge, or perhaps just more or less rational belief, of what universals there are. Hence the term '*a posteriori*' realism. The theory of universals may have to be developed in an *a priori* manner. But the theory of what universals there are must be an *a posteriori* matter. And even the theory of universals should be relatively *a priori* only. We shall see in the sequel how scientific considerations may incline us toward certain answers to certain questions in the theory of universals.

It may be noted that a trope theory can be, indeed should be, developed in the same *a posteriori* manner as the theory of universals.

3.4 PREDICATES AND PROPERTIES

Something that more or less follows from the empiricist epistemology of universals just adumbrated, and that is also a well-worn theme in previous writings, is that the semantic relations that hold between predicates and properties are many-many. A predicate that is one, semantically one, may apply to different particulars in virtue of different universals. Adapting Wittgenstein's remarks on games (1953, secs. 66 & 67) to the current purpose, 'game' may be such a predicate. The predicate 'e', however, when used to pick out the charge of the electron, may apply to the particulars it applies to in virtue of a single universal. The current state of physics gives this some plausibility. Given that there are no uninstantiated universals, (something that is still to be argued for) then to a predicate such as 'phlogisticated' no universal or universals correspond because the predicate applies to no particular. Contrariwise, to the one property many semantically distinct predicates may apply, for instance 'gravitational rest mass M' and 'inertial rest mass M'. There might only be one predicate corresponding to one particular property, although further predicates could always be manufactured. Finally, a property might be totally unknown, and so no predicate would exist. The possibilities just enumerated are diagrammed in the table below.

one predicate has corresponding to it	many properties (being a game)
	one property (charge of the electron)
	no properties (phlogisticated)
one property has corresponding to it	many predicates ('gravitational rest mass M' and 'inertial rest mass M')
	one predicate (though further predicate easily created)
	no predicate (completely unknown property)

3.41 Rejection of disjunctive and negative properties

It is a very important part of this theory of universals that, given distinct universals F and G (it is essential to note that F and G are universals here), to the predicates 'F or G' ('FvG'), 'not-F' and 'not-G', in general at least, no universals correspond. There is nothing wrong with these predicates:

there will usually be many things to which the predicates apply truly. There may even be universals that happen to have the very same extension as these predicates. But the predicates are not, as we may put it, 'property-predicates'.

This result, as I take it to be, follows fairly directly from a very simple but very illuminating analytic truth about universals, a truism that we shall have much occasion to recall, as should all who think about universals: that universals are strictly identical in their different instantiations. The disjunctive case is pretty straightforward. If *a* is F but is not G, while *b* is G but is not F, then the predicate 'F or G' truly applies to both particulars. Yet that seems no ground for thinking that the particulars have something in common. The giveaway is that such disjunctive predicates are so easily manufactured *a priori*. It is true, as Herb Hochberg has pointed out to me, that it would beg the question against disjunctive universals to say that there definitely is no identical universal, F or G, that both particulars instantiate. But it is hard to see that there *has* to be one. Rather, it seems plausible to say, the predicate 'F or G', when applied to a particular, has two possible truthmakers, the particular's being F and the particular's being G. The existence of just one of the truthmakers is sufficient for truth.

The case of negation is perhaps not quite so clear. There are some pressures towards accepting negative properties. Yet consider all those particulars – a miscellaneous lot – that lack charge *e*. Is it very plausible to think that each of these particulars have an identical something in virtue of which 'not-*e*' applies? I suggest not. (For a more extended treatment of disjunctive and negative properties, see Armstrong 1978b, ch. 14.)

What is true, however, is that the attempt to extrude negation from the foundations of the world is not an easy enterprise. It certainly cannot succeed without introducing into this metaphysic something more than first-order states of affairs. At least one higher-order state of affairs is required, the state of affairs that the totality of all other states of affairs *are* the totality of the states of affairs. To get rid of *not* you have to accept the presence of *all*. This difficult matter will be taken up again at 8.7 and in chapter 13.

But in any case, further qualification is necessary. We said four paragraphs back that the rejection of disjunctive and negative properties holds 'in general'. The reason was this. In the spirit of *a posteriori* realism, our conclusion should be no more than: there are no *a priori* reasons for thinking that disjunctions of universals and negations of universals are to be taken as universals themselves. But might we not consider *selected* disjunctions of universals and *selected* negations of universals? Might it not be legitimate to account these as universals *if the development of the natural sciences appeared to demand this*?

The present state of quantum physics comes to mind. Before the so-called 'collapse of the wave-packet' we have, it may be argued, a probabilistic smear of values, say for the position of some photon, and the smear can perhaps be presented as an exclusive disjunction of a range of values. This *might* be interpreted within a theory of universals as the instantiation of a disjunctive universal. No firm thesis is being advanced here. Perhaps in such a case we should postulate disjunctive universals, but it is a perhaps only. Again, exclusion laws, such as Pauli's exclusion principle, might be thought to require negative universals. (But see 15.4.) In the spirit of *a posteriori* realism, options about disjunctive and negative properties should be kept a little open.

Conjunctive universals are a different matter. Provided that F and G are both instantiated by the very same particular, there seems no reason to reject this species of complex universal. See 3.7, to come.

3.5 UNIVERSALS AS STATE-OF-AFFAIRS TYPES

It will be argued in this section that universals are state-of-affairs *types*. To argue for this thesis is already to trench upon the theory of states of affairs. But, as already warned, it does not seem possible to develop this ontology, and perhaps any other, without in some degree anticipating and presupposing parts of the argument that, in the serial order on the page, still lie ahead. Metaphysics is a serpent that has itself by the tail.

The phrase 'state-of-affairs types' is not intended to mean that universals are themselves states of affairs. They are not. They are mere constituents of states of affairs. The word 'types' is here a *modifier* of the expression 'state-of-affairs', changing the expression's force in a way to be explained shortly. The phrase is clumsy, but it has proved hard to find anything better. Notice also, that the word 'types' must be taken in a very narrow way here. The demand that universals be strictly identical in their different instances, the 'powerful truism', entails that for two instantiations of the same universal, the sameness of type involved must be strict identity.

Now to explain our phrase. If particular *a* has the property-universal F, then the state of affairs is *a's being F*. For convenience we may continue often to refer to the universal by the mere letter 'F'. But it is best thought of as *_'s being F*. Similarly, we have *_'s having R to _*. The universal is a gutted state of affairs; it is everything that is left in the state of affairs after the particular particulars involved in the state of affairs have been abstracted away in thought. So it is a state-of-affairs type, the constituent that is common to all states of affairs which contain that universal.

This contention will at once recall Frege's doctrine of the unsaturatedness of his 'concepts'. I happily acknowledge the influence, and, indeed, think of his concepts as close relatives of my universals. Frege's view is criticized by Reinhardt Grossmann in his 1983 (sec. 59). Grossmann argues that Frege has wrongly identified properties (in Frege's language, concepts) with a complex structure (a propositional function) that contains not only properties but also the copula, that is, the bringing together of particulars and universals in facts (our states of affairs).

But it seems that Grossmann fails to see that Frege is really offering a different conception of the copula, a different one, a defensible one, and, it may be thought, a preferable one. The universal, the state-of-affairs type, has one or more blanks as part of its nature. That makes it unsaturated. Frege's copula is the *bringing together* of a particular or particulars, on the one hand, and 'concepts' on the other, by inserting the particulars in the unsaturated structure. The 'bringing together' or 'inserting' is something relation-like, which is the traditional conception of the copula. We are given a rather good linguistic image of the copula when we fill in the blanks of the unsaturated expression that stands for the universal, filling them in with the names of the particulars involved in this state of affairs. Grossmann, perhaps, has let himself be deceived by the word 'is'. It is traditional to use this word to represent the copula, but it wrongly suggests to the imagination (which can be so hard to restrain in philosophy) that the copula is thing-like rather than something relation-like.

This conception of universals as state-of-affairs types seems right in itself and also brings out the dependence of universals upon states of affairs. As such, it should at least incline us to accept the primary position of states of affairs and to be sceptical about the reality of uninstantiated universals. Again, it greatly simplifies and clarifies the defence of the doctrine, to be defended at a much later stage in this work (15.2), that laws of nature are relations of universals, a doctrine that brings great ontological advantages but which is thought by many to have a mystery or unclarity at its centre. These are systematic considerations only, and do not constitute a direct argument for the Fregean conception. But coherence is an important virtue in a philosophical system, and so one that, to a degree, recommends that system.

3.6 UNIVERSALS AS WAYS

David Seargent (1985, ch. 4) has argued that the correct way to conceive of universals is not as *things*, or even, he says, as *entities*, but rather as *ways*. Properties are ways things are, relations are ways that things stand to each other. He even suggests that it is a category mistake to treat them in any other manner.

I demur at his suggestion that properties and relations are not entities. Seargent would not deny that universals exist, and it seems convenient to say that whatever exists is an entity. But I do accept that it is wrong to *substantialize* universals. To think of them as ways that things are or stand to each other is to *de*-substantialize them. What is more, it seems plausible to say that to substantialize them, as, for instance, does the theory that particulars are bundles of universals (and *mutatis mutandis* the theory that particulars are bundles of tropes) is to make a category-mistake.

Ayer spoke of sense-data as 'junior substances', and this excellent phrase might also be applied to universals conceived of in the substantializing manner. How is such a conception to be shown to be a category-mistake? Seargent suggests that this is done by Bradley's regress. Once properties and relations are conceived of in a thing-like way, then they will need real relations to attach them to their particulars (in a substance/attribute theory) or to attach them to each other (in a bundle theory). These relations will in consistency have to be conceived of as substantial also, and the regress is off to infinity. By contrast, *ways* things are or *ways* things stand to each other seem to form so much closer a unity with the things involved, that perhaps further relations are not required. One begins to see the force in talking about the copula as a 'non-relational tie', self-contradictory as it sounds.

At the same time, *pace* Laurence Goldstein (1983), talk of properties and relations as 'ways' does not derogate from their ontological reality. They are real features of things, real joints in reality, some of which are grasped in approximate fashion by everyday perception and others of which are uncovered *a posteriori* by deep scientific investigation. It is to be noted also that the conception of universals as ways stands in no opposition to, indeed quite naturally goes along with, the important Fregean idea, argued for in the previous section, that universals are 'unsaturated' entities, an idea that was linked in that section with the doctrine that universals are state-of-affairs types. It may also be noted that there is nothing to bar, and much to recommend, treating property tropes and relation tropes as ways. They will be unrepeatable ways, of course, as opposed to universals which are repeatable ways. Such a conception of tropes will mandate, or at least push towards, a substance/attribute trope theory rather than a bundle theory. That, in my view, is all to the good.

3.7 COMPLEX PROPERTIES

3.71 The existence of complex properties

In this section the existence of complex properties will be argued for. To some this may seem a work of supererogation. But there are philosophers who hold that all universals are simple (e.g. Grossmann, 1983, secs. 58–61), and in any case the theory of complex properties is of great interest and importance.

Consider conjunctions of universals. If there are complex universals at all, then conjunctions of universals should qualify. We are inclined to deny that there are disjunctive and negative universals. But conjunctive universals seem much more acceptable. Given that F and G are distinct universals, then F&G can be a universal, provided always that a particular exists at some time which is both F and G. With this *co-instantiation condition* in place, the key requirement of identity, strict identity, in different instances is met in a way that it is not met, or not clearly met, in the disjunctive and negative cases. Indeed, one who accepts universals but rejects conjunctive universals may be challenged to say what further condition must be added to this strict identity to yield a universal. It will be question-begging to say that the missing condition is that the universal should be simple.

(It is to be noted that although the property F, the property G, and the property F&G are all different, they are not wholly different. They are *partially* identical, although the partial identity is not *quite* simple mereological overlap. The notion of partial identity has already been introduced and defended in 2.32. It is of great importance for the theory of complex universals.)

But, it may be objected, if there are complex properties, then they must be complexes of simple properties, or at least complexes of simple properties and relations. If it is also maintained, as this work maintains, that all universals are instantiated, then any complex property can then be replaced in each of these instantiations by a conjunction of states of affairs involving simple properties and relations. The alleged conjunctive property, or any other complex property, will supervene on these states of affairs. And then what need to recognize anything but the complex of states of affairs involving nothing but simple universals?

This retort has a presupposition, however, a presupposition that is controversial. How do we know that there are any simple universals at all? May it not be, for instance, that *every* universal is a conjunctive universal? F&G has F and G as its constituents. But F and G, perhaps, are each of them mere conjunctive universals, and so for the new conjuncts, and so perhaps 'all the way down', with simple universals nowhere to be found, even at the end of an infinite road. How can we rule this out?

Conjunctive universals may still be resisted. Michael Tooley has suggested to me a possible source of resistance. It is a matter of 'ease of detachability'. If a pen lies on a desk, it is natural to say one has two material objects here, as opposed to one – pen+desk. This is because it is so easy to detach the pen from the desk. Similarly, if some object has a certain specific mass and a certain specific shape, that, on my view, gives a conjunctive property. But the object can lose one property without losing the other. They are detachable, they form no natural unit. I suggest, however, that for our ontological purposes, the ease of detachability that is to be found in many cases of co-instantiation of properties should be no bar to saying that co-instantiation is sufficient for a conjunctive property. Cases where the properties together are 'synergistic', bestowing a power that is less or more than the sum of the powers bestowed by one conjunct in abstraction from the other, are merely the more interesting sort of conjunctive properties.

Leaving conjunctive properties, we pass to *structural* properties, which involve both properties and relations. Instantiation of the universal F may come to this. To be an F a particular must be made up of just two non-overlapping parts, one of which instantiates universal G while the other instantiates universal H, with the G part and the H part linked by the (external) relation R. To be an F is thus to be a certain sort of structure, so F may be called a structural property. Even a conjunctive property could be called a structural property, but it is a structural property where the constituents, the conjuncts, are properties of the very same particular that has the conjunctive property. In a paradigm structural property, this is not so. The constituent properties and relations are instantiated by particulars that are proper parts of the particular that has the structural property. (For a more extensive, earlier, discussion of structural properties, see Armstrong, 1978b, ch. 18.)

Returning to our structural property F, suppose that G and H are also structures of the same sort, with structures all the way down, and that a similar situation holds for all other properties. After what has transpired in the search for atoms, what scientific realist, at least, can conclusively rule such a possibility out?

If every universal, property and relation, dissolves in some way into some sort of complex structure, then, it may be said, every universal dissolves into complex state-of-affairs types. I accept this, but see no intellectual difficulty in it. Indeed, it would seem to be a very attractive, if quite speculative, prospect for one who holds that the world is a world of states of affairs. It would not seem to involve the denial of universals. Different particulars could still instantiate the strictly identical complex structure.

It may *perhaps* be a contingent matter whether there are or are not simple universals in the world. But what is not a contingent matter, although it is an empirical question, is whether a particular universal is or is not simple. Equally, if it is not simple, it is not a contingent matter just what its structure is. In my 1978b (ch. 15, sec. 1), I failed to appreciate this necessity, but corrected the mistake in 1989b (ch. 5, sec. 1). The argument is yet another application of the powerful analytic truth, the 'powerful truism', that a universal is strictly identical in its different instances. Suppose that a certain universal is in fact simple. It may well be an *epistemic* possibility that it is complex. 'For all we know', the universal is complex. But how can this be a non-epistemic, an ontological, possibility? The latter would involve the simple universal being complex 'in some other possible world'. But it is evident that it would then be a different universal.

But the epistemic possibility is there. And that epistemic possibility seems by itself sufficient justification for accepting the reality of complex universals. If, at the bottom, any complex universal is a complex that contains nothing but simple universals, then the latter may well be called the fundamental universals, just as the ultimate constituents of particulars, if such constituents exist, are the fundamental particulars. And just as one day natural science may give us reason to think that fundamental particulars have been identified, so also it may give us reason to think that the fundamental universals – the fundamental properties and relations – have been identified. But even then, what is non-fundamental is not therefore non-existent. Macroscopic particulars do not fail to exist if it turns out that they are assemblages of fundamental particulars! In the same way, complex universals exist even if they turn out to be assemblages of fundamental universals.

3.72 Complex properties as state-of-affairs types

But let us now see how an account of *complex* properties can be given using states of affairs and state-of-affairs types. We may take as our example the property of *being methane* which David Lewis uses in his article 'Against structural universals' (1986a). (See also Armstrong, 'In defence of structural universals' (1986) and Lewis, 'Comment on Armstrong and Forrest' (1986d).) Methane is a *kind* of thing, a kind of substance, and so perhaps not really a property, but that complication seems not important here. Methane's structure is familiar:

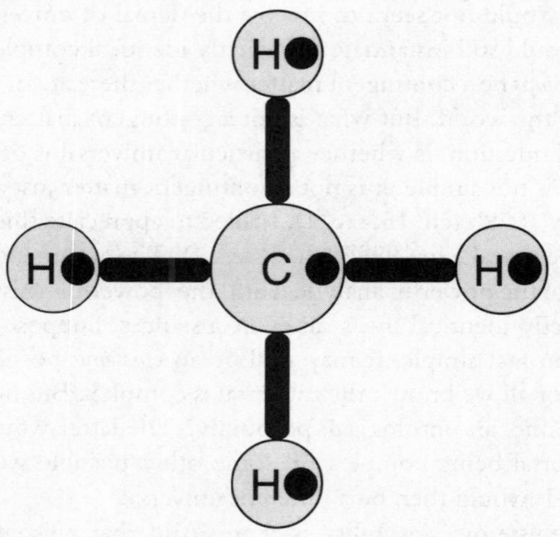

The above is a diagram which represents a particular, a token, methane molecule. It is a thing with parts – mereological parts – *a*+*b*+*c*+*d* (the hydrogen atoms)+*e* (the carbon atom). Let us assume, for simplicity's sake, that these parts are not merely non-identical, but that they involve no overlap. (Overlap would complicate the story, but would not change it essentially.) Of *a, b, c* and *d* it is the case that they are each of them hydrogen atoms. So we have states of affairs H*a,* H*b*, H*c* and H*d*. The object *e* is a carbon atom. We have the state of affairs C*e*. Between the carbon atom and each of the hydrogen molecules the relation B (bonding) holds. So we have *a*B*e*, *b*B*e*, *c*B*e*, *d*B*e*. If and only if all these states of affairs obtain, then the particular, *a*+*b*+*c*+*d*+*e* , is a methane molecule.

(John Bigelow has pointed out to me, though, that if there were further states of affairs, for instance further bondings to other atoms, the particular might not count as a methane molecule. If so, the definition of methane involves a negative element. Let us, for the sake of a relatively simple example, bracket this awkward point. The problem can be dealt with in our metaphysical scheme by introducing a higher-order state of affairs. It will be a totality state of affairs. Perhaps it has the form: that these particular atoms enter into these sorts of bonding (at that time) with no atoms besides their four partner-atoms. See ch. 13. States of affairs of totality are ubiquitous in the world.)

With this difficulty pushed aside, and allowing for the sake of the example that H, C, and B are all universals, then an ontological analysis of what makes this object a methane molecule has been given. The form of the analysis is this. It is *a conjunction of states of affairs*. A thesis may now be put forward. In every case where a particular has a complex property (in this case the particular [$a+b+c+d+e$] having M – where M is *being methane*) this state of affairs is identical with a certain conjunction of states of affairs.

(Is the thesis convertible? Is it the case that, for every conjunction of states of affairs, the mereological sum of the constituent particulars has a structural property determined by the states of affairs involved? If *a* is F and *b* is G, then, given permissive mereology, the particular $a+b$ must exist. It is further entailed that this particular has a very trivial sort of structural property: it is made up of an F-part and a G-part. But to get an interesting structural property the F-part and the G-part must be related by some external relation R. It is not a necessary truth that any two particulars must be related by some external relation, although if it is true that the world is a single spacetime, such a relation will always in fact exist.)

A conjunction of states of affairs is what is called in the literature a species of *molecular* fact or state of affairs. For us, denying disjunctive and negative states of affairs as we do, such a conjunction is the *only* sort of molecular fact or state of affairs. The interesting thing about this sort of conjunction is that provided the conjuncts, the 'atomic' states of affairs, are taken as unanalysed atoms (atomic states of affairs in the *loose* sense, 3.1), then the conjunction behaves in a mereological manner. More precisely: the conjunction, &, is identical with mereological addition, +. Two such conjunctions (including the 'unit conjunction', that is, the 'atoms' of the conjunction) can be disjoint, can overlap, or can stand in the mereological relation of part to whole. This suggests, what seems obviously true, that a conjunction of states of affairs supervenes upon the totality of its conjuncts and that the conjuncts supervene upon the conjunction. If this is correct, then the principle of the ontological free lunch can be applied: there is no ontological cost involved in admitting such molecular states of affairs.

What we have got so far is an analysis of what it is to be a certain methane molecule. We have not yet reached the complex universal *being a methane molecule* which, after all, knows nothing of the particulars *a*, *b*, *c*, *d*, and *e*. But may we not arrive at the universal easily enough? Here, one may suggest, is a picture of it, with the particulars replaced by unsaturated blanks:

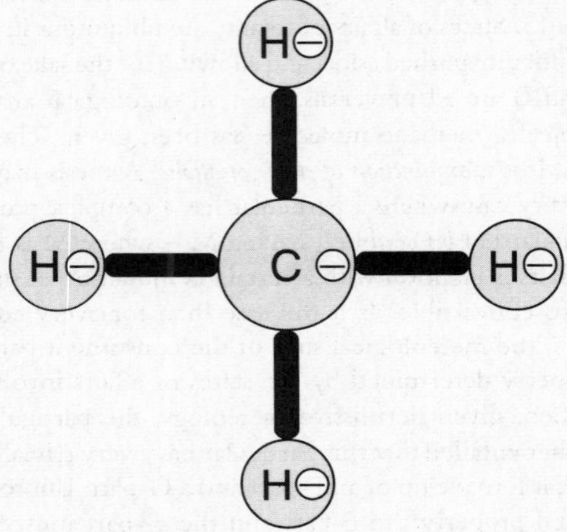

Can we not say that what this pictures is no more nor less than a conjunction of state-of-affairs types? And will not such a conjunction behave in the same simple mereological manner?

This is not quite enough, though. The complex universal is a conjunction (a mereological sum) of state-of-affairs types, and to that extent it behaves in the same manner as the states of affairs that make up an individual methane molecule. But it is something more. A simple case will be best to illustrate the point: the conjunctive property P&Q. The requirement of co-instantiation means that this must be more than the mereological conjunction of *_'s being P* and *_'s being* Q. We need to add that it be *the very same particular* that 'fills the unsaturated space' in each universal. (The analysis of the individual methane molecule provided this feature, though in a way that did not call attention to itself.) Without this addition, the conjunctive universal falls apart and is no more than a mereological conjunction of universals. Universals P and Q might be instantiated at opposite ends of the universe. But in all complex universals there must be this *welding together* of the state-of-affairs types. And notice that it is not always simply a welding by means of the ontological correlate of a binding existential quantifier. It may be necessary, in order to give the correct structure of a particular complex universal, to specify whether the particulars involved are identical, wholly distinct *or standing in part/whole or overlap relations.* Mereology, that is, comes in again for the identity-relations of the particulars involved.

But this having been said, a complex universal *is* a conjunction of state-of-affairs types (or at least this is the claim) even if it is subtly more than such a conjunction. And considered as no more than a conjunction, it will stand in mereological relations to other complex universals.

3.721 *Lewis's objections to such a scheme*

It may be useful here if we anticipate the later course of the argument, and explain why David Lewis would be, is, dissatisfied with an analysis of this sort. What he denies is the lynch-pin of this scheme: states of affairs. He has two reasons. The first is his acceptance of the Quinean view that predicates, *qua* predicates, need not have ontological correlates. Just by itself this would not prevent him recognizing the existence of universals such as H, C and B. But if he were to recognize them, then the true form of e.g. *a's being H* would, according to him, be I(a,H). The symbol 'H' would not be in predicate position, but rather in subject position. The two-place predicate I ('instantiates') would then become something that for him lacked an ontological correlate (except the class that would be its extension) and there would be no state of affairs: *a's having the instantiation relation to H.*

Lewis's second reason is that states of affairs (as opposed to conjunctions of states of affairs) have something that, according to him, is impossible for anything to have: a non-mereological sort of composition. The state of affairs of *a's being H* is not just *a*+H, but according to Lewis there is no other sort of composition besides mereological composition. We will look further into these matters when states of affairs become the explicit subject of discussion.

3.722 *Complex universals involving succession*

We have shown how to analyse *being a methane molecule* as a certain state-of-affairs type. The structure involved is a synchronous structure. It is important to note that there can be structures involving succession. At a certain place and time a billiard-ball hits another billiard-ball, which is followed by the latter moving. We can give this the rough formal representation: *a* has property F, has relation R to *b*, and *b* comes to have property G. Here we have what is natural to call a (token) event, analysed in terms of states of affairs. Clearly, we can abstract from this to reach an event type, that is, a certain complex state-of-affairs type involving succession. We leave this matter for the present, but it becomes of the first importance when we arrive, eventually, at the topic of causality, with one state of affairs bringing about a succeeding state of affairs.

3.8 UNINSTANTIATED UNIVERSALS

We have argued for a conception of universals, both properties and relations, as state-of-affairs types, *unsaturated entities* in Frege's phrase, entities hungry for a certain definite number of particulars, the number corresponding to the -adicity (degree) of the universal. We have also advocated a conception of universals as ways, ways things are and ways things stand to each other. Neither of these conceptions of universals encourage the postulation of uninstantiated universals. An unsaturated entity is naturally seen as a mere abstraction from actual states of affairs, saved from being a vicious abstraction only because there are always saturating particulars. Again, if universals are ways things are, or ways things stand to each other, then it seems implausible to assert that there are entities, the ways, with no thing to be that way or no things to stand that way to each other.

Sydney Shoemaker has objected to this last point that it is at least equally natural to characterize universals as ways things *can* be, a conception that does not rule out uninstantiated universals. But this would have the consequence that universals would then be necessary beings, whereas it is fundamental to the system being developed here that they, like particulars, are contingent beings.

I recognize, however, that the contentions that universals are state-of-affairs types, that they are ways, that they are contingent existences, contentions that together suggest quite strongly that uninstantiated universals should be rejected, are all pretty controversial doctrines. To bring these conceptions of universals against the existence of uninstantiated universals is, to a degree, to beg the question at issue. So here we will first criticize arguments that have been put forward for asserting the existence of uninstantiated universals, and then advance an argument which is intended to give an independent reason for denying their existence.

3.81 Criticism of arguments for uninstantiated universals

At one time uninstantiated universals might have been postulated in order to provide objects to be the meanings of meaningful and non-self-contradictory predicates. But, as Wittgenstein in particular taught, meanings are not objects. A somewhat more persuasive argument is furnished by empirical possibilities that are never realized. Consider the following case. It is known that certain sorts of chemical structure make a chemical a powerful solvent. It may therefore be predicted that a certain compound, which could be manufactured, would be such a solvent. But because of expense, or danger, or the fortuitous collapse of civilization, the compound is never manufactured. Does not this structure exist (it might, after all, be frequently referred to by chemists), and is it not a candidate for an uninstantiated complex property?

I suggest, however, that such reference is but pseudo-reference. Pseudo-reference is common enough with respect to particulars, especially in the case of events. We can speak about that meeting that never took place, and draw out what its consequences would have been. Ontologically, though, we give the meeting no more respect than the present King of France. Science, even science as it is conceived by scientific realists, is full of what can plausibly be construed as convenient fictions. (See Keith Campbell's 'Selective Realism in the Philosophy of Physics', 1994.) A phase-space in physics, for instance, is a 'space' of empirical possibilities, possible boundary-conditions, most of which may never occur. It has turned out to be a most helpful instrument in physical analysis. But the phase-space has no causal power, nor has the uninstantiated chemical structure. So is there any need to assert the existence of either?

This is not the end of the dispute. Evan Fales (1990) argues that there are universals, but that they cannot be brought down into spacetime. Universals are necessarily *transcendent*. If this is correct, then, as he says, it is a rather persuasive, though not conclusive, reason for thinking that uninstantiated universals are *possible*. After all, with universals transcendent, particulars and universals are so easily detachable in thought. A Combinatorialist or a Humean about possibility would certainly want to say that here is a possibility. To go beyond the mere possibility of uninstantiated universals to their actuality, Fales relies on a certain argument of Michael Tooley's. But Tooley's argument depends upon considerations about the nature of laws and, in particular, considerations about uninstantiated laws. It will be some time before we can broach that topic in this essay, but I shall be arguing that Tooley's case does no more, at best, than show the *unrealized possibility* of uninstantiated universals (16.3). If I am right about this, then Tooley's argument does not significantly advance Fales' argument.

But if we want to uphold Naturalism, yet at the same time admit universals, we must also deny the first step in Fales' argument: that universals are transcendent. An important step, one already adumbrated in 1.31, is to argue that the hypothesis that the world is a world of states of affairs, with universals as constituents of these states of affairs, is compatible with the hypothesis that the world is exhausted by the spacetime system. So far from being removed from spacetime, universals will, on this view, help to constitute spacetime. They do this by helping to constitute the states of affairs that in turn constitute spacetime. Spacetime is a vast conjunction of states of affairs.

Another line of thought that might lead one to the postulation of uninstantiated universals is the consideration of mathematical entities. It seems that in this metaphysic these entities will, in general, have to be universals. Yet, perhaps, some of these are uninstantiated. Consider, in particular, very large infinite cardinals. We do not know whether there is a finite or an infinite number of first-order particulars in the universe. And even if the number is infinite we do not know how large an infinity it is. Indeed, unless it is the case that for *every* infinite number (and there is an infinity of such infinite numbers) there exists that number of first-order particulars, then there are infinite numbers which number no class of particulars, or at any rate number no class of first-order particulars. These infinite numbers are candidates for being uninstantiated universals.

It may be said against this that it will always be possible to find entities that *instantiate* these infinities. Set theory will see to it. Given just one ultimate individual, one can build up sets of sets that have any desired cardinality. They will ensure that all infinite numbers are instantiated.

But this is a reply that I do not wish to avail myself of. The sets upon sets that are used to create classes with the right cardinality are things manufactured *a priori*. It is not at all clear that here we have genuine instances falling under genuine universals. (See the discussion of classes to come in ch. 12.) Instead I prefer to meet the argument to uninstantiated universals from the infinite numbers by arguing for a deflationary doctrine of mathematical existence. (Already defended in Armstrong, 1989b, ch. 9.) For a mathematical entity to 'exist', according to this view, is for it to be a *possible* property or relation (not necessarily a universal, see 3.9), one that could be instantiated. One great advantage of this theory is that it enables us to understand how it is that mathematics can proceed in the *a priori* fashion that it does. Some mathematical properties, structures and relations will be genuine properties or relations. These will be cases where the mathematical entities are actually instantiated in the physical world, or in any other particulars that really exist. Others, of which the bigger infinite cardinals may be instances, are merely possible properties or relations, and do not exist any more than anything else that is *merely* possible. We will return to this question in chapter 11.

A final argument for uninstantiated universals is that they fill in gaps. Let us suppose that the 'missing shade of blue' is never instantiated. Postulating its existence gives continuity to a family of universals, in something the way that postulating the continuous existence of an unobserved physical object may correlate what is observed at one time with what was observed at a previous time.

The argument must be given a little force, but I doubt whether the postulation of an uninstantiated universal ever has any *explanatory* value. This makes it very different from the unobserved physical object, which serves to explain a good deal. We will not expect anything else in the world to be different because the universal exists. (See the immediately following 3.82.) That being so, we appear to have no more than an argument from neatness. I am assuming, of course, that universals, like particulars, are contingent existences. But I know of no good argument for their necessity. It is true that it is open to us to treat universals as I have just suggested numbers are treated. We could take the 'existence' of universals to be no more than the *possibility* of their instantiation. But what is *merely* possible does not really exist, although it may be convenient to talk about its existing in certain contexts.

3.82 The eleatic argument against uninstantiated universals

If uninstantiated universals exist, they are entities that are nowhere and nowhen. Given this, the (metaphysical) hypothesis that uninstantiated universals exist contradicts Naturalism as it is defined in this work. It contradicts the *negative* portion of that thesis: that there is nothing over and above the spacetime system. The following argument, which concludes that we have no good reason to postulate such universals, has been dubbed by Graham Oddie (1982) the Eleatic Principle (after the Eleatic Stranger in Plato's *Sophist*). Adapting a suggestion made to me by Michael Pendlebury it may be formulated thus:

Everything that exists makes a difference to the causal powers of something.

The wording is meant to get round annoying counter-instances to the simpler formula that everything that exists has causal power. For instance, it can be argued that it is wrong to attribute causal power to properties, instantiated or uninstantiated, on the grounds that it is things, particulars, that have causal power. But we can certainly say that it is in virtue of the properties of particulars that the particulars have the powers they have. The properties make a difference causally. Again, does the causal relation itself have causal power? Perhaps not, but without the relation nothing else could have causal power! It makes a difference.

It may be that the Principle should be widened to allow for any irreducibly non-causal laws that there are, and so that making a difference to *nomic* power should be substituted for, or inserted alongside, causal power. But however that may be, the argument for the Principle seems to be epistemic and even pragmatic. If an entity makes no difference to the causal powers of anything, then there would never be any good reason for postulating that thing's existence. Our whole experience, including all our thinking, would go on in exactly the same way whether or not the entity existed. So why postulate it?

But what is the truthmaker for the Eleatic Principle, if it is true? Is it just the totality state of affairs that there is nothing that fails to make some sort of causal contribution, nothing that is epiphenomenal in any way? Or could it be a basic *law* of the world that there are no epiphenomena? The latter would be attractive, but I will have to leave this question as too hard. It is a distinct, if related, question from the epistemic question what reason we have to accept the Principle.

In any case, Michael Tooley has pointed out to me that although the Eleatic Principle would serve to outlaw uninstantiated universals, it seems that a somewhat stronger principle is really wanted. For consider a counterpart of David Lewis who restricts Lewisian realism about possible worlds to ones where the Eleatic Principle holds sway. The Principle would not rule out this postulation, yet our whole experience would go on in exactly the same way whether these worlds of powerful things existed or did not exist. It seems that we really want to outlaw things that have no causal power, actual or potential, *in relation to the actual world*. That, though, is getting a little too close to a new Verification Principle, although it would not have to be taken as a semantic Principle, a principle about what statements make sense. I do not know what to say here, and will again leave the matter in uncertainty.

It is worth noticing, though, that the Eleatic Principle cannot be used against some of the entities postulated by non-Naturalists. A transcendent Deity is outside spacetime, but has causal power (and power in our spacetime) if anything has.

Could uninstantiated universals be defended by being credited with causal powers? Plato may have thought that they had such powers. (See the *Phaedo*.) But it would not be easy to turn this into contemporary scientific doctrine. The most plausible way of trying to endow uninstantiated universals with causal powers would appear to be this. One could say that *if* such a universal had been instantiated (by hypothesis it never was or will be) then the particulars instantiating the universal would have certain powers in virtue of this instantiation. In effect, the uninstantiated universal would be put forward as the ontological ground or truthmaker for this counterfactual.

While this looks to be the best one can do for uninstantiated universals in face of the Principle, the *evidence* on which such a counterfactual could be asserted must all come from the powers bestowed by instantiated universals. The uninstantiated universal would have to be, say, a 'missing value' of some functional law. The question arises, then, whether the truthmaker for the counterfactual cannot be found in the *instantiated* values of the function. It will be a reduced truthmaker, but perhaps sufficient for all that. The matter will have to be resolved at a later point (see 16.22), but it is to be hoped that a sufficiently plausible truthmaker can be pointed to which enables one to continue to uphold Naturalism and reject uninstantiated universals.

This whole section (3.8) has left a good deal of unfinished business. Some have alleged that there are, or that there could be, laws of nature that require postulation of uninstantiated universals. It has further been alleged by others that it is impossible to 'bring universals down to spacetime', something that, as Fales has pointed out, would at least strengthen the case for uninstantiated universals, and which would in any case greatly weaken the credit of universals with me. These allegations still have to be adjudicated. The Eleatic Principle looks attractive, but raises some unresolved problems. But, even so, the case for all universals being instantiated seems quite strong.

3.9 'SECOND-CLASS' PROPERTIES, RELATIONS, AND STATES OF AFFAIRS

The world is no more than a world of states of affairs, and these states of affairs have as their constituents particulars, properties and relations, the properties and relations being universals. It is natural science which tries to identify the universals for us. This is the thesis. But, of course, philosophy and other disciplines, not to mention ordinary discourse, have endless occasion to speak about properties and relations which, from the standpoint of an *a posteriori* realism about universals, have little claim to be universals. This essay itself is not able to stick to the austere standard that it appears to have embraced. From time to time it is necessary to talk about properties and relations that are not universals. There are, for instance, good *a posteriori* reasons for thinking that colour-qualities, together with many other perceptual qualities, are not universals.

I shall therefore distinguish between first-class, second-class and third-class properties (and relations). This distinction is relativized to the particulars that have these properties, or between which these relations hold. (From this point on, I will speak only of properties. Extension to relations seems straightforward.)

The first-class properties of particulars are the universals they instantiate. The second-class properties of particulars have the following necessary and sufficient condition. They are not universals, but when truly predicated of a particular, the resultant truth is a contingent one. The rationale behind this is, first, that second-class properties are to be thought of as constituents of (second-class) states of affairs, and states of affairs are all contingent. Second, with contingent attachment of a property to a particular, *and only with contingent attachment*, do we have increase of being over the particular that the property attaches to. The italicized clause of the second thesis is controversial, of course, and in chapters 9 and 10 we will confront the genuinely strong intellectual pressures there are to abandon it. But I seek to uphold it. It is linked to the contention that all states of affairs are contingent.

Where increase of being is lacking, we will speak of third-class properties of particulars. *Being identical with a* is undoubtedly true of *a*. But there is no state of affairs involved, no genuine 'is' of predication. So it is a third-class property of *a*.

We turn back now to the second-class properties of particulars. What is their status? Will it be said that they do not exist? That will be a difficult saying, since it can hardly be denied that innumerable statements in which these property- and relation-words appear are *true*. Some bridge between the universals, which are the first-class properties and relations, and the second-class properties and relations, is urgently required.

The suggested bridge is a thesis of supervenience. (It is, of course, a thesis only, and so is disputable.) Second-class properties, as we have said, require second-class states of affairs, contingent states of affairs where second-class properties truly attach to particulars (which may themselves be in some way second-class). The supervenience thesis is this. Given all the first-class states of affairs, all the second-class states of affairs supervene, are entailed, are necessitated. This will involve the supervenience of all second-class properties that can be truly predicated.

Qs supervene on Ps if and only if there are P-worlds and every possible P-world is a Q-world. Alternatively put, worlds that are not Q-worlds are not P-worlds. No difference in what supervenes without some difference in the base that it supervenes upon, with absolute necessity. Take the totality of all first-class states of affairs. Any world that has *just* these states of affairs, with their constituent properties that are all universals, will exactly agree in all second-class states of affairs with their second-class properties. That is the thesis.

To this is added the thesis of the ontological free lunch. What supervenes in this strong sense is not something that is ontologically anything more than what it supervenes upon. The second-class states of affairs are no addition of being to the totality of first-class states of affairs. And the second-class properties are not properties ontologically additional to the first-class properties.

Why should we accept this thesis of supervenience and with it the thesis that the supervenient second-class states of affairs are no ontological addition? Principally, it would seem, because of its superior simplicity. If it really is true that the world is a world that contains (first-class) states of affairs, then the natural way to develop this hypothesis is that these states of affairs do not require a further set of states of affairs, ones whose properties are often suspiciously predicate-dependent, suspiciously oriented towards human classifications.

The second-class states of affairs are no addition of being. So the second-class properties are not properties additional to the first-class properties. But it is to be emphasized that this does not make the second-class properties unreal. They are real and cannot be talked away. They can properly be said to bestow causal efficacy on the particulars that they are properties of, even if such speech must be taken with a small grain of salt. (Such causal truths have second-class states of affairs as their preliminary truthmakers.) There is emphatically no possibility of *semantic* descent from these properties to the first-class properties by means of conceptual analysis, a descent that Wittgenstein seems to envisage in the *Tractatus*. What is more, *in the order of knowledge*, the second-class properties actually come first. They are the perceptual properties, the properties of the 'manifest image'. Indeed, it is only relative to the arcane discipline of ontology that they can be called 'second-class'. But in the order of being, so the claim is, they are not something more than the first-class properties.

To illustrate, let us suppose that microreductive physics turns out to be able to give us a complete scientific theory of the nature of the world. (This view is here neither endorsed nor rejected. Physicalism, which *is* upheld in this work, does not entail microreductive Physicalism.) But given the truth of microreductive physics, the ultimate particulars are the truly fundamental particles. Their ultimate properties and ultimate relations are the ultimate universals, thus yielding us the ultimate states of affairs. All the properties, relations and states of affairs recognized in less fundamental sciences and in ordinary discourse will supervene on these ultimates, and so, according to the argument, will be no addition of being.

Before leaving the topic of the supervenience of second-class properties on properties that are universals, a special but interesting case of the supervenience of *universals* on universals is worth mentioning here. Suppose it to be the case that every property-universal is nothing but a structure of property-universals in relation, a supposition that sets up an infinite regress of dissolution of properties. A consequence that ensues under this supposition is that *every property is supervenient* (relative to some base). This sounds very strange, but is not really particularly difficult.

The point to appreciate is that, as we have defined it (2.1), supervenience can be symmetrical. P can supervene on Q, and Q on P. And in such a case, I contend further, we have identity. Our present case is one of symmetrical supervenience, and, fairly obviously, identity. As we go down the infinite regress of structures, we are doing no more than analysing the original universal more and more deeply, even though the analysis can have no termination. The ubiquity of the supervenience then seems harmless. There is an asymmetry, but it is an asymmetry of depth of analysis.

The present importance of this is that if the supposition is coherent, then this helps to remove the suspicion that the supervenient is unreal, lacking in causal power and so on. It is no *increase* of being, but that does not make it non-being. This applies to the second-class properties as much as to first-class properties, the universals.

A final note. We have rejected disjunctive and negative universals, with the possible exception of ones admitted selectively, on *a posteriori*, scientific, grounds. But there will be no objection to admitting disjunctive and negative properties, and admitting them promiscuously, provided it is recognized that they are at best second-class properties.

The third-class properties are, of course, supervenient also.

4

Properties II

4.1 RESEMBLANCES AMONG UNIVERSALS

4.11 Introductory

The topic of properties is not easily disposed of! We come now to consider one of the most difficult issues in the theory of universals. Not only do particulars resemble, but so do properties and relations. And just as particulars may resemble each other more or less closely, so the same is true of properties and relations. Thus: all the colours resemble each other, and a consideration of red, orange and yellow, and again red, purple and blue, shows that one colour can resemble a second colour more than it resembles a third.

Before getting on with our main topic, it is interesting and important to notice that these very same resemblance relations appear among the tropes. Suppose that the colours spoken of in the last sentence of the previous paragraph are not universals, but are particulars, tropes. Any red trope resembles any orange trope more than it resembles any yellow trope, and any red trope resembles any purple trope more than it resembles any blue trope. What we have is a further parallelism between universals and tropes. We will not, however, take the matter further here. (But see Armstrong, 1989a, ch. 6, sec. V especially.)

Resemblance orderings of universals are not subjective phenomena. This is obvious in the case of most of the great orderings of properties into classes. The class of the lengths and the class of the masses (taken as universals, the yard, the kilometre, the kilo, the ton and so forth) quite obviously go together and our whole science would not be objective if these were not objective orderings. Degrees of resemblance may perhaps be thought to be less objective for such classes as the colours or the shapes. But for the classes of the lengths or the masses their one-dimensional ordering seems perfectly objective, and even the more recalcitrant cases seem more a matter of alternative and complex objective orderings than genuine subjectivity.

Certain attempts to reduce these resemblance orderings of universals to truths about ordinary first-order particulars are known to fail. Here one can build on the work of others. Frank Jackson has shown that 'Red is a colour', although it entails 'All red things are coloured', cannot be reduced to the second statement (1977). Previously, Arthur Pap (1959) pointed out that 'Red resembles orange more than it resembles yellow' does not reduce to 'Each red thing resembles any orange thing more than it resembles any yellow thing'. (This second statement is not even true.) These results, incidentally, form part of the case for accepting the existence of properties, although they do not show that these properties must be universals (Armstrong, 1978a, ch. 6).

4.12 Determinables and Determinates

The resemblance of universals can to a great degree be organized using W. E. Johnson's scheme of *determinables* and *determinates* (1921, ch. XI). Properties such as having length, having mass and having colour are determinables. Absolutely specific lengths, absolutely specific masses and absolutely specific shades of colour are (lowest) determinates. We should pay attention to no fewer than five features of the relation between determinable and determinate.

(1) If an ordinary particular has a determinable property, then it is entailed that it has some determinate property, some more particular length or mass or colour, right down to the absolutely determinate lengths, masses or absolutely precise shades of colour. (Here we will not concern ourselves with the intermediate determinates, the ones that fall between highest determinables and lowest determinates.) Possession of the determinable property, however, does not entail possession of any *particular* determinate among the ones that fall under that determinable.

(2) But to have a determinate property entails having the corresponding determinable. If a particular is of length one metre exact, of mass one kilogram exact or of some absolutely precise shade of red, then it is entailed that it has length, or mass, or colour.

(3) If a particular has a determinate property, then it cannot have a further determinate falling under the same determinable and at the same level of determinates (e.g. at the lowest level). Thus, a particular cannot, at one time, have two different lengths, or two different masses, or two different colours at the very same place. (For some classes of properties that would rather naturally be classified as determinates falling under a

single determinable, this feature *may* be absent. Consider, for instance, the tastes.)

(4) The determinable/determinate relationship is to be distinguished from the superficially similar genus/species relation. The reason for this is that a species can be defined *per genus and differentia*, where the genus and differentia are two distinct properties that can be instantiated in independence of each other. But there seems to be no way that a determinate can be defined by means of its determinable plus some independent differentia.

(5) Finally, let us not forget the point from which this section started: the resemblance of universals. Inside a class of determinates falling under a single determinable, there are systematic resemblances between the determinates. In particular they can be *ordered*, ordered in such a way that there are different degrees of resemblance between different determinates. A metre in length falls between an inch and a mile, a pound in mass falls between a gram and a kilogram and orange falls between yellow and red. Determinables (highest determinables) exhibit no such order among themselves.

It can be seen that the relationship between determinables and determinates is a very complex affair. It is also rather a mysterious one. How are we to explain all these facts, as I take them to be? It is not a very attractive idea that we should just accept these features with natural piety, and declare them not to be further analysable. At the same time, the complexity of the relationship may help us in the search for an explication of its nature. Any theory about what determinables and determinates are which can plausibly explain *all* the five features that attention has just been drawn to, must have quite a lot going for it.

Some preliminary reflections. Properties that are lowest determinates, that is, that are not at the same time determinables to still lower determinates, are good candidates for universals. One can appeal yet again to the powerful truism that universals are strictly identical in their distinct instantiations. Exact sameness of length, exact sameness of mass, exact sameness of colour shade, all these suggest strict identity. (A trope theory would equally find them plausible cases of exact resemblance.) I am not saying that here are knock-down cases. Scientific investigation might discredit claims for strict identity, for instance in the case of colour. But we have here good *prima facie* cases of strict identity, and for the purposes of the present investigation it will do no harm to accept such cases at face value.

But it is not so clear that determin*ables* are universals. For it is not at all obvious that when two things have different lengths, then there is something *identical* that both the things, or perhaps both the lengths, have. The same doubt applies to things with different masses or different colours. The (epistemic) possibility of identity is not to be ruled out, and, indeed, at a later point (16.13) we will argue that in certain central cases identity really is present, as a property possessed by each member of a class of determinates. But it should not be automatically ruled in. A point to consider very seriously is that because determinates entail the corresponding determinable, the determinable supervenes upon the determinates, and so, apparently, is not something ontologically more than the determinates. This may make us suspect that, often at least, determinable *predicates* are applied to first-order particulars, or to determinate universals, in virtue of nothing more than the fact that the determinate universals form a certain sort of class of universals.

What sort of class might this be? What links the members of such a class of determinate universals? What gives the class its unity if not a common property? Resemblance is the obvious first answer, but it cannot be exact resemblance. Different universals cannot resemble exactly, because if they did, then they would be the same universal. (This, I think, is the point behind Plato's rather obscure 'Third Bed' argument in the *Republic* (597). He argued that there could not be two Forms of the Bed, because, if there were, one Bed would appear above them, and that would be the Form.) We have noted also that resemblance is an internal relation, so the resemblance of universals must flow from the nature of the universals themselves. Again, less than exact resemblance admits of degrees. (Recall the different degrees of resemblance among members of a class of determinates.) Indeed, for universals, exact resemblance can be thought of as an unreachable limit to which inexact resemblance can approximate.

Should we treat resemblance as a primitive notion? A philosophy of universals will not easily be content with this. But how are we to avoid it? Traditionally, upholders of universals analyse resemblance as resemblance in a respect, and the respect they think of as a property, and the property they think of as a universal. Given this way of thinking, consider the class of determinates falling under a certain highest determinable. The class will be very numerous. Any two of these determinates resemble each other, at least to some degree. So each of these resemblances will require universals. A huge number of extra universals will be required, one for each resemblance-pair, and the nature and status of these universals is unclear. If we want to get away from primitive, unanalysable, resemblance, as I think we should want, some other analysis of resemblance seems preferable for the case of resembling determinates. (Peter Forrest has pointed out to me that since a trope philosophy admits resemblance and its degrees as a primitive, it could unite a class of determinates falling under a single determinable simply by appealing to resemblance.)

My suggestion for a theory that works with universals rather than tropes is that we should explain such resemblance in terms of *partial identity*.

4.13 Determinates linked by partial identity

We have already introduced and briefly discussed the notion of partial identity (2.32), which, it will be remembered, is quite different from the notion of loose or Butler/Geach 'identity'. The present idea is that the resemblance of determinate universals is constituted by partial identity, where the greater the resemblance the greater is the degree of identity.

I will first set out the suggested analysis in an abstract way, and then illustrate it by considering a particular case. We will consider a class of determinates, lowest determinates, all and only those falling under one highest determinable. We will take it that each such determinate is a universal, though we should not overlook the possibility that there are determinates that are 'second-class' properties and relations, ones that are not universals (3.9). But confining ourselves here to determinates that are universals, what is the uniting principle of such a class?

Since different such classes of determinates do not intersect, it is likely that what we have here is an equivalence class, falling under some particular equivalence relation. Without trying to specify this relation directly (it may differ from determinate to determinate), my proposal is that it is a complex relation involving partial identities, ones which hold either directly or recursively between any two members of the one equivalence class. In the best sort of case, found in one-dimensional quantities such as duration and mass, each member stands directly in a partial identity relation to every other member of the class. Probably this is not a necessary condition for all classes of determinates.

The partial identity here is the sort of partial identity that can hold between universals. To take simple cases, it is the sort of partial identity that holds between the conjunctive universal P&Q and P, or between P&Q and Q&R. We have noted that this relation is close to, but is not quite, a purely mereological relation. It is internal, flowing from the nature of the universals involved, and it admits of degrees.

The claim is that every class of determinates falling under a determinable is held together by partial identities. I am not claiming that this proposition is convertible. There may well be classes of universals where the members are linked by partial identity but it is not the case that the class-members fall under a common determinable. Furthermore, as already noted, it remains possible that *some* of these classes are unified in a more direct manner. It is possible for some of these classes that to the determinable *predicate* there corresponds a property, a determinable universal. But this possible mode of unification of a class of determinates, important for understanding functional laws, will not concern us until chapter 16. The present concern is to expound and defend the partial identity thesis.

Two *simple* things cannot be partially identical. They must be wholly different or not two at all. So if the resemblance of determinates is to be partial identity, the universals involved must be complex. We have already proposed in the discussion of the methane molecule (treated for the sake of the example as the methane universal) that we give an account of complex universals as *conjunctions* of state-of-affairs types (3.72). They are conjunctions of unsaturated entities, state-of-affairs types, which latter, be it remembered, are not fully states of affairs. They are, rather, truncated states of affairs, states of affairs considered apart from ('abstracted from') the particulars that, when the latter are 'added' to the state-of-affairs types, make them into states of affairs. This insight, as I take it to be, I did not have fully available in previous treatments of this topic (1978b, chs. 21 & 22 is the most extended of these). It is to be hoped that this Fregean conception of universals will make things clearer here.

We can now make the argument more concrete. Start with a simple case. Consider the relationships of three universals: three units of duration, two units of duration and a single unit of duration. Call the three universals 3T, 2T and 1T. Consider now 3T. This duration is a certain state-of-affairs type. It is identical (strict identity) with all sorts of conjunctions of state-of-affairs types. As David Lewis has put it to me, it has 'multiple parsings'. We here select one of these parsings. It is identical with a conjunctive or molecular state-of-affairs type: the conjunction of three states of affairs. Each conjunct is of the following type: some particular or other having duration 1T, and where the three particulars have no overlap, that is, are not even partially identical, but together make up an instance of the original 3T type of particular. One conceivably needs to add a further condition that the three particulars (which in this particular case can be thought of as events) form a *continuous* larger particular. But it does not seem that this extra condition plays any special part in our present argument, so it will be given no further notice here.

Now consider the relation that holds between the three universals, that is, state-of-affairs types, *a particular's having duration 3T* and *a particular's having duration 2T* and *a particular's having duration 1T*. (Remember that the phrase *a particular* in these three formulae stands for an unsaturated blank.) A relation of partial identity holds. (It is the part to whole as opposed to the overlap sort of partial identity.) Complex, that is, molecular, state-of-affairs types are quasi-mereological complexes of atomic or relatively atomic state-of-affairs types. They are conjunctions of state-of-affairs types, conjunctions of unsaturated entities. We have seen in 3.72 that complex state-of-affairs types, that is, complex universals, are something subtly more than *mere* conjunctions of simpler state-of-affairs types. There has to be a linking together of the blanks for the particulars involved in the state-of-affairs types, a linking that gives a definite and united structure. (For instance, in the methane molecule the four hydrogen atoms have to be linked to *one and the same* carbon atom.) But this extra condition does not abrogate the simple mereological relations that hold between the state-of-affairs types.

Let us now see how the analysis of this example can deal with the phenomena to be explained: the intricate connections of determinable and determinate properties laid out at the beginning of 4.12.

(1) We can say, in part at least, what a determinable is and why it entails that some determinate or other must be instantiated. For a particular to 'instantiate' a determinable is (at least) for it to instantiate just one of a class of universals united in a certain way by partial identities. In the case of duration these partial identities hold between *any* two members of the class of duration universals. So, in the way I have sought to explain two paragraphs back, enduring for ten years is partially identical with enduring for ten seconds.

(2) It follows from our analysis that having one of the determinates entails that the particular having it also has the determinable 'property'. For having the determinable property entails no more than having one of the determinate properties. It may be remarked here that we have to be a little careful about the extension of the class of the determinates, the extension in terms of which the determinable is characterized. After all,

instantiation of one determinate does not entail that any of the other determinates exist, at any rate if they have to be instantiated to exist, as I hold. So the class of the actual determinates falling under a particular determinable may be a sub-class of the class of the *possible* determinates falling under that determinable.

(3) It can also be seen why the determinates exclude each other, that is, why different determinates falling under the same determinable cannot instantiate the same particular at the same time. There are complex universals, complex state-of-affairs types, such that a universal that is a proper part of these universals cannot qualify the very same particular that the complex universal qualifies. To see that this is so, consider, by way of *contrast* with the partial identities that we are at present considering, the universal P&Q and the universal P and the universal Q. The former is a matter of some particular being P and the very same particular being Q. (Remember as ever that the 'same particular' here is an unsaturated blank.) Something's being P and something's being Q are proper parts of the conjunctive universal. But in the case of the duration-determinates which are our present concern, the particulars involved in any two of these state-of-affairs types are such that they, the particulars, are partially identical only. One of the two particulars is a whole of which the other is a proper part. For two of the determinates to qualify the very same particular, that particular would have to be identical with its proper part, which would make it non-identical with itself.

There is a tricky point here. If a thing endures for a day, there is a sense in which it endures for each lesser unit of time. If a thing has mass of one pound, there is a sense in which it has all lesser masses. If asked if one has a pound of potatoes, it would be a little strange to reply that, on the contrary, one had five. This suggests that we ought to say that a certain particular endures for a day, or has a mass of one pound, *and no more*. And this in turn suggests that totality states of affairs must be introduced in deriving incompatibilities of determinates.

It seems, though, that if we have determinate properties (and relations) in our ontology, then this is not necessary. A certain particular instantiates the duration of one day. It is *other particulars*, some of which are proper parts of the original particular, that instantiate other durations. A particular has the mass of five pounds. It is other particulars, some of which are proper parts of the original particular, that instantiate other masses.

(4) It also becomes reasonably clear why the determinable/determinate relation is different from the genus/species relation. The species is defined

by means of the genus and an independent differentia. If one tries to define a certain determinate duration by reference to its determinable, no independent differentia can be found which, when added to the determinable of duration yields the determinate. There is the determinable, there is the class of the determinates, and there is nothing else available in the situation to add to the determinable with which to reach the individual determinates.

(5) Finally, different degrees of resemblance between determinates under the one determinable are explained. The resemblances of all the determinate durations under a single determinable is a matter of partial identity. Since partial identity, including partial identity of universals, of state-of-affairs types, admits of degree, the resemblances in question admit of degree.

4.14 Difficult cases for this analysis

Lengths, durations and masses seem to yield to this sort of treatment sketched in the previous section fairly readily. They are remarkably unified classes of determinates. Given any two determinates under the same determinable, one universal, one state-of-affairs type (one determinate) is partially identical with the other universal, the other state-of-affairs type (the other determinate). Again, if a determinate universal U is instantiated, then each particular that instantiates U will have, for every 'lesser' determinate, at least one proper part that instantiates that determinate. Thus, an event of duration D will, for each determinate duration less than D, contain at least one event that instantiates that duration. A tightly-knit class of universals indeed!

Evan Fales, however (1990, p. 231), objects that an account of this sort cannot be generalized to *shapes*. He was working with earlier formulations of mine (1978b) which left something to be desired. It may be conceded at the outset that the unity of the class of shapes is a much messier affair than the lengths, durations and masses, which all arrange themselves as simple one-dimensional arrays. But with the three clues of (1) states of affairs, (2) universals as state-of-affairs types, and (3) the idea that complex properties break down into quasi-mereological conjunctions of state-of-affairs types, it is at least plausible that cases like that of the shapes can be dealt with.

Let us start by giving ourselves the notion of a Euclidean flat plane, a notion that it seems could be cashed out in terms of a state-of-affairs type, perhaps involving arrays of points, and then consider some shapes in that plane. What is it to be a triangle? It is to be a thing enclosed by boundaries having just three parts, each of which is a straight line. Here we have three non-overlapping particulars, each of which has the properties of being straight and being a line. I lack the mathematical knowledge to give a further account of these properties, but lines involve *length* and that is a determinable of a type that I have claimed to give an account of. These three lines are related to each other. Each of the lines meet the other two at their end points and there form an angle. There seems nothing here that cannot be spelt out in terms of properties of the three boundaries and relations of the three boundaries to each other. This can then be spelt out as a conjunction of state-of-affairs types involving the three parts. What is it to be a quadrilateral? Here four boundaries are required, again they are straight lines, and they are connected by the lines meeting at an angle at end points, the lines being linked up in cyclic and non-intersecting fashion. The difference between the two shapes lies in the difference between three straight lines and four straight lines (which ensures that a triangle cannot be a square) while the resemblance lies in the fact that the parts involved are three and four *straight lines*, lines which are connected up according to the same formula. The series of triangle, quadrilateral, pentagon . . . obviously does not exhaust the shapes, but a beginning has been made with some simple ones. The formal relations between the determinates, the different shape universals, are obviously more complex than those that obtain in the case of the simple one-dimensional cases. But it is submitted that the resemblance of universals has begun to look a lot less mysterious for the case of shape, as does the relation between the determinable *shape* and the determinate shapes.

Another difficult case, put to me by Peter Forrest, is that of directions in space. Consider the directions from a certain point. They form a family of determinates under a determinable. These determinates resemble in different degrees. Thus, E–N–E is more like N–E than S–W. Is there partial identity there?

It seems that there is such identity. Consider the relation of radial angle, a universal, that separates any two of the directions. Such angles differ in size. The angle between E–N–E and N–E is greater than the angle between E–N–E and S–W. The first angle has two proper parts of which the second angle is one. So, without going into details, it seems that the complex universals involved, and their logical relations, can be analysed along the same general lines.

The analysis of complex universals is a probably endless business. It involves both logico-conceptual and mathematical analysis, and, more importantly, *a posteriori* scientific investigation. As a result, the hypothesis that complex universals may be analysed as conjunctions of state-of-affairs types is difficult both to confirm and to disconfirm conclusively. But perhaps it has been given a certain plausibility here. Provisionally, it looks as if determinable properties are not universals, or more cautiously, need not be universals, but are classes of universals united by all sorts of complex partial identities. To attribute a determinable property to a first-order particular is to assert that the particular instantiates one member of that class.

There are at least two important threats to an analysis of determinable/determinate relationships along these lines that require discussion. The first threat comes from the (epistemic) possibility that there are quantities that are irreducibly *intensive*. Discussion of this is postponed until 4.22. The second difficulty will receive our immediate attention.

The second threat has already been touched upon. If there are good reasons to think that simple, or near simple, properties could stand in the determinable/determinate relationship then the theory adumbrated above would have to be abandoned. For it is only if the universals involved are complex that determinates can be exhibited as overlapping state-of-affairs types. In practice this means that much hangs upon what might be called the pride and the sorrow of analytic philosophy. I refer, of course, to the colours. What attitude we take to the colours in turn hangs upon what weight we give to *phenomenology*.

4.141 Colour

(This rather lengthy discussion could be omitted, especially by convinced physicalists.) The phenomenology of colour appears to tell us this: these properties are simple or relatively simple; and they are completely distinct from the primary properties of things in the environment, or possibly in the brain, with which the colours are correlated. Primary properties show promise of being analysable in terms of complex universals, complex state-of-affairs types, in a way that will make the relations between determinables and determinates reasonably transparent. (See the accounts already given of duration, length, mass and the gestures toward an account of shape.) But how is the same trick to be worked for the relation of the determinable *colour* to the individual *colours* if colours are as their phenomenology tells us they are? Their simplicity or at least relative simplicity will forbid any analysis in terms of long conjunctions of state-of-affairs types.

While feeling the force of the phenomenological case, I wish to resist it. The prospect of theoretical unification held out by the theory of the resemblance of universals just sketched seems too tempting. A physicalist account of the colours seems required for this theoretical unification, so here is a point where the thesis of Physicalism becomes a premiss on which a portion of the metaphysics of this book rests. Furthermore, there are some relatively independent reasons for rejecting the phenomenological case. One consideration is the difficulty of working out a satisfactory theory of *perception* if colours are really as they appear to be.

To expand. There are good reasons for holding a theory of perception that is (i) Cognitivist and (ii) Direct Realist. By 'cognitivist' is meant that a satisfactory theory will hold that perception is essentially the acquiring of information (a term which is here understood to cover misinformation) about the world. Perception is propositional (though obviously not linguistic) and so, incidentally, it conforms itself to a world of states of affairs. By 'Direct Realist' is understood that the information is, from the beginning, about the current state of the perceiver's environment and body together with their relationships, and not about the state of the perceiver's mind or brain. (See Armstrong, 1968a, ch. 10, and for a more recent defence of a direct realism about colour see my 'Reply to Campbell' in Bacon, Campbell and Reinhardt, 1993.) All this fits in naturally with a view of perception as a biological function of organisms. What organisms need is information about the way things are presently arranged in their environment and in their own body, and how that body is at present related to the environment.

Now consider the perception of colour from this perspective. Colour presents itself as a property of physical surfaces and in some cases volumes. It seems clear from what is now known about the perception of colour that the causal chain from surface or volume to the eye is set in train by very small-scale physical processes in these objects, processes whose nature and physical action are governed by ordinary physical laws. These physical processes are very complex, unlike the colours as they are perceived. Yet they are correlated – in a complex and apparently very disjunctive manner – with the colours and with the differences perceived among the colours. Under these circumstances, I submit, despite the disjunctiveness, we have good reason to identify the colours with physical states of the objects, or with processes in these objects. The relative simplicity of the content of colour perception is to be explained as a failure to perceive all there is to perceive about the nature of these processes or states, including a failure to perceive their disjunctivity. The disjunctivity entails that colour is a 'second-class' property, that the colours are not universals.

The direct realist who rejects this identity view will have to argue that the colours are distinct from, though correlated with, the physical processes. But now let such a *non*-reductive direct realist consider the hypothesis that the colours as he or she conceives them (out in the world, unreduced) do not exist, but that the physical processes, laws, etc. are unchanged. Why would the *experience* of colour be any different from the experience actually had? Same causes and laws, same effects. This goes some way, not the whole way obviously, but some way, to suggest that a reductive account of colour ought to be correct. (Alternatively, much less attractively I think, it suggests an Eliminativist account of colour. Colour would be a 'false imaginary glare', to use a wonderful phrase of Berkeley's for a view that he, of course, rejected. See his *Second Dialogue*, p. 74.)

Some direct realists who reject the reduction of colour-properties to physical properties of external objects may be attracted to the expedient of saying that colour is a property of our perceivings rather than what is perceived, of our experience not of what is experienced. (Some philosophers suggest that colour is a *relation* holding between our minds and external objects, but this is mysterious in the extreme.) Colour, a property of our perceivings, is then 'projected' onto, that is, erroneously attributed to, external objects.

I am inclined to think that supporters of the projection theory have not really thought it through. The other instances of projection that are cited as precedents are various strong attitudes, whether of attraction or revulsion, which, as we all experience, seem to invest things or events with an objective correlate of the attitude. Hume, in a wonderful conceit, spoke of the mind's disposition to spread itself on external objects. (See the *Treatise*, bk 1, pt. 3, sec. XIV. See also the *Enquiry concerning Morals*, Appendix 1, last para, on the mind's 'gilding and staining' all natural objects. David Stove drew my attention to the latter passage.)

But this spreading is surely very vague and imprecise. It creates a good or an evil aura around things, but it is something hard to pin down. In sharp contrast, the boundaries of the colours of physical things are in the great majority of cases very exact. Nothing is easier than to get non-collusive agreement between different perceivers that one colour is found up to a certain line of a surface and another colour beyond it. It is impossible not to think that at that point there is an objective change in the surface. The projection story must be that the eye is able to pick up a physical differentiation at this boundary (without perceiving it *as* a physical differentiation!), and then clothe the difference with colour qualities that are instantiated in the mind only, colours which the mind precisely but erroneously substitutes for the physical difference. Not self-contradictory, perhaps, but that seems about the best thing that can be said for the story!

I think that the moral of this is that those who want to use the colours as a reproach to a partial identity account of the resemblance of determinate universals cannot be direct realists in perception. A representative theory seems inevitable, presumably with the postulation of sense-data or something similar to be the bearers of the colour-qualities. Not very attractive, at least for the physicalist. Unreduced colours, we then see, are not cheaply bought, though some may be willing to pay the price. I suggest that the price is too high, and that we ought instead to accept a physicalist *and objectivist* account of colours.

But the phenomenology is there. It seems that the colours present themselves as at least relatively simple, and as *other* than any primary properties to which a physicalist may hope to reduce them. Can these presentations be explained away? The headless woman illusion is certainly of importance here (Armstrong, 1968b). What it shows is the naturalness of an illegitimate transition from a failure to perceive something (that the woman has a head) to a 'perception' of something unreal (the woman has no head). The illusion is rather easily brought about by presenting the woman against an illuminated black background with a black cloth over her head. A source of the power of the illusion seems to be that failure to perceive something is very often a reliable way of ascertaining that the thing is not present. (If it had been there, we would have been able to see it.) So our failure to perceive the identity of the colours with certain primary properties, and our failure to grasp their full complexity, could actually generate the illusion that we could *observe* that they are not identical with any primary properties and that they are objectively relatively simple. Here a phenomenological result, the headless woman, is used to try to tame phenomenology.

If colours are really complex physical properties, then our perceptual grip on them is weak indeed. Yet it does not appear to be weak. If there is anything that we seem to have a perceptual grip on, it is the internal nature of colours. How can this be explained? Here I suggest that the very complex relations of resemblance and difference between the whole array of the colours, with its three 'dimensions' of hue, saturation and intensity, relations which are so vividly presented in visual perception, creates in us the impression that we are given in perception the qualities from which these resemblances flow. After all, it is common enough for what are really relational entities to present themselves as something non-relational. Up and down is a relative notion, but it presents itself to us as absolute.

If all this is correct, then the determinables and determinates that colour-perception presents us with will be much, much, messier affairs than those to be found in the agreeable cases of length, duration and mass. But they need not be any different in principle, except that the properties involved are very unlikely to be universals, and instead are 'second-class' properties.

4.15 Fales' causal account of determinates

This defensive operation concerning colour may serve as a model for a treatment of all the secondary qualities. But before leaving the topic of the resemblance of universals I should like to consider an interesting suggestion about determinables and determinates put forward tentatively by Evan Fales (1990, ch. 9.3). For Fales, physical universals may be differentiated from each other by the causal relations in which they stand to other universals. Different universals, different causal powers. (These causal powers constitute for him the laws of nature.) This is a plausible enough starting point. Consider now the set of determinates falling under the one determinable. Associated with each member of the set will be its own peculiar set of causal relations to further universals. Associated with the determinable will also be a set of causal relations. Fales' suggestion is that this further set is a proper subset of *each* of the sets associated with each determinate. It is this, according to him, that explains why instantiation of any of the determinate universals entails instantiation of the determinable. The ordering of the determinates in terms of closeness of resemblance can also be explained in terms of degree of overlap in their associated sets of causal relations. Why does instantiation of a determinable ensure that a determinate universal is instantiated? Fales suggests further that the ground for this, in some cases at least, is the fact that the subset of causal relations associated with the determinable is nomically insufficient for independent existence. That is to say, it may be nomically impossible for any particular to instantiate these causal relations and these alone. Fales holds that causal relations between universals are necessary, so on his theory instantiating the determinable will *entail* instantiating some determinate, just as it ought to.

It is not so clear how one such as myself, who holds that causal laws are contingent, can get this intuitively desirable result. Perhaps, if I were to go along the Fales path, which certainly has its attractions, I ought to modify his idea and merely work with overlaps in the classes of causal relations associated with each determinate, leaving determinables as mere predicates. The treatment of determinates would be like the treatment of determinates already sketched, but with sets of causal powers associated with each determinate substituted for an internal analysis of the structure of the determinate universals.

It is to be noted that Fales does not see his suggestion as giving a reductive account of the determinate/determinable distinction. He thinks of the determinables as genuine universals, over and above the determinates. He also has phenomenological scruples. Are we not directly aware of the logical relationships between determinables and determinates while apparently unaware of the causal relations of these putative universals? This makes him think that the logical relationships cannot be *identified* with relations between the sets of causal powers associated with the various properties.

If I adopted Fales' causal theory I would, as already indicated, like to develop it in a reductive way, without the automatic need to postulate determinable universals. As the previous discussion of colour will perhaps have indicated, I would be hopeful of explaining away the phenomenological difficulties. In this reductive version of Fales' theory, when we classify universals together in the determinable/determinate way we are reacting to and registering causal facts about the universals involved, causal facts of the sort pointed to by Fales. But we are not necessarily aware of what it is we are registering and reacting to. One attraction of this view for me is that it does not demand that it be possible to give a *physicalist* account of the unity of classes of determinates, which my own account in terms of partial identity did appear to demand for the case of colours. Even if Physicalism is false, it may still be possible to give an account of the unity of classes of determinates in terms of overlapping classes of the causal relations associated with each determinable. This would ease the worry about basing very general metaphysical hypotheses upon a particular, if high-level, scientific speculation, the thesis of Physicalism.

4.16 Functional laws as determinables

A final note before ending this long section. It is interesting and important to note that in the case of functional laws of nature we have the determinable/determinate relation recreated. Consider Newtonian gravitation: $F=K(M_1 \times M_2)/D$. Each of F, M and D are determinables, under which fall as determinates specific forces, masses and distances. But more than this: if determinate values of F, the Ms and D are substituted in the equation then we reach a law which stands as a determinate to the original, determinable, law. The determinate laws form a class of laws, a class that may have 'missing values', that is, uninstantiated values, reminiscent of Hume's 'missing shade of blue'. Thus, supposing that the universe has a finite mass, M_u, then the determinate gravitation laws involving greater total masses than M_u will be uninstantiated. We will return to this in 16.12.

4.2 QUANTITIES

No scientifically oriented philosophy, as this one purports to be, can neglect the topic of Quantity. For us, the matter is very closely intertwined with the topic of complex universals, and also the determinable/determinate distinction. Quantities provide at least the most obvious examples of classes of properties where the determinable/determinate distinction is naturally drawn. As a result, most of our work has already been anticipated by the discussion of that distinction in the previous section.

If we consider determinate as opposed to determinable quantities, and if we exclude minimum quantities, if such there be, then we could say that a determinate quantity is a complex universal, a state-of-affairs type, a molecular or conjunctive state-of-affairs type, whose constituents have a certain monotony. The monotony gives that universal a certain simplicity and a certain nomic importance. We have already discussed the structure of duration, length and mass, which are one-dimensional quantities. But some issues remain.

4.21 Properties or relations?

In the discussion of length, duration and mass in the previous section, it was tacitly assumed that these are monadic, if complex, universals. It was assumed that they are properties as opposed to relations. Bigelow and Pargetter, though, have argued that they should rather be taken as relations, mathematical relations of proportion (1988 and, more cautiously, 1990, ch. 2). These relations of proportion obtain, of course, but what seems to be overlooked by Bigelow and Pargetter is that the relations are *internal*, flowing from the nature of the terms that have these relations.

These natures will have to be properties of the terms. Just possibly they will be *relational* properties of the terms, but they will have to be relational properties that are prior to the relation of proportion holding between the terms. It is these properties that appear to constitute the quantities. (See my reply to Bigelow and Pargetter's article, Armstrong, 1988.)

4.22 Are there fundamental intensive quantities?

We will illustrate this topic by taking the example of mass once again. If we take a mass-universal of the sort instantiated by macroscopic bodies, then it can be exhibited as a structure of smaller bodies of lesser mass. It is thinkable that this sort of decomposition continues *ad infinitum*. If it does, then mass may be said to be *a purely extensive quantity.* It is an interesting hypothesis that all the fundamental quantities are purely extensive. It seems possible, epistemically possible, however, that mass, though perhaps fundamental, is not purely extensive. For instance, electrons are often thought of as points, and as such would not have spatial parts, yet they have a mass. If all point-masses had the same mass, then one would have the plausible speculation that every body of greater mass was composed of differing numbers of such point-masses. It seems, however, that other point-like particles have different masses. Supposing this to be so, then we are faced with what may be *purely intensive* differences of mass.

This, however, is a problem, at least given our account of the way that determinates falling under the same determinable are linked together. Suppose that Q_1 and Q_2 are purely intensive and determinate quantities falling under the same determinable Q, and Q_2 is the greater. There seems to be no way that one can break up Q_2 into a conjunction of Q_1 and the result of subtracting Q_1 from Q_2. The notion of a part does not seem to get a foothold with purely intensive quantities. That being so, I take courage and declare that this metaphysic has no place for such quantities. They are as objectionable as determinable/determinate relations holding between *simple* properties.

If there were an irreducibly intensive quantity, then one would certainly wish to associate with it a difference in potential effect, a difference correlated with the intensive difference, and such a difference in effect would presumably be measurable along some extensive scale. But unless the intensive difference can be *identified* with its potential effect, and so really got rid of, we would still be faced with purely intensive differences in the causes.

Hypotheses are available that would restore extensiveness. Unlike universals, particulars that are not at the very same place at a certain time cannot be wholly identical. But it is not so clear that different particulars cannot be at the very same place at the same time. Suppose that the latter is possible. Then one might explain a difference of mass in different point-particles by saying that the particles in question contained a different number of unit-mass particulars 'piled on top of one another'. One could even hypothesize that 'inside the point', as it were, there was no fundamental unit-mass, but that one point-particle could be more massive than another in a continuous fashion. The bigger particle *a* would contain a proper part, *a*′, that had the same mass, say, as another particle *b*. But the proper part *a*′ would be 'inside' *a*, with both *a* and *a*′ wholly at the very same point in spacetime. One might think of these sorts of 'extensive quantities within the same point' as involving a further dimension orthogonal to the ordinary three, or else as involving bare numerical difference.

If, however, science finally declares for irreducibly intensive quantity, then here, as elsewhere, a cherished metaphysical thesis must be abandoned, or modified, in the light of empirical enquiry.

4.3 KINDS

Properties, as opposed to relations, are monadic or one-place universals. But are they the only sort of monadic universals that there are? There is an important tradition, going back as far as Plato and Aristotle, that would recognize *kinds* in addition. A particular may be a man or a horse, a methane molecule or an atom, or it may be a quantity of stuff such as wood or gold. It sounds strange to speak of the *property* of being a man or the property of being a quantity of gold. At the same time these kinds are repeatables and so have a *prima facie* claim to be a particular sort of monadic universal. One striking candidate for a kind that has recently been suggested (Bigelow, Ellis and Lierse, 1992) is the spacetime world itself. It does seem to be an object that is to a degree a physically unified thing. (Presumably it is, *qua* kind, a repeatable, although we have no particular reason to think that it is actually repeated.)

Stuffs are perhaps not very important for a scientific realist ontology that also accepts the existence of universals. The reason is that stuffs, though regularly appearing homogeneous 'within the manifest image of the world', turn out to be assemblages of particulate, countable, things such as molecules and electrons. It may turn out, of course, that homogeneity or something like it is to be found once more within spacetime and in fields, and that we should not treat electrons and other such particles as little objects. But let us here concentrate on countable substances. Consider the traditional example. Is there a universal of humanity of which each member of the human race is an instance?

Biologically considered, human beings are extremely complex structures. And it is sufficiently obvious that, despite resemblances, these structures will not be *identical* (strictly identical) in all, or indeed in any two, human beings. Using once again the powerful truism that a universal must be strictly identical in each instance, it seems that there is no biological structure that will serve as the universal required. The genetic structure of human DNA is perhaps the nearest thing to an identical structure that can be pointed to, and instances having that structure are the only things that can give rise, in suitable circumstances, to human beings. Furthermore, there may well be a sufficiently abstract description of that structure which is necessary and sufficient for human DNA. But is there any reason to think that this abstract description picks out a universal? Such a universal will clearly have to be some very complex determinable. The only reason that I can think of for postulating such a universal is that things answering to this description play some unique and irreducible causal or nomic role in the workings of the world. But while this is a possibility, or at least a conceivability, there seems no reason to think that it is anything more. The causal work in producing and maintaining a human being is surely done by constituent molecules, and more complex structures, that act in virtue of their determinate properties.

But if the universal of humanity is not a determinable biological structure, what is it? In the Aristotelian tradition one has the impression that this universal broods over the whole and somehow, a 'somehow' perhaps linked with final causes, keeps the individual human being within its biological limits. But how can the contemporary scientific realist who wishes to combine scientific realism with a recognition of universals conceive of this universal if not as a determinable biological structure? From the substance-universal, as we may call it, the ordinary properties of human beings must somehow flow. But what have we here but vague gesture?

Consider also the Bigelow–Ellis–Lierse suggestion that being a spacetime should be considered a kind or substance-universal. The same sort of difficulties that have just been noted for the putative kind-universal of being a human being apply here also. The detailed structure of different spacetimes would presumably differ from instance to instance. This detailed structure is, again presumably, largely determined by causal interactions of the individual entities to be found in spacetime. These individual causal interactions are determined, we ordinarily think, by the particular *properties* of the interacting things. How is the kind-universal of spacetimeness to get into the act? 'The sun will not overstep its measures' Heraclitus wrote. Does the kind, a determinable universal, lay down measures which serve as a limit beyond which the causal interactions of the things within a spacetime cannot go? I certainly do not want to say that no intelligible story can be told here, and perhaps turn out to be true. But I say that the story is still to be told.

There is, of course no objection to the hypothesis that a spacetime has a certain property or properties and that this property or these properties play an important causal or nomic role in determining what happens within a spacetime. This may be so and it may turn out to be an immeasurably important correction to the microreductive drive in many of the explanations given by fundamental physics. But kinds, as I understand them, are conceived of as universals that are both other than mere properties and in some way govern properties.

But perhaps being human and being a spacetime are simply bad examples of kinds? Perhaps we should look for the true kinds among the fundamental building blocks of the world. The electron is not at present thought of as having any structure and all electrons are thought of as identical in nature. Perhaps, then, we should recognize a kind: electronhood?

It would *appear*, however, that a reductive account is available of electronhood. Unlike an ordinary macroscopic object, or even a molecule or atom, the electron is not credited with very many properties. And for properties to make it an electron there are required only mass, charge and the absolute value of the spin, properties that are identical in all electrons. Why, then, should not electronhood be identified with the property that is the conjunction of these three properties?

It is, of course, a great fact about the world that it contains kinds of things, individual objects that lend themselves to being gathered together into classes that in many cases do not overlap. This holds within the manifest image of the world and, though some lines are re-drawn, it is not repudiated in the deeper, truer, scientific image. The kinds mark true joints in nature. But it is not clear that we require an independent and irreducible category of universal to accommodate the kinds.

It is one of the hypotheses of this work that the deepest, most absolute, of joints are given solely by property and relation universals, linked together by nomic relations. We may perhaps render this as a thesis of supervenience. Given all the states of affairs, where these are conceived of as involving nothing but particulars ('thin' particulars, mere individuators) properties and relations, then, it may be hypothesized, all the *kinds* of thing that there are, supervene. And if they supervene, they are not an ontological addition to their base.

5

Powers and dispositions

5.1 INTRODUCTORY

Given properties and relations in our ontology, one great issue is whether they are repeatables (universals) or unrepeatables (tropes). We have opted for universals. But another large question in the theory of properties and relations demands our attention, an issue in great degree independent of the dispute between universals and tropes. It is an issue of equal importance, though perhaps less well canvassed. Concentrating, for convenience, on properties as opposed to relations, we think of them as bestowing *powers* upon the particulars that have them. A property that bestows no power will not be easy to detect! Conversely, if a particular has a power, either to act or be acted upon, then that is a property of the particular. The question arises, therefore, whether a property's nature is *exhausted* by the powers that it bestows, or whether instead the property, in itself, is to be distinguished from those powers. To discuss and come to a position on this issue is the main business of this chapter.

Properties (and relations) are thought of by some philosophers as having a nature that is self-contained, distinct from the powers that they bestow. We shall call this position *Categoricalism*. Others think of them as having a nature that essentially looks beyond the particulars they qualify, outward to potential interactions with further particulars, and where this nature is exhausted by these potential interactions. This view may be called *Dispositionalism*. As one might naturally expect, there is a *Two-sided* view which holds that properties have, essentially, both a categorical and a power side to their nature.

This chapter will criticize Dispositionalism, defend Categoricalism, and rather briefly criticize the Two-sided view, leaving a fuller discussion of this third position to a later chapter. But preliminary brief discussion of dispositions, of the distinction between transeunt and immanent causation, and of propensities (probabilistic powers) will be in order before we embark on the issue between Dispositionalism and Categoricalism.

5.2 DISPOSITIONS

There is a traditional distinction between the active and passive powers of a particular. A particular has an active power if when it is in, or comes into, a certain relation to a particular sort of thing, it has some effect on the second thing. This effect may be a *change* in the properties of the second particular or it may be a mere *sustaining* of properties of that particular. A dose of opium makes a person sleep, thus changing the person's state. A table supports a book, thus sustaining the book in this position. Note that there may be a still more radical form of active power, where a particular in certain circumstances actually creates a second particular.

A particular has a passive power if, when some further particular of a certain sort is in, or comes into, a certain relation to it, certain of its properties are changed or sustained. The brittleness of a glass is a passive power of the glass. A radical case here is where the original particular ceases to exist.

The term 'disposition' is most naturally applied to passive powers, with such properties as brittleness and solubility as paradigms, although in contemporary philosophical usage the word is sometimes applied to active powers also. We ourselves will not be particularly careful to restrict the term to passive powers.

Our concern is with an individual particular, a token that has the property of, say, brittleness. We distinguish, orthodoxly enough I suppose, between (1) the property itself, (2) its *manifestation*, the object shattering, a manifestation that need not occur, and (3) the *initiating circumstance*, a suitable striking of the object, a circumstance that also need not occur.

A particular may have a disposition or power, but may fail to *manifest* that disposition or power. This, indeed, is the normal thing. One would suppose it to be the case that *no* particular ever manifests all its powers, and perhaps most particulars fail to manifest most of their powers during the span of their existence. When a particular has an unmanifested power, then the particular cannot be *related* to the potential manifestation of this power because the instantiation of a relation demands that all its terms exist. It is true, of course, that the particular still has the power (whatever be the truthmaker for this truth, a matter still to be investigated). But, by hypothesis, the manifestation does not exist, so the particular cannot be related to it. This is of the first importance.

Suppose, however, that a particular does manifest a power that it has. This is always a case of *causation*, singular or token causation. (Earlier explicit endorsement of this causal account of dispositions is to be found in Mackie, 1978.) For a brittle object to manifest its brittleness, the striking of the object, in conjunction no doubt with suitable standing conditions or other circumstances, together with the brittleness itself, must *bring about* the shattering of the brittle object. We can add the totality of the suitable circumstances to the initiating cause, further add the brittleness, and speak of all these taken together as the *total* cause of the manifestation.

I take singular causation with full ontological seriousness (*contra* the Humeans), although elaboration and defence of this position must be postponed until chapter 14. Notice also that with the rejection (or near rejection) of negative universals (3.41), the absence of some factor is not accounted a cause, ontologically speaking. From nothing, nothing comes. We do of course say things like 'Lack of water caused his death' and such statements can well be true. But, my position is, the truthmaker for such a statement is not a causal relation between the absence and its 'effect'. (David Lewis has pointed out to me that the opium example might not be a strict case of causation. For suppose it works by blocking stimuli that would otherwise keep one awake. It would then be like the lack of water case.)

If singular causal connection is missing, then the disposition has not been manifested, even if, because of some other cause, or for no cause at all, the shattering still occurs. A thought experiment brings out the force of this. A brittle glass is suitably struck. But before the striking can cause the shattering, the glass is hit by a pre-emptive lightning strike which causes it to shatter. This lightning strike, however, is such that it would suffice to shatter even a *non-brittle* object. Has the glass's brittleness been manifested? Not, it seems.

A further point that may be noted is that the total cause acting upon the brittle glass must bring about the manifestation *in some standard way*. If the causal chain from striking to shattering is a 'deviant' one, then the shattering will not be a manifestation of the brittleness. An example is not easy to construct. But suppose that, in peculiar conditions, the striking caused the brittle glass not to be brittle. (See C. B. Martin's '*electro-fink*' which, when a charged wire is touched, makes the wire go dead if and only if it is touched. Martin, 1994, p. 3.) But suppose also, that the striking added to the previous brittle condition triggers the lightning strike envisaged in the previous paragraph, a strike that shatters even non-brittle objects and which shatters this glass. The glass was not manifesting its brittleness, even though striking plus the brittle condition caused the shattering.

Looking forward to the Dispositionalist thesis, the thesis that the properties of particulars are nothing but powers, it may be noted that if a (singular) causal relation is necessary for the manifestation of a disposition of a particular, then, however this causal relation is analysed, a Dispositionalist account cannot be given of that relation. So Dispositionalists had better, on pain of falling into circularity, exclude the relation of causality from their Dispositionalist thesis. Causality must be categorical.

It is to be noted further that, given this causal account, the consequents of the conditionals that are in some way associated with dispositions must be causal statements. 'If this glass had been suitably struck, it would have shattered.' The consequent should be interpreted as 'this would have caused it to shatter'. I hold that it is not possible to analyse out this causal component so as to remove the causality. If so, there will be no question of *analysing* causality in terms of conditionals.

5.21 *The impotence thesis*

In what has been said so far, it has been assumed that Dispositional properties are causal factors, joining with the properties of the initiating cause to produce the appropriate manifestation. Prior, Pargetter and Jackson (1982), however, argue that brittleness, for instance, is a *second-order* property of the brittle object. It is, they say, the object's property of having some first-order property, where it is the latter property that is the causal factor. This second-order property is not a causal factor, hence dispositions are impotent.

These authors raise a difficulty for my sort of position. Given that the laws of nature are contingent, as they and I assume, then in some world where the laws of nature are different, it would be possible for the brittle object to have just the first-order properties that it has and yet not be disposed to shatter if struck. A certain bonding of molecules that produces the shattering in this world would not play that causal role in another world. An identification of brittleness with such bonding would make 'brittle' no more than a *non-rigid* designator of the disposition. As such, it cannot claim to catch the Dispositional essence. Hence the need to identify the disposition with the second-order property, which, however, is impotent.

The point is certainly valuable. I used to argue that a certain bonding of molecules in the brittle object could function as the truthmaker for the truth that the object is brittle. But this is certainly wrong if the relation of truthmaker to truth is an internal one, with the truthmaker necessitating the truth, a premiss that will be argued for in 8.11. The truthmaker ought to be the bonding of the molecules *plus* the relevant laws of nature. The impotence thesis is a way of coming to terms with this point.

But it may still be defensible to identify the brittleness with the bonding. Consider that the first-order state plus the laws will, in the given conditions, be sufficient to entail (or give a certain objective chance) that a suitable striking will shatter the object. (The higher-order property which Prior, Pargetter and Jackson champion as the disposition supervenes on this situation.) Given this, cannot one say that, *relative to the laws*, the first-order state is the disposition, and then leave this relativity in the semantic background? I find this preferable to the impotence thesis, though decision one way or the other may not be of major importance.

It is to be noted that the identification of disposition with first-order state here defended, the causal theory of dispositions, can be token-token, or perhaps more realistically (sub-type)-(sub-type). The brittleness of *a* and the brittleness of *b* could be different sorts of state.

5.3 TRANSEUNT AND IMMANENT CAUSALITY

Active and passive powers are manifested, if and when they are manifested, in causal processes. Characteristically, these involve the causal action of one particular upon another. Using W. E. Johnson's terminology (1964 [1924], Part III) we may call this *transeunt* causality. It is a 'going across'. By Newton's Third Law, such action will always be accompanied by a reaction. That is, the action will always be one side of an *interaction*. This ensures that in all such action active and passive powers of both particulars are involved.

But the world may contain another, more controversial, sort of causality, which Johnson calls *immanent* or 'remaining within' causality. Certain wholes maintain their stability by the interactions of their proper parts. In general, that holds for social wholes, such as nations. That is transeunt causality. But it may also be that there is a form of causality which remains confined to a single particular and that, further, does not proceed by interaction between sub-particulars. This will be immanent causality.

Where, if anywhere, is immanent causation to be found? Spontaneous radioactive decay is a possible case. Nancy Cartwright says:

> In treating [radioactive] decay, quantum physics employs two different concepts – that of stimulated emission and that of spontaneous emission. Stimulated emissions have some assignable cause . . . spontaneous emissions are random and uncaused events.
>
> (1989, p. 109)

I suggest that spontaneous emissions are better understood as immanent causes. There is, by hypothesis, no external cause. One could suggest that the remainder of the atom acts on the particle, causing it to be emitted. This would be transeunt causality. In default of this, though, the causation would appear to be immanent. The particle as a whole, and in a certain state, brings about the decay. A still 'quieter' form of immanent causation may be involved in the way that an electron, which may be a simple particular, one having no parts, goes on existing and retains the same mass, charge and absolute value of spin while it remains in existence.

What makes me think that the cases of spontaneous emission and the electron continuing to exist are causal is the combination of two doctrines which can be indicated here, but can only be discussed and defended in the discussion of particulars, to be embarked upon in chapter 7. The first doctrine is the contention that particulars which exist for a period of time, which are not mere instantaneous existents, have temporal parts just as, if they are not spatially atomic, they have spatial parts. The second doctrine arises out of the problem set if it is accepted that such persisting particulars have temporal parts. The problem is to give 'principles of unity' by which non-overlapping temporal parts of the one particular are welded together to constitute the single thing that exists through time. Mere spatial and temporal continuity, together with resemblance of temporal parts, can be shown to be insufficient. Indeed neither sort of continuity seems even to be necessary. (See 7.2 and references there.) What seems necessary in addition is the actual *bringing into existence* of later by earlier temporal parts.

(This, if correct, shows that not all causality is a matter of *forces* in the physicist's understanding of the latter term. No forces are involved in the mere continuing existence of an electron. It may well be, however, that all *interactive* causality involves forces.)

5.4 PROPENSITIES

We should give brief consideration to the question of merely probabilistic powers and dispositions, sometimes spoken of as *propensities*. If our argument has been correct, this is identical with the question of 'probabilistic causality'. It seems a very reasonable assumption (though I am unaware of any proof for it except the somewhat uncertain verdict of experience) that each token of the causal relation (each case of *this* causing *that*) should be governed by some law (or laws) of nature. But it by no means follows from this that the laws in question are *deterministic*. It may be (epistemic 'may') that some or all of these laws are irreducibly and objectively probabilistic. The rule of law need not be the rule of deterministic law. Suppose that all or some of the fundamental laws that govern ordinary active and passive powers and also immanent causation, if it exists, are of a probabilistic nature. How much, if at all, would we then need to modify what has already been said?

Not very much, it appears. Certain powers and so on associated with particulars will have to be scaled down, as it were, to allow for the empirical possibility that, even where all the conditions for the manifestation of a power are present, there may still *be* no manifestation. Symbolically, this can be done by associating with every power a number ranging from 0 and 1, but with 0 itself excluded. A deterministic power will take the number 1. (With 1 minus an infinitesimal *not* set equal to 1. Infinitesimals are dealt with in non-standard analysis. They are perfectly respectable, despite the conservative term 'non-standard'.) The number measures the objective probability of the effect occurring. The peculiar cases are then those where the power is non-deterministic, and the 'total cause' occurs – all conditions for manifestation are present – but on a certain occasion the manifestation does not occur. What ought we to say about such cases? In particular, are they cases of causation?

I think that we should deny that these are cases of causation. Causation is a relation, fundamentally a dyadic relation, and, *pace* R. Grossmann, 1983, secs. 78–83, no relation exists without its full complement of terms. Causation that is law-governed, but where the law is probabilistic only, exists only when, as one may say, the state of affairs falling under the antecedent of the law 'fires', that is, the potential cause actually brings about its effect. The moral to be drawn from this is that an irreducibly probabilistic power or disposition does not involve 'probabilistic causality' but rather a certain (objective) probability of common-or-garden, two-termed, causation. 'Probabilistic causality' should rather be thought of as a *probability of causing*, a probability that is irreducibly probabilistic. That is what a propensity is.

5.5 DISPOSITIONALISM

We turn to the Dispositionalist theory of properties. In a thoroughgoing Dispositionalism, all properties, and in particular the properties of the total cause, the properties in virtue of which the manifestation occurs if it does occur, have a nature that is exhausted by their possible (*empirically* possible) manifestations. This has a fascinating consequence. Given the total cause, the effect, the manifestation, necessarily occurs, or, in the case of a mere propensity, the total cause necessarily has a certain objective propensity to bring about the manifestation. It is contingent that a particular has the particular properties that it has. But granted that it does have certain properties, then, because of the Dispositional essence that constitutes properties on this view, there is a necessary, or a necessarily probabilifying, connection between property and manifestation.

Sydney Shoemaker (1980) and I think Chris Swoyer (1982) are Dispositionalists. Shoemaker, in a postscript to his 1980 paper added in his 1984 collection, does include 'backward looking' causal features in his causal theories of properties. These are a matter of a property being such that its instantiation is caused in a certain way. I cannot see that this makes much difference to the critique of Dispositionalism to be mounted here. Shoemaker does think that there is a distinction to be drawn between dispositional and nondispositional properties, but on his view even the latter are analysed as a cluster of conditional powers. Swoyer gives an account of properties in terms of laws rather than causes, but again this does not seem an important difference in the present context. But in a recent personal communication, however, he has told me that he does not want to give a Dispositionalist account of *all* properties. More recently, we have Brian Ellis and Caroline Lierse (1994), who provide a valuable survey. Ellis and Lierse, however, explicitly except spatiotemporal properties from their Dispositionalism, and would presumably except spatiotemporal relations also. This involves some qualification of their avowed Necessitarianism about cause and effect. Suppose that *a* is at a certain distance from *b*. This will be a categorical relation, one that presumably can have causal effects. For instance, the effect on *c* might have been different if *a* and *b* had been at a different distance. Will it not be contingent just what different effects flow from different distances? Ellis and Lierse, at any rate, cannot demonstrate any necessity in such a case. So for them some causal relations will be necessary and others contingent, which seems a bit messy.

In order to see the force of Dispositionalism it is particularly useful to consider the nature of *vectors*, physical as opposed to merely mathematical vectors. We are interested here in such vectors as velocity, acceleration and force, although our discussion will restrict itself to velocity and force. What follows builds on the work of Michael Tooley (1988), Denis

Robinson (1989) and John Bigelow together with his co-author Robert Pargetter (1990, 2.6). The argument has two steps.

Vectors have both a quantity and a direction. They are *attributed* to bodies at instants. A question, though, is whether we should take this attribution at face value. Suppose that at a certain time a certain person was thirty-seven years old and (because of nothing particular about the person in question at that time) doomed. He died shortly afterwards as a result of being hit by a meteorite. These attributions, thirty-seven years old and doomed, have as their subject that person at that time. They are nevertheless true in virtue of the person's past and future. Are vectors like that? Philosophers disagree. Bigelow and Pargetter point out, indeed, that the dispute was alive and well among the Scholastics. Ockham, in particular, as one might expect, took the more positivistic view that attributions of velocity at an instant, for example, should not be thought of as attributing a property that really qualifies the particular at that instant. His view seems to have prevailed (among philosophers) until quite recently. But as Tooley, Robinson, Bigelow and Pargetter all show, such a view is quite difficult to defend.

A simple, but powerful, example is given by Bigelow and Pargetter (p. 72). A meteor crashes into Mars, making a crater. The size of the crater is proportional to the force exerted on impact, together, of course, with whatever Mars happens to be doing at that instant. But if that force is not something, a property presumably, that the meteor has *at the moment of impact*, then how is the particular size of the crater to be explained? Is it to be thought that the meteor, at the moment of impact, 'remembers' the velocity that it was travelling at before the impact? Surely it is the mass of the object, *and its velocity at the instant of impact*, together with the current state of Mars, that determines the rest of the causal process? So the velocity had better be a property that really qualifies it at that instant. (It may be a *relational* property, involving a relation to Mars as it was at that instant, but that does not seem to destroy the force of the point.)

Although physically unrealistic, the thought experiment of the absolutely uniform but rotating disc is also very instructive. The disc (or sphere) was introduced into current philosophical discussion by Saul Kripke (1979) and independently by me (1980, original paper presented 1976). But it was Robinson who spotted the link between this case and the notion of a vector. We imagine two absolutely homogeneous discs that are in their two natures absolutely identical *except* that one is stationary, the other rotating. When I first thought of this case as an undergraduate at

Sydney University, I assumed that the non-relational properties of the discs were constituted by *qualities* that the two discs instantiated. So conceived, there seemed to be no difference between the two objects. With the rashness of youth I drew the conclusion that there *were* no non-relational differences. The discs are identical in their non-relational properties. Yet this conclusion can hardly be sustained. Why should it not be a fact that there is a difference, and a non-relational difference at that? Consider the difference in counterfactuals that apply to the two discs. A mark applied to the stationary disc would also stay stationary. A mark applied to the rotating disc would rotate. Must there not be a difference in truthmaker corresponding to this difference in truths? As Robinson in effect points out, it seems that we just have to accept it as a fact that, at any instant, any point on the rotating disc has the vectorial property of a certain radial velocity with a constantly changing direction, a property *intrinsic* to the disc at that instant.

The Mars case and the case of the two discs constitute the first step in the argument. This step does not by itself lead to a Dispositionalist account of these vector-properties. It simply leads to the conclusion that attribution of such vector properties to bodies at certain instants must be taken with ontological literalness. But, of course, vector-properties are identified in terms of what they do, in terms of their effects. No doubt this was an important motive, in the not too distant positivist past, for many philosophers not taking the attribution of vector properties to bodies at instants with ontological seriousness. But if we do start taking such vectors-at-an-instant seriously, must we not also start taking seriously a Dispositionalist account of them? For we seem to have no handle on these properties except via their effects. And once we do this, it will become attractive to take a Dispositionalist view of mass, charge, energy and so on for all fundamental physical properties.

Vectors, therefore, pose an important challenge to the Categoricalist, the upholder of self-contained properties that are only contingently connected with their effects. Can we provide categorical bases for all physical vectors? It may even be that the dispute will have to be settled by science rather than philosophy.

In the meanwhile I offer an inexpert suggestion. Could the relativistic contraction in the direction of motion point to some categorical property, presumably a structural property, perhaps a relational as well as structural property, of the moving object? It is to be observed though, as pointed out to me by Michael Tooley, that this would, at best, deal with the problem of the *quantity* of motion. It is less clear how *direction* of motion, also involved in the vector property, is to be catered for.

But now to consider two important difficulties for Dispositionalism. The *first* difficulty springs from the fact that a disposition as conceived of by a Dispositionalist is like a congealed hypothetical fact or state of affairs: 'If this object is suitably struck, then it is caused (or there is a certain objective probability of it being caused) to shatter.' It is, as it were, an inference ticket (as Ryle said), but one that exists in nature (as Ryle would hardly have allowed). That is all there is to a particular disposition. Consider, then, the critical case where the disposition is not manifested. *The object still has within itself, essentially, a reference to the manifestation that did not occur.* It points to a thing that does not exist. This must remind us of the *intentionality* of mental states and processes, the characteristic that Brentano held was the distinguishing mark of the mental, that is, their being directed upon objects or states of affairs that need not exist. This intentionality of the mental undoubtedly exists. But for physicalists such as myself it presents a *prima facie* problem. If the mental has intentionality, and if, as Brentano thought, it is also *ontologically irreducible*, then there is something here that would appear to falsify Physicalism. Physicalists about the mind are therefore found trying to give some ontologically reductive account of the intentionality of the mental. But if irreducible dispositions and powers are admitted for *physical* things, then intentionality, irreducible intentionality, has turned up in everything there is.

Is this not objectionable? Does it not assimilate the physical to the mental, rather than the other way around? But more to the point, how can a state of affairs of a particular's having a property enfold within itself a relation (of any sort) to a further first-order state of affairs, the manifestation, which very often does not exist? We have here a Meinongian metaphysics, in which actual things are in some way related to non-existent things.

Some bite the bullet, though. John Burnheim (*c.* 1968), C. B. Martin and K. Pfeifer (1986), and U. T. Place (1988) have argued, in Place's words:

> that physical dispositions and their descriptions bear all the marks of intentionality mentioned by such philosophers as Elizabeth Anscombe, Roderick Chisholm and Bill Lycan.

As a result, Place goes on:

> we reach the conclusion that intentionality is the mark, not, as Brentano thought, of the mental, but of the dispositional.
>
> (p. 210)

Here the result that appears objectionable to me is accepted by Place in the spirit of natural piety.

Perhaps, however, dissatisfaction with Dispositionalism can be articulated in the following way, which constitutes my *second* criticism of the theory. (See also Swinburne, 1983, criticizing Shoemaker, 1983.) Suppose that a thing acts and as a result some further thing gains a new property. Unless this property is a spatiotemporal one, which Ellis and Lierse, at least, would allow to be non-dispositional, the new property will itself be purely dispositional. If and when this new property has its effects, these too will be a matter of gaining, losing or sustaining purely dispositional properties. Is this acceptable?

As George Molnar has pointed out to me, we do have a *prima facie* model for this situation. A magnetizable thing may become magnetized, yet to be magnetized is a dispositional property. But can we generalize from Molnar's case? Can it be that everything is potency, and act is the mere shifting around of potencies? I would hesitate to say that this involves an actual contradiction. But it does seem to be a very counter-intuitive view. The late Professor A. Boyce Gibson, of Melbourne University, wittily said that the linguistic philosophers were always packing their bags for a journey that they never took. Given a purely Dispositionalist account of properties, particulars would seem to be always re-packing their bags as they change their properties, yet never taking a journey from potency to act. For 'act', on this view, is no more than a different potency.

Perhaps accepting that the purely spatiotemporal properties are categorical will give enough categorical basis to blunt the force of this criticism. But the trouble then is that admission that there are such things as categorical properties weakens the Dispositionalist case. We have already seen that causality must be categorical. Why not other properties besides the spatiotemporal ones?

5.6 CATEGORICALISM

The Categoricalist goes to the other extreme. All true properties, the true universals if the universals account of properties is preferred to the trope theory, are non-dispositional. This view is to be found in Armstrong (1968, ch. 6, sec. VI & 1973, ch. 2), Mackie (1978), Pargetter and Prior (1982), Prior, Pargetter and Jackson (1982), Prior (1985). Properties are self-contained things, keeping themselves to themselves, not pointing beyond themselves to further effects brought about in virtue of such properties.

The main problem for such a view is to explain the powers and dispositions that we predicate of particulars and regularly associate with properties, particularly the properties that are no more than theoretical posits. It cannot be denied that we associate many different dispositional *truths* with the properties that we credit things with. If a thing has a certain mass, it is certainly true that it is disposed to act in certain ways. The problem is to find *truthmakers*, entities in the world that correspond to these truths, without the aid of properties conceived as the Dispositionalist conceives of properties.

Great emphasis will have to be placed on *laws of nature*, meaning by these not true law-statements but whatever it is in the world that makes such statements true, the correspondents in the world of true law-statements. In the situation where a power or disposition is actually manifested, there is no problem. Put in an utterly schematic way, suppose that there is a law that links properties F&G with H (that is, a law that F&G→H). The object that has the power or disposition is an F (perhaps has its molecules organized in a certain way), further conditions G are present (say a striking in suitable conditions), and H (shattering) occurs. H is then no more than the instantiation of the consequent of the law. The puzzling cases, however, are those where the object is F but conditions G, and so manifestation H, fail to obtain. We want to say that the object has the disposition, power or potential to produce H under conditions G, but, as Categoricalists, we do not want to say that it has a property that of its essence points to the non-existent outcome H under conditions G.

What is to be done? We do have to embrace a somewhat *deflationary* doctrine of unmanifested powers and dispositions. We may compare the situation to the Soft Determinist in the freewill debate, who must produce a somewhat deflationary doctrine of what it is to possess freewill; or to the Copernican in astronomy, who must produce a somewhat deflationary doctrine of what it is for the sun to rise. Deflationary doctrines are to be *contrasted* with eliminativist ones. Of course, deflation is a matter of degree, and too much deflation becomes elimination. But the doctrine of unmanifested powers now to be advocated seems not too deflationary. The Megarian philosophers of old were Eliminativists about unrealized possibilities. The view now to be advocated is to a degree Megarian in spirit. But it is an eirenic Megarianism. (Compare Soft Determinism.)

We need first the possession by the particular of relevant properties, say the property F. We need the relevant law or laws of nature, say the law that with the addition of G (and perhaps the *absence* of factors J, K, etc.) the manifestation H will occur. We need it to be *empirically* possible that the particular should have the extra property, G (with J and K absent), which would allow for the instantiation of the total cause. That is to say, the false supposition that the particular be G (and in addition not J or K) must be compatible with the laws of nature. Summing up, what we need is that the particular should have the property F, together with the totality of the relevant laws of nature, because it is laws that give us empirical possibility. These states of affairs, I suggest, give or take some fine tuning, are sufficient as truthmakers for truths of unmanifested powers and dispositions. For the unmanifested power would appear to *supervene* upon these truthmakers. That is to say, given these truthmakers, the particular's having a certain property, plus the relevant laws, it is entailed that the particular has the power or disposition. We might call this a Soft doctrine of powers.

Not a sufficiently full-blooded truthmaker? I have a suggestion why some metaphysicians want more. They may be unconsciously dominated by the *practical* attitude. When human beings plan, and it is a special feature of human animals that they can and do plan quite thoroughly, they have to take various empirical possibilities, many of which never become actual, very seriously. They have to represent the various possibilities to themselves, to image them perhaps, and in general to invest mental energy in them. If they do not do all this, it seems, they lack the emotional and intellectual drive to think about these possibilities effectively. It helps in this planning to reify dispositional possibilities. It helps to think of the undrunk poison as having death lurking within it, a death which philosophical reflection can only think of as an unreal death, yet an unreal death to which the poison is somehow related.

In my 'soft' account of powers and dispositions much weight falls on the laws of nature. How should the Categoricalist think of them? In Chapter 15 it will be argued that they cannot be mere uniformities in nature, even if the uniformities are restricted to the systematic and coherent ones. 'Strong' laws are required, and an intelligible theory of such laws is required. But the laws, although strong, will have to be contingent. The contingency of laws seems to follow from the self-contained nature of the Categoricalist's properties, just as the necessity of the Dispositionalist's laws follows from the unself-contained nature of the latter's properties. Suppose that the Categoricalist's laws are necessary. It will have to be a necessity discovered *a posteriori* because, for any law of nature, it seems that not only can we conceive it to be false, but we can never find any self-contradiction in the proposition that it fails to hold. If there is a necessity here, a necessity linking 'distinct existences', it will be one whose necessity can never become 'transparent', nor, indeed, would there seem any way to give positive arguments for the necessity. It would be a truly 'brute necessity', comparable to brute contingencies. It would be necessary, furthermore, to qualify severely the natural Combinatorial approach to the theory of metaphysical possibility. All of which seems to constitute at least a strong case for taking the Categoricalist's laws to be contingent.

Martin Tweedale (1984) has argued that unless laws are necessary they would be unable to 'sustain counterfactuals', or, as we can also put it, laws would be unable to explain the attribution of unmanifested powers and dispositions. For myself, I think that strong but contingent laws can do the job. The Categoricalist account of such attributions given does not appear to be too adversely affected by the laws involved not being necessary. (See 16.5.) But it is the way that Tweedale continues his argument which is of present interest. He asks how it is possible that laws should be necessary, and then suggests that this is *only* possible if the antecedent universal is dispositional. His idea, presumably, is that at that point the necessity becomes transparent, obvious, and so intelligible. The moral is that Dispositionalists should have necessary laws, but Categoricalists should have contingent ones.

So in this section a defence of the Categoricalist position on properties (and by implication, on relations) has been given. It is clear, though, that there is a certain intellectual pressure to accept a Dispositionalist account of many properties, especially of vector properties. The matter is more evenly balanced than once I would have thought. But it does seem that the second difficulty proposed for Dispositionalism, the difficulty that potency is never able to translate itself into genuine act (non-potency), is a more serious disadvantage than any facing Categoricalism.

5.7 THE TWO-SIDED THEORY

If the two previous sections are a fair account of the present state of play, then it will be natural to wonder if there is a middle way or ways between these theories of the nature of properties. One way to do this, as Ernest Sosa pointed out to me, is to have a mixed theory with both Categoricalist and Dispositionalist properties. On this view, some laws of nature would come out contingent, others necessary. In default of further motivation, though, it seems unattractive to introduce laws with different modalities.

One important middle way is argued for by C. B. Martin (1993). I originally read Evan Fales (1990, ch. 8) as taking the same line as Martin, but he has informed me that this is an (excusable) misreading. So let us concentrate on Martin. In his 'Power for realists' Martin argues that every property has two 'sides' to it, a categorical and a power side, both sides ultimately real and irreducible to each other. The great weakness of Dispositionalism, that the properties of things each become a potency whose manifestation is itself nothing but mere potency, is done away with. In Martin's theory, every property and every manifestation of a property has a categorical side. Furthermore, provided that the same sort of powers can be systematically linked with the same sort of categorical side, the powers will serve as a substitute for the Categoricalist's laws of nature. Martin takes properties as tropes rather than as universals, and so must apparently appeal to a *resemblance* principle to explain the uniformity of nature. Like categorical sides have like power sides, and so like causes like. For myself, I think he would do better to substitute universals for tropes. That the same universal should everywhere bestow the same powers (an *identity* principle) seems a more solid principle than Martin's, even if, once Dispositionalism is rejected, not a necessary truth. The laws of nature could then *be* the fact that each universal bestows its own unique set of powers.

This view seems clearly preferable to Dispositionalism, and close consideration of it is best left until chapter 16, when cause and law have been much more fully explored. In the meanwhile I call attention to one central problem. What is the status of the connection between the categorical 'side' of the property and its dispositional 'side'? Does the categorical side necessitate the dispositional side, or is the connection contingent only? If C, the categorical side, is only contingently linked with P, the dispositional side, which in turn necessitates M, the manifestation under suitable conditions, then we appear to be back with laws that are fundamentally contingent. And then perhaps we can cut out the middleman P. But if C necessitates P which necessitates M (in suitable conditions), then presumably C necessitates M (with the same restrictions). But then we seem to have necessary connections between distinct categorical properties. And can this be? I am inclined, with Hume, to set my face against such connections.

6

Relations

6.1 PROPERTIES AND RELATIONS

Properties, as opposed to relations, are monadic universals, the only species of monadic universal, as has been argued (4.3). The term 'relation' covers all *polyadic* universals: dyadic, triadic, . . . *n*-adic. Properties then emerge as a limiting case of a universal, though no doubt a limiting case of quite particular importance. *Being a universal* becomes a determinable with being a monadic, dyadic, . . . *n*-adic, universal as its determinates. This in turn suggests that a particular universal can only have one -adicity. The latter conclusion is in any case mandated by the powerful truism that a universal is identical, strictly identical, in its different instantiations. Consider a relation such as *is surrounded by.* Such relations take a variable number of terms in their different instantiations. (They have been called *multigrade* relations – Leonard and Goodman, 1940, p. 50 – and also *anadic* relations – Grandy, 1976.) But it seems that they cannot be universals, because they would differ in their essential nature in these different instantiations. How could a three-term relation be strictly identical with a two-term relation? Indiscernibility of Identicals would seem to forbid it. We may call this result the Principle of Instantial Invariance (see Armstrong 1978b, ch. 19, sec. VII). I will not venture an analysis of *is surrounded by*. But it will be a 'second-class' relation (3.9) that the surrounded particular has to a number of other particulars. The relation will supervene, for the most part, upon the spatial relations of the particulars involved, relations that are universals.

It is, of course, a matter to be decided *a posteriori* and also, it would seem, it is a contingent matter, whether there really are relation-universals having a particular polyadicity. It might be, for instance, that all ontologically fundamental relation-universals are dyadic. Again, thinking of properties as merely the monadic case of universals, one might wonder whether it is a possibility for all fundamental universals to be polyadic. Perhaps all property-universals are constructed out of relations.

The form of the construction may be this. Start with basic particulars that have no non-relational properties. (It is not at all clear that there can be such particulars, but then again it is not quite obvious that such particulars must be excluded.) They will be bare particulars, or at any rate particulars that are internally bare, bare of non-relational properties. They may be conceived of, or at least imagined, as points, whether spatial points or as spacetime points. They will stand in various relations to each other. By hypothesis, the points are not different from each other in intrinsic nature, because they have no intrinsic nature. All objects that do differ from each other in nature will be made up of pluralities of these particulars, pluralities differing in the number and/or pattern of relations in which the members of the pluralities stand. On this view the electron, for instance, cannot be a *basic* particular, unless perchance all its properties – mass, charge and so on – are really relational. It would seem that this hypothesis of internally propertyless particulars can be confirmed or disconfirmed, although no doubt not *conclusively* confirmed or disconfirmed, by scientific investigation.

From a metaphysical point of view, the advantage of this hypothesis is its promise to solve the problem how one can come to know the intrinsic nature of things, a stick that Dispositionalists try to beat Categoricalists with. The only information that we have about the nature of things comes as a result of their action upon us. Scientific investigation has, it seems, entirely discredited the pleasant idea that this action takes the form of a migration of the sensible species from the object to the perceiver. All we can know of the world, commentator after commentator has bewailed, is its structural features. This would not be so sad if particulars generally had *nothing but* structural features and the basic particulars had no intrinsic features at all. (For another suggestion for solving this problem, see 10.41.)

The disadvantage of the hypothesis is this very notion of a particular without non-relational properties. The basic particular would not be an absolutely bare particular but its clothing would be no more than its (external) relations to whatever other particulars existed. Given this, it would be hard to deny the metaphysical possibility, at least, of a particular that lacked non-relational properties *and* had no external relations at all to any other particular. (Though other particulars might exist.) The main thesis of this work, that whatever exists is a state of affairs or a constituent of one, would then be at best contingently true. This inclines me to reject the absolutely bare particular. A particular that is of no sort or kind, a particular that has no nature, is a very strange conception. It is dubious even as a mere possibility. We will assume, then, that such an attempt to construct properties out of relations does not succeed.

6.2 INTERNAL AND EXTERNAL RELATIONS

This distinction is one of the fairly substantial number of pillars of the argument of this work, and has already received mention in 2.1 and at other points. I have also discussed the distinction on previous occasions (1978b, ch. 19, sec. IV, and 1989a, ch. 3, sec. 2, in particular). We should therefore try to avoid too much repetition. To summarize. An internal relation is one where the existence of the terms entails the existence of the relation. Given our definition of supervenience, it follows that the relation supervenes on the existence of the terms. Using the picturesque extensional model provided by possible worlds, in every world in which all the terms exist, the relation holds between them. If, as I further contend, what supervenes is not something ontologically more than what it supervenes upon, then, once given their terms, internal relations are not an addition to the world's furniture. External relations are those that are not internal, and are therefore the ontologically important relations. It should not be overlooked, however, that given this purely negative definition of 'external', some external relations, on analysis, resolve into a mixture of internal and purely external components.

The distinction between internal and external relations is to be found in Hume, *Treatise,* bk. 1, pt 1, sec. V, 'Of Relations' and pt 3, sec. I; *Inquiry,* sec. IV, pt 1. (In the *Enquiry* he introduces the rather clumsy terminology of 'relations of ideas' and 'matters of fact'.) But the interesting thing about his discussion is that he offers a taxonomy of relations which seems very plausible (give or take a few details), yet classifies relations under just seven heads. Four of them are species of relations of ideas, that is internal relations. These species are resemblance, quantity and number, degrees of quality and 'contrariety', which last is asserted by Hume to apply only to the ideas of existence and non-existence. We should add to this list identity and difference and what Donald Williams (1963) called the 'partitive' relations of overlap and part/whole. In 2.32 of the present work the partitive relations were argued to be relations of identity also, although the identity involved is *partial* only. The peculiar significance of the partitive relations will emerge in the next section.

It is to be noted that for the relations on Hume's list of 'relations of ideas' to fall under our definition of internal relations, the particulars involved must be taken as having their non-relational properties. Resemblances, for instance, depend upon the properties of the resembling things. If we abstract away from the properties of particulars, then almost no relations between particulars are internal. What is needed is the *thick* as opposed to the *thin* particular, the particular with its non-relational properties upon it. See 8.3, to come.

The matter is still more interesting when it comes to the external relations. Here Hume can find only spatiotemporal relations, 'identity' and causation. By identity in this context he is referring to the identity of changeable objects over time, which he is very far from considering genuine identity. (In the terminology of this essay, derived from Joseph Butler, it is 'loose' identity. See 2.31. Hume calls it a 'feigned' identity.) Since he analyses this loose identity in terms of resemblance, spatiotemporal continuity and causation, he really only admits two fundamental sorts of external relation: spatiotemporal relation and causality. And even the latter, at least according to the current orthodox interpretation of Hume, he reduces to regular succession. I resist the reduction of causality to regular succession, but it is a plausible *a posteriori* thesis that all external relations are either spatiotemporal or causal. (See also Fales, 1990, ch. 10.) If there are laws of nature that are irreducibly non-causal, then nomic connection of this non-causal sort will be a further species of external relation. But it may well be that the *fundamental* laws are all causal, so that Hume's minimalist thesis is not falsified by the existence of laws.

In this work, however, we part from Hume by holding that there is one further species of external relation. It will be argued in ch. 13 (following Russell) that states of affairs, or facts, of *totality* are required to complete a states of affairs ontology. (A great advantage is that they will relieve us of the need to accept negative states of affairs.) These facts, it will be argued further, are best conceived of as a totality or T relation, an external relation, holding between a suitable term, such as *being an elephant* and a certain aggregate, a certain mereological whole (the aggregate of the elephants).

But setting aside states of affairs of totality, it seems to be true that all other external relations may be analysed in terms of spatiotemporal and causal relations. It does not follow from this that the latter are ontologically fundamental. There is first the question whether one of the species can be analysed, conceptually or empirically, in terms of the other. As we have just noted, Humeans, as the term is understood today, will seek to give an account of causality in terms of regular succession. They do require universally quantified states of affairs, and these are actually totality states of affairs. But, even conceding this, for Humeans causality is eliminated as a fundamental species of relation. More attractive, I think, is the attempt to give an account of some, or, just possibly but not very plausibly, all, spatiotemporal relations in terms of causality. In particular the direction of time – from the past to the future, a direction that has no parallel in the case of space – may perhaps be analysed in causal terms.

But we are not limited to the attempt to give an account of spatiotemporal relations in terms of causal relations, or causal relations in terms of spatiotemporal ones. It may be the case (epistemic 'may') that one or both of these sorts of relation are constituted by still more fundamental relations, picked out perhaps by theoretical terms in still to be developed theories. The spatiotemporal relations (and, more generally, spacetime), rather than causality, seem the natural candidates for such scientific analyses. If, among the (external) relations that we are actually acquainted with, any is ontologically fundamental, then I suspect it to be causality. Perhaps it really is the cement of the universe. The relation between causality and laws of nature remains to be spelt out in the final chapters of this essay.

6.3 THE TRUTHMAKERS FOR INTERNAL RELATIONS

The truthmakers for internal relations, it was argued, are nothing more than the terms of the relation. An hypothesis is now advanced. In every case of an internal relation, the relation is determined by nothing more than the *identity* or the *difference* of these truthmakers. The identity may be mere *partial* identity, which is, of course, at the same time mere partial difference.

Thus, consider resemblance. For those of us who accept universals, in the simplest case this is a matter of the resembling particulars instantiating the same, the identical, universal. The resemblance supervenes on these states of affairs, and it seems easy to accept that the resemblance is no ontological addition to the states of affairs themselves.

Things become more controversial where, say, two determinate universals resemble by falling under the one determinable predicate. But if no determinable universal corresponds to that predicate, then, we argued in 4.13, the truthmaker for the resemblance is the partial identity of the determinate universals. It was the difficulty of taking this line for fundamental intensive quantities that led us, in 4.22, to cast doubt on the existence of such quantities.

What can be said at least, though, is that very many internal relations are grounded on nothing more than the identity or difference of their terms. A challenge may be issued to those who think that there are internal relations (as we have defined them) that are not so grounded. The challenge is to give an account of the truthmakers for these special internal relations. Are necessary states of affairs required?

A challenge may also be issued to those who would substitute exactly resembling tropes for identical universals. It is natural to take the tropes involved as truthmakers for the truth that they resemble exactly. The exact resemblance appears to supervene on the tropes. But can it be an ontologically costless supervenience as it is in the case of universals? It does not seem so. The tropes cannot be identical, they must be different. How, then, do they support the exact resemblance in the special cases where there is exact resemblance? It seems that 'brute necessities', *un*transparent necessities, will have to be postulated *in re*.

6.4 TWO SORTS OF EXTERNAL RELATION

Dyadic relations may be either symmetrical, asymmetrical or non-symmetrical. Asymmetrical relations will be left aside here because, as will be argued in chapter 9, there is reason to think that among the external relations, which are the ones to be taken seriously ontologically, none of the relations in the true states of affairs are asymmetrical of necessity. This leaves symmetrical and non-symmetrical external relations to consider. It appears that they are very different sorts of affair.

We may begin by considering Grossmann's claim (1983, sec. 67), following Russell in *The Principles of Mathematics* (1937 [1903], p. 97) that every relation has a *direction*. (Russell calls it a *sense*.) The alleged fact that Russell and Grossmann are pointing to is that, in the latter's words: 'A relation comes with a definite order among its places.' Such an order is clearly visible in the case of non-symmetrical relations. There is all the world of difference between *a* loving *b*, and *b* loving *a*.

But it seems wrong to say that *every* relation has a direction, at any rate from the distinctly economical standpoint taken in this book, in particular given the contention that what supervenes is no increase of being. For us, the state of affairs of *a's being a mile from b* supervenes upon *b's being a mile from a* and vice-versa. This commits us to saying, what philosophical commonsense in any case dictates, that what we have here is no more than one state of affairs which language allows us to refer to in two different ways. And so for all relations that are symmetrical by necessity. In Fregean terms, there is no *order* in the places for particulars provided for in the unsaturated entity that is the relation. David Lewis has suggested to me that an appropriate symbolism for a necessarily symmetrical relation is a predicate with a plural subject: *they* (*a* and *b*) are a mile apart.

It may be noted in passing that if *a* has a relation to *b*, then, by the usage of logicians, *b* automatically has the *converse* relation to *a*. There is no increase of being here either.

So relations that are symmetrical by necessity lack direction. But non-symmetrical relations do have a direction. Consider *loves*. If we write *a* L*b*, then this formalism does not tell us who loves and who is beloved. This is to a degree concealed in ordinary language because the word 'loves' indicates that the name before the relation-word is to be taken as the name of the lover. But to make the same point in a formal symbolism we need, say, to subscript the blanks: $\_{_1}L\_{_2}$. It then becomes clear that symmetrical and non-symmetrical relations are, ontologically, two different sorts of relation.

This is not the only difference between these two sorts of relation. Consider a typical external and symmetric dyadic relation such as *being a mile distant from*, a relation, moreover, that appears to be reasonably fundamental ontologically speaking. Contrast it with a relation such as *before*. (It will be argued in ch. 9 that this latter relation is not necessarily asymmetrical. If time is linear, then it is asymmetrical *de facto* and if time is circular it is symmetrical *de facto*. But in its essence it is non-symmetrical.) Distance is a quantity, and might even be thought of as a non-relational *property* of the stretch between its terms. But *before* cannot be thought of as a property. In general, the non-symmetrical relations seem to be, if one may so put it, the more truly relational relations.

It is likely that there is much, much, more to be said about the ontology of relations, although my own inspiration is exhausted at this point. For the reasons mentioned in 1.2, relations, as distinct from relational properties, have come upon the scene very slowly. As a result, their ontology is not a topic about which very many positive conclusions have been reached.

6.5 RELATIONAL PROPERTIES

There is a quite important distinction, not so important ontologically but important in the stating and discussing of many issues, to be made between relations and relational properties. A relation is polyadic in nature, holding between two or more terms. We may confine ourselves here, for simplicity's sake only, to relational properties associated with dyadic relations. Such a relational property is, on the surface, something monadic: it attaches to a single particular. Thus, *being a father* is a relational property, while *fathering* is a relation.

A relational property of this sort is to be contrasted with a non-relational, or, as it is sometimes put, an intrinsic property. (Though there is always a tendency for philosophers to understand 'intrinsic property' as *essential* property, a notion of which the present metaphysic will make only limited use. This moves me to prefer, and use, the clumsier-sounding phrase 'non-relational property'.) It is often very important to distinguish non-relational from relational properties in certain ontological enquiries, for instance, in discussing the thesis or theses of the Identity of Indiscernibles, the idea that sameness of all properties yields sameness of the particulars having the properties (see Armstrong, 1978a, ch. 9, sec. 1). It is also often very important to discover (science or philosophy or both may be involved) whether a particular property is or is not a relational one, for instance whether *size* is a relational or a non-relational property.

A further point is this. As we have noticed, both Greek and Scholastic metaphysics found it very difficult to focus upon relations, and constantly tried to assimilate the holding of relations to the possession of relational properties by the related terms. But it seems that this assimilation is right for the case of *internal* relations. Given that such relations supervene upon the existence of their terms, given, that is, that the relation is necessitated by the terms, it is right to think of such a relation as assimilable to properties of the terms (taken together). The only trouble is that internal relations, because of their supervenience, are not the sort of relations we should be focussing on in ontology. If this is correct, then the Greek/Scholastic error was based upon a degree of real insight, so becoming the more excusable.

But just as internal relations supervene upon their terms, so do relational properties supervene upon states of affairs. Indeed, two different sorts of relational properties may be distinguished, and both supervene. If *a* has R to *b*, and *b* is a G, then *a* has the relational property of *having R to a G*, with this property supervening upon these two states of affairs. If R and G are both universals, then this relational property would appear to be a universal itself. It could even be a property that had important causal effects. We may call it a *pure* relational property. But *having R to b* could also be, and often is, described as a property of *a*. It is not a universal because it essentially involves the particular *b*. But it does, or may, have *one* of the important properties of a universal. It is 'predicable of many'. If R is a universal, the relational property is even strictly identical in its various 'instantiations'. Yet it supervenes upon any state of affairs where something has R to *b*. We can call it an *impure* relational property.

A relational property that is usually of special *un*importance ontologically is one 'generated' by an *internal* relation. (For instance, 4 having the relational property of *being greater than 3*.) This is to be expected if internal relations are not anything over and above their terms. A sort of double supervenience occurs. The relational property supervenes upon the holding of the internal relation, and the internal relation supervenes upon its terms.

A useful bit of terminology has been introduced by Andrew Newman (1992, p. 197). He speaks of a relational property of something as a *monadic reduction* of that thing's relation to something further. We shall follow his usage from time to time. It is especially useful in cases where it is controversial whether we are dealing with a genuine property, or merely a relation to something further. Newman thinks that the *force* exerted by a body is a monadic reduction of its causal relation to the effect of the force. True force, he holds, is the force-relation. We have, in effect, disagreed with him, arguing in 5.5 and 5.6 that the force *is* a property of the force-exerting body, though a property either semantically picked out *via* its potential effects (Categoricalism) or even essentially linked to such effects (Dispositionalism). But that dispute about the facts does not make the terminology any the less useful.

6.6 THE EPISTEMOLOGY OF RELATIONS

We have noted the ontological confusion about relations to be found in the whole Western philosophical tradition until quite recently. Indeed, it was suggested that this confusion was responsible for the tardy emergence of Factualist ontologies. A natural result of this ontological confusion was that the epistemology of relations fell into confusion also. In particular, it proved difficult for philosophers to acknowledge that relations are as directly perceived as qualities.

But with the ontological mistake corrected, the epistemology can be corrected also. William James was the pioneer, as I learnt from John Anderson in my undergraduate days. In Essays II and III of his *Radical*

Empiricism (1943 [1912]) James argued that relations are given in experience as much as qualities. That was the 'radical' aspect of his Empiricism. We can translate this as: states of affairs involving relations, polyadic states of affairs, are given in experience as much as subject-attribute states of affairs, monadic states of affairs. In Essay VI James argued that even the relation of causality is directly experienced and we shall follow him in this (14.6).

7

Particulars

7.1 TRYING TO DISPENSE WITH PARTICULARS

We are attempting to develop a theory of states of affairs, to be followed up by arguing that states of affairs are all there is to reality. States of affairs, we said, involve properties and relations, properties and relations which are universals rather than particulars (tropes). We now turn our attention to the particulars which instantiate these universals.

The question that immediately arises is whether we really need to recognize an independent category of particularity. May it not be possible to give an account of particulars in terms of properties and relations alone? Various intellectual motives may drive such a strategy. First, there are the epistemological difficulties thought to be involved in postulating particulars which are surplus to their properties and relations. The properties and the relations can be known. The bearer of properties and relations, it is alleged, cannot be known. Why then postulate a bearer? Second, the postulation of bearers appears to lack ontological as well as epistemic economy. Once we have admitted properties into our ontology, we presumably have the bundle of a particular's properties. Why have a bearer in addition? The postulation of a bearer of *universals* may be thought to be uneconomical in special degree, because a Dualism of particulars and universals has been introduced at the bottom of reality. For some or all of these reasons it may be thought better to construe particulars as bundles of properties.

7.11 *Epistemological difficulties about particulars*

We begin by replying to the epistemological difficulty. It seems plausible to say that the particularity of particulars is actually given in experience. What we need to do here is to look at perception, considering it as an event in the mind. So taken, perception is always perception *that* something is the case. Perception need not always be veridical, and whether veridical or not, the content of the perception may be overruled by higher cognitive faculties so that there is no simple relation between the content of perception and the acquiring of beliefs. But the content is always *that* something is the case. It is propositional. (And as a Direct Realist about perception I claim that what is putatively perceived is always some state of affairs external to the mind.) One might call this a *propositional* account of perception, provided that this is not taken to suggest any link with language. (See Armstrong, 1968, ch. 10.) One could also call it a *states of affairs* account of perception although the states of affairs need not exist and the properties and relations involved are pretty much certain to be 'second-class' properties and relations, that is to say, not universals. (See 3.9 for these ontologically second-class citizens.)

Now consider the content of a perception. Basic perceptions (as opposed, for instance, to perceptions of absences, which are more sophisticated) would seem to take the form 'This has certain properties' and/or 'This has certain relations to that.' In a visual case it may be a matter of an object having a certain shape and colour and having a certain spatial relation to other things. Will it not be natural to take the 'this' and the 'that' as referring to particulars, particulars which are not wholly constituted by their properties and relations? If so, then it can be claimed that the particularity of particulars, the fact that they are not exhausted by their properties and relations, is part of the content of perception.

Misunderstanding is easy here, and must be guarded against. It is not being claimed that this point of metaphysics can be settled by a propositional theory of perception plus a perfunctory phenomenological inspection. The claim being made is much weaker. Perhaps the point can best be put cautiously by saying that it is not *obvious* that all that is given to us in perception is mere properties and relations. But if it is not obvious, what is the standing of the *epistemological* argument against irreducible particularity? The argument would seem to beg the question by assuming from the beginning that only properties and relations are perceived. If it is conceded that the question is being begged in this way, then the epistemological argument is surely neutralized. The question whether there is or is not irreducible particularity in the world then becomes a matter to be settled on *ontological* grounds.

7.12 Ontological critique of bundle theories

What then of the more serious, because ontological, arguments? Here it is a matter of assembling a profit-and-loss account and arguing that, although it is true that there is a certain lack of economy in accepting the irreducibility of particularity, this disadvantage is quite outweighed by some of the consequences of adopting the reductionist or bundle position.

Embracing a bundle position involves substituting a fundamental relation between properties – often spoken of as compresence – as a substitute for the fundamental tie between particular and property. These properties that go to make up a particular on this bundle theory are, presumably, all and only the non-relational properties of the particular in question. If the truthmaker argument for states of affairs succeeds for a metaphysics that recognizes particulars and universals, as will be argued in detail in the next chapter, then it would seem that bundle theories should also recognize states of affairs, states of affairs that weld constituents of the bundle together. These states of affairs, however, have laws of composition that are somewhat different from the particular/universal theory. (Particular/attribute is asymmetrical, compresence of attributes is symmetrical.) External relations between different bundles, that is, ordinary external relations between ordinary particulars, will come out as relations between bundles, that is, as states of affairs. The bundles will be bundlings of properties, and so will also be states of affairs. As a result, the relations between these bundles will be states of affairs involving relations between states of affairs. The latter case is not all that different from our own states of affairs involving relations, although in our theory higher-order states of affairs are not required for the analysis of the holding of first-order relations. (A minor lack of economy in the bundle theory.)

A bundle theorist must choose between making the constituents of the bundles universals or particulars, that is, repeatable or non-repeatable properties. Choosing universals makes the task very difficult. In order to see this, first consider the position of a bundle theorist who works with non-repeatable properties, that is, with tropes. For that sort of bundle theory, each ordinary particular such as a stone is a bundle of non-repeatable entities. The compresence relation is symmetrical, and, it is plausible to say, transitive. Different ordinary particulars may overlap or be proper parts of each other. But it seems that the tropes that, on this theory, make up the ordinary particular will be tropes of that particular alone. As a result, the bundling relation that holds between the non-repeatable entities that constitute a single stone or whatever will, as it were, keep all the bundled items in the same place.

By contrast, universals are identical in their different instantiations, so the bundles of universals that constitute different ordinary particulars will overlap wherever the particulars have a common property. Such overlap would not matter if the theory contained, as a distinct but linked constituent, thin particulars that instantiated these overlapping universals. Such particulars would secure the numerical difference of things. But the only particulars that a bundle of universals theory can countenance are ones constructed *from* the universals.

Consider, for instance, that on this bundles-of-universals theory two different things could not be exactly alike. For if they were exactly alike, they would be the same bundle of universals and so would not be different. The theory must therefore pronounce what at least seems to be a distinctly arbitrary ban on such likeness. (Unless, indeed, the one bundle of universals could have two numerically different bundling-relations.) But there is much more trouble than this. The principal problem is given by the relation of compresence. Each property of a particular will, by definition, be compresent with every other property of that particular. Suppose that two of the properties are F and G. But suppose that another particular has properties G and H, where H is a property that the first particular lacks. Since G is a universal, it is the very same property in both particulars. So the one entity G is compresent with both F and H, and the compresence relation, although symmetrical, turns out to be not transitive. This means that, for the bundle of universals theory, compresence is not an equivalence relation, as it is for the bundling relation holding between properties that are particulars. Without an equivalence relation, it is not possible to divide the field of universals into non-overlapping bundles. How is such a relation to be specified? Russell made an attempt (best seen in his 1948, pt 4, ch. 8), which Goodman showed to fail (1966, 5.3). Goodman in turn suggested a repair which, however, may have difficulties of its own (1966, 6.4 & 6.5). But the discussion will not be taken further here. See Armstrong, 1978a, chapter 9; and 1989a, chapter 4.

Once properties and relations are taken to be particulars, a bundle theory becomes at least quite attractive. Contrariwise, if one chooses a bundle theory, then that is a strong motive for taking the constituents of the bundle to be particulars rather than universals. It should therefore be noted carefully, as it has already been noted at 3.23, that it is possible to combine a substance/attribute account of particulars while holding that the attributes are particulars. This was probably the view of Locke, and the view is explicitly held in our own day by C.B. Martin. (See his 'Substance Substantiated', 1980.) It is arguably a superior view to the more usual 'bundle of particular attributes'. At any rate, it is for the present author the position one should fall back to if universals have to be given up.

For there is a fundamental difficulty with all bundle theories. It is that properties and relations, whether universals or particulars, seem not suitable to be the ultimate constituents of reality. If they are the ultimate constituents, then, it appears, completely different (non-overlapping) properties and relations will be 'distinct existences' in Hume's sense of the phrase: entities logically capable of independent existence. But are properties and relations really capable of independent existence? Can a certain determinate mass, for instance, whether the universal of that mass or the trope mass of this particular body, exist in logical independence of anything else? It hardly seems so. The case against the possibility of independent existence for relations seems even stronger. If one thinks of properties as *ways* things are and relations as *ways* things stand to each other, as already argued in chapter 3.6, one has a particularly strong motive for denying the possibility of such independent existence. How can ways exist by themselves, whether universals or particulars?

The alternative is to argue that ways are, after all, distinct existences, but to permit relations of necessity, full metaphysical necessity, to hold between such distinct existences. The properties and relations come accompanied by others or they do not come at all. A certain amount of bundling (how much?) is necessitated. There seems to be no conclusive argument against such a position. But it would, for instance, require considerable qualification of an independently attractive theory of what *possibilities* there are: the Combinatorial theory of possibility.

At any rate, in this work it will be taken that particularity cannot be accounted for in terms of the properties and/or relations of particulars, whether these properties and relations be universals or particulars.

7.2 TEMPORAL PARTS

7.21 *Arguments for temporal parts*

There may be particulars that occupy no more than a spatial point. But whether or not there are such particulars, there certainly are particulars that have spatial parts. Where spatial parts of particulars are non-overlapping, the parts in question are wholly mereologically distinct particulars, although they may be nomically bound together. (They may instantiate the very same universals. But they can be wholly distinct existences in the

Humean sense that it is possible for either to exist in the absence of the other.) Again, there may be particulars that exist for no more than an instant. But whether or not there are such particulars, there certainly are particulars that exist for a time. Do such particulars have *temporal* parts, parts which, if non-overlapping, constitute wholly distinct particulars? Here, temporal parts will be argued for.

There is, or perhaps only was, a rather disgraceful tendency to try to settle this question against temporal parts by doing no more than appealing to the authority of ordinary thought and language. 'He's the very same person as the one we saw yesterday, isn't he? So we are seeing *him*, not a mere temporal part of him.' Some philosophers who have used this argument ('ordinary language spoken in a plonking tone of voice' – F. Knöpfelmacher) were aware that other metaphysical issues cannot be settled in this all too easy way. But the phrase 'the very same' seems to cloud judgment. It may be helpful to consider the proverbial blind men who came at the one elephant from different directions. All had hold of *the very same* elephant. Yet it was different parts of the elephant that they had hold of. It may equally be that when we see the same person on different occasions we are seeing wholly distinct temporal parts of that person (ontology) *and* seeing the very same person (ordinary discourse).

An illuminating way of putting the problem is in terms of the distinction made at 2.31 between strict and loose identity. If this distinction is well-founded, then where we have what ordinary discourse speaks of as the very same entity at different times, there is still the question whether this identity is strict or loose. It seems that to maintain that the identity is strict is to deny temporal parts in these cases; to maintain the identity is loose is to uphold temporal parts.

Consider now a particular, not a particular considered in abstraction from all its properties, but the particular taken along with its *non-relational* properties. (This is the *thick* particular. See 8.3.) Let it be a particular that changes over time. Consider two times, t_1 and t_2, at which the particular has incompatible non-relational properties. Perhaps it is hot at one time, cold at another. It seems that the particular at t_1 cannot be (strictly) identical with the particular at t_2. The identity can be loose only, a matter of two different temporal parts of the one particular. For how can strictly the same thing have incompatible properties?

Consider by way of contrast a classical atom. The non-relational properties of such atoms never change while the atom exists. Such lack of change is a necessary (though not sufficient) condition for strict identity over time. I think that classical atomists thought of their atoms, so far as they thought about the matter, as strictly identical over time. I think their position was coherent.

But, it will be objected, what about the *relational* properties of the atom? Will not the atom be at one distance from another atom at one time, but at a different, incompatible, distance at another time? And how can that be if the parallel argument from incompatible non-relational properties is sound? In fact, however, the cases are different. The classical atomist can maintain that the atom is strictly identical at all times and has to its environment *all* the relations that it enters into while it exists. (It is important here that the negations of relations are not relations.)

The case of universals is helpful here. A universal is exactly the same, it cannot be different, in its different instantiations. Each instantiation is differently environed. That, I take it, is not a difficulty for the existence of universals. The universal has *all* these environments. In exactly the same way, the classical atom, strictly identical at all times, has all its environments.

Changing particulars, though, demand temporal parts (see also my 1980). The same position has been upheld by David Lewis (1986, pp. 202–4 and 210). He calls it the problem of temporary intrinsics, temporary non-relational properties as I would put it. Peter van Inwagen in an article 'Four-Dimensional Objects' (1990) discusses Lewis's argument, appreciates the problem, but still wishes to defend the rejection of temporal parts for a wide class of changing particulars. Taking the particular case of the philosopher Descartes, who he thinks like other human beings and animals to be strictly identical through time, he says that when we say Descartes was hungry at t_1:

> we are saying either (take your pick) that this object bore the relation *having* to the time-indexed property *hunger-at-*t_1, or else that it bore the time-indexed relation *having-at-*t_1 to hunger.
>
> (p. 247)

What van Inwagen is doing is adjusting the theory of properties, in one case, or adjusting the theory of the connection between things and their properties, in the other, with the object of evading the Lewis argument. Does 'take your pick' mean that the two theories are equivalent? Whether it does or not is perhaps not so important, because the fundamental adjustment seems the same in both cases. In each case it is said that Descartes does no more than bear a *relation*, an external relation as I suppose, to the properties. So, I take it, van Inwagen's position entails that the properties lie *outside* Descartes' being. He seems to be saying, therefore, that Descartes himself, the true Descartes, does not change intrinsically, nor does any other animal. It is a possible view, perhaps, but I see no reason to adopt it. I take it, on the contrary, that Descartes himself changes, and so I conclude that Descartes has temporal parts.

Given what has already been said about loose identity in 2.31 we will expect that there is a reasonably salient relation that will sort the different temporal parts of such objects as animals and stones into what are at least roughly equivalence classes. Probably these approximate equivalence classes should not be identified with the objects, but the *aggregates* or *fusions* of their members (the mereological sums of their members) can be so identified. The exact nature of this equivalence relation we have still to discuss (see 7.23).

It is an argument for an account of identity over time in terms of equivalence classes that it is real or imagined cases of fission and fusion, splitting and coalescing of objects, that make us particularly uncertain whether the original thing continues to exist after its division, or whether the original things continue to exist after they have fused together. All sorts of ingenious puzzle cases have been proposed. But it is just in such cases that relevant and salient equivalence classes are difficult to find. If particulars that exist over time are cut off from each other, then it is easy to see that their temporal parts fall into classes that do not overlap, and so that there will be salient equivalence relations which produce just these classes. But once there is overlap, as there is with fission and fusion, equivalence classes become a problem. That it would in these circumstances become difficult to decide questions of identity over time, a loose identity as has just been argued, is exactly what is to be predicted if loose identity is a matter of common membership of a relevant equivalence class.

Van Inwagen does note a consequence of accepting a doctrine of temporal parts which he thinks may be some embarrassment to its upholders. If a thing that exists over time is a sum of its temporal parts, in the same way that a thing at a time is the sum of its spatial parts, then this sum of parts will apparently have to be essential to the thing. This seems to make it tricky to say, as presumably we want to say, that Descartes, for instance, might have died before he did or lived longer than he actually did. Herbert Hochberg has pointed out to me, however, that this is a point that is regularly brought up in connection with any theory that identifies a thing with a bundle or collection of its constituents. Van Inwagen himself remarks that the situation can be dealt with if we are prepared to embrace the view that possible Xs may be mere counterparts of actual Xs. He remarks further that this need not involve accepting a full-blown ontology of counterparts such as that of David Lewis. For us, given the distinction between strict and loose identity, there is the possibility of treating counterparts as the 'same' as the actual thing that they are counterparts of, but the same in a loose sense only. We will come back to this when we come to discuss the theory of modality. See 10.42.

7.22 *Things that have duration yet do not change*

We have seen that the argument to temporal parts from non-relational change fails for things whose non-relational nature does not change. Such objects *may* have temporal parts but it would seem possible to hold that they are strictly identical, strictly the same, objects during the time that they do not change.

I have already suggested that classical atoms were thought of as strictly identical in this way. Bishop Butler was contrasting such atoms with the gradually changing conglomerations of such atoms that he thought constituted a human body existing over time. The latter was loose identity, and if, as I have suggested, loose identity is a matter of approximate equivalence classes under a salient equivalence relation, then one can see that the succession of such conglomerations would be an equivalence class under a salient equivalence relation. (Allowing that the *analysis* of this apprehended relation may still be a tricky and controversial matter.)

The classical atomic theory is scientifically dead. But it may still be that physics will wish once again to postulate unchanging constituents (perhaps of more than one species) at the bottom of the universe. Such particulars could be taken to have strict identity over time. But it may also be that all particulars are subject to internal change, and so that any particular existing for a time lacks strict identity over time.

David Lewis, however, has a further argument that would, if good, be very damaging to the hypothesis (which we have here entertained speculatively only) that our world of change contains a plurality of particulars that are strictly identical for the whole time that they exist (1986b, p. 205, n. 6). It is a re-use of the argument from change. Consider two Newtonian atoms that have strict identity over time. It would not be possible, Lewis argues in effect, for them to have, say, different distances at different times. Assuming that distance is ontologically a two-place relation, then the two atoms would have to be at the very same distance from each other at all times during which they both exist. Yet this conclusion seems absurd. Lewis calls this the problem of *accidental external relations.*

It seems that the metaphysics of states of affairs (to which, of course, Lewis objects on independent grounds) is able to deal with this problem. We must distinguish between the whole formed by the two atoms in abstraction from any (external) relations that they may have, and the 'larger' whole formed by the two atoms related by whatever external relations relate them (where these relations are ones that involve the two atoms and nothing else). The first of these two wholes is a mereological one, and nothing more. Being nothing but the mereological sum of two strictly identical, and therefore unchanging, things, it itself cannot change except by annihilation of parts. But the second whole is something more. It is a succession of states of affairs, atomic or molecular states of affairs which have as their constituents the two atoms *plus* the genuinely dyadic relations that hold just between them at different times. Those relations are an addition of being to the two atoms. This second whole is an object that has temporal parts, and hence lacks strict identity over time. Granted states of affairs, then, the strictly identical things can change their relations over time without paradox.

7.23 *How are particulars unified over time?*

But there are particulars that change internally, even if just by rearrangement of parts, and it seems that *their* identity over time can only be loose identity. Accepting temporal parts, for these cases at least, we can go on and ask what is the particular equivalence relation, the principle of unity, that binds together the temporal parts of a physical thing: a stone or a human body. An answer that has in recent times commanded assent from some is that it is, roughly, a matter of spatiotemporal continuity plus the resemblance of adjoining portions of the spacetime line. This answer may be more or less extensionally correct, but there are difficulties in taking it to constitute the essence of continued existence in the light of the following cases. The cases may not be actual, but they seem to involve no contradiction.

First, it seems possible that things should exist intermittently. Consider, in particular, a case where a person disappears at a certain time and after an interval a very close counterpart of the person appears (it may not even be at the same place) and shows every other sign of being that person. Even though certain temporal parts are as it were missing, it does not seem that we would automatically rule out a claim of identity as involving contradiction. Intermittent existence seems possible. If so, then spatiotemporal continuity is not an essential necessary condition for identity (loose identity) across time.

It is true, of course, that we could have puzzle cases where not just one but two internally indiscernible counterparts appeared simultaneously. In such a situation, we might be unable to give any clear answer to the question which of these counterparts was (loosely) identical with the original object. But that is one of the cases where, as has been indicated in 7.21, it may not be possible to construct the required equivalence classes.

Second, spatiotemporal continuity seems not to be an essential sufficient condition for cross-temporal identity. Apparently possible cases have been suggested by Shoemaker (1979), Lewis (1983a, 1986b, ch. 4) and myself (1980), where an object is annihilated at a certain place and time, and another object just like it is created at the very same place and time so that spatiotemporal continuity is preserved. Provided that there is no connection between the annihilation and the creation, provided, that is, that the whole affair is an accident, we seem to have, not continuity of existence, but replacement of one thing by another.

What does seem to be essential is that there should be a causal, or at any rate nomic, relation between past and future temporal parts. A continuing thing must grow out of its past. This view is to be found in Hume and in Russell's neglected late work, *Human Knowledge* (1948), where a continuing thing is described as a series of events forming a *causal line* (pt VI, ch. V). It is clear that not any sort of causal line will do. Russell himself thinks of it as a more or less self-determined process (*immanent* as opposed to *transeunt* causality) which may be regarded as the persistence of something – a thing replacing itself. He says that it is, in a sense, an extension of Newton's First Law of Motion. We can think of it as a temporal part of a thing bringing about, causing, a later part of the thing.

What it seems can be added with advantage, and was perhaps intended by Russell, is that the causal line be *information preserving*. Perhaps this can be spelt out by using David Lewis's notion of *counterfactual dependence* (see Lewis, 1986c, pps. 164–5). Consider some ordinary physical object such as a stone or a tree. It is a complex mass or structure of much smaller objects. Each of these smaller objects is itself a causal line, projecting itself into the future, while more or less maintaining the various relations that it has to its fellows, in particular to its nearest fellows. Just what the nature is of the causal line projected by the constituent objects depends on what happens to the constituent object both as a result of action upon the object and, if it has parts itself, the effect of the interaction of these parts. A vast mass of conditionals will have to be true of these constituent objects. If they are acted upon in one way, the line of their future will have a certain nature, if acted upon another way their future will be systematically different. In this way the stone or the tree reflects in its current constitution what has happened to it in the past. And so the causal line may be said to be information-preserving. Just how much information is preserved that one might have thought was gone for ever, contemporary science is discovering for us every day.

We must, of course, as already argued at 5.1, be prepared to adopt a wide conception of causation. The continued existence of things that have temporal parts need not, or need not necessarily, involve the interactive causality that is to be found where there are *forces* operating. (Newton's Third law ensures interaction wherever forces operate.) Again, causation has been identified with *transfer of energy* (Fair, 1979). Where is the transfer of energy in mere continued existence? Perhaps, however, if continued existence is a continual succession of temporal parts then we do have a form of transfer of energy. The 'transfer' is a transfer from earlier to later. Even so, it is clear that the causation involved is a different sort of thing from the ordinary causality that involves interaction. That is recognized when the phrase 'immanent causation' is introduced. How different a thing? Provided we are thinking in terms of temporal parts, as Russell obviously is, the difference is not so very great. In each case something is succeeded by something, a succession of a regular sort, and so presumably governed by a law. If one rejects an account of ordinary causality in terms of mere regular succession, holding out instead for a 'strong' theory of laws such as the one advocated in this work, then the difference is no more than the difference between laws of immanent succession and laws of transeunt succession. If one thinks that in ordinary causation there is a production or bringing into being in some strong sense, then it would seem natural to hold that earlier temporal parts of things produce or bring into being later temporal parts of the same thing in just the same sense. It seems that, given temporal parts, immanent and transeunt causation are naturally taken to be different species of relation falling under the same genus. Nor does there seem to be anything particularly paradoxical about this conclusion, anything that would give occasion for a *modus tollens* directed against the idea of immanent causation.

So for particulars that exist for a period of time (particulars taken along with their non-relational properties), the doctrine of temporal parts is accepted. (A reservation is made for the case, at least a thinkable one, of atoms of some sort that do not and cannot suffer internal change.) Perhaps temporal parts divide in the end into instantaneous parts, and of these instantaneous parts there may be just a finite number or else there may be some infinite number. Or there may be no ultimate parts at all, with division *ad infinitum*. But I suggest that this question of parts, like the question of the ultimate structure of space, is not one for philosophers to dogmatize over. If it can be settled at all, it will be settled by physics and/or cosmology.

7.3 THE NATURE OF PARTICULARITY

The position being taken is that the particularity of particulars is not to be accounted for in terms of universals, or, indeed, in terms of properties taken as particulars. It is an irreducible feature of particulars, distinct from their properties. How can we characterize it further?

A technique that I found useful in earlier work (1989b, ch. 4, sec. 2) is to begin the discussion with quite small and simple worlds, where different positions (though not necessarily the grounds for deciding between these positions) emerge with greater clarity. Consider, then, a world containing just two simple individuals, *a* and *b*, with the first having just the one simple property F and the second having just the one simple property G. For the Factualist, that world is like this:

(1) F*a* & G*b*.

The conjuncts are states of affairs. Because the constituents are all simple, with the particulars lacking any spatial, temporal or other sort of part, and the universals lacking any constituent universals, there are only the two first-order states of affairs. We do, I believe, and will later argue, require a higher-order state of affairs: that these are the *totality* of lower-order states of affairs. But that is not of present importance, and we can let it be shown, as opposed to its being said, by the absence of any further symbols for states of affairs in formula (1). If it is thought (as I do not think) that the mere conjunction of two monadic states of affairs involving distinct atomic particulars will have the effect of dividing this world into two different worlds, then we can add a further state of affairs, R*ab*, with R simple and symmetrical. Again, the matter is not of importance here.

Now consider the world:

(2) G*a* & F*b*.

The question to be considered is whether world (1) is the same world as world (2), or different? In my 1989b I argued that all we have here are just two verbally different formulations to which no ontological distinction corresponds. I called this position anti-haecceitist. A haecceitist was thus defined as one who holds that the two worlds are genuinely different. Carnap would have said that we have here two state-descriptions but only one structure-description: a world of two simple objects, one having the simple property F, the other having the simple property G. My position in effect was that the identity-condition for worlds was: having the same structure-description. Or, putting it another way: indiscernible worlds are the very same world.

Discussion with Michael Tooley has made me think that I made the wrong choice here. I have never had any objection to indiscernibility *within* worlds. If we consider the world:

(3) F*a* & F*b*

then I know of no argument against such a world, although *a* and *b* are perfectly indiscernible. Suggested counter-examples to the Identity of Indiscernibles (same properties → same thing), such as Max Black's indiscernible spheres (1952) or an endless exact repetition of the events in the world, seem to be too plausible to reject (see my 1978a, ch. 9, sec. 1).

Such cases can, however, be manipulated a little to produce plausible counter-examples to the anti-haecceitist position. Suppose, for instance, that after the two indiscernible spheres have existed for a period of time, one of them just goes out of existence. Are there not two possibilities here: *a* ceasing to exist and *b* ceasing to exist? Yet the structure-description for the two apparent possibilities would be identical. One could make the case more poignant by substituting for the spheres twin earths, exactly twin, with a full range of human activity. Is there not a real question which set of persons ceases to exist? So I now think that my anti-haecceitism was too extreme. The two state-descriptions did describe two different possible worlds. I owe apologies to Brian Skyrms, who held to the haecceitist position all along. See his 1981.

But in any case, even if haecceitism returns, this does not mean that any extreme haecceitism need be embraced either. (As Skyrms would agree, personal communication.) There is certainly no call to think of haecceity as a unique inner nature or essence possessed by each particular, something property-like, although a property necessarily limited to one thing. When we have said that different particulars are numerically different, then we appear to have said all that can be said about the nature of particularity. The *nature* of a thing is given exclusively by its properties, in particular by its non-relational properties. And one thing should be noted especially. It was argued in the previous section that changeable particulars have temporal parts. Consider, then, two non-overlapping temporal parts of the one particular. Each will have its own haecceity, which, though, is to say no more than that they are numerically different particulars.

Holding as they do that nothing exists but the spatiotemporal system, Naturalists may be tempted by the idea that difference of haecceity, difference of particular, is given by difference of spatiotemporal position. This suggestion, though, seems multiply flawed. First, it only drives us on to ask what constitutes difference of spatiotemporal position. It is hard to find any plausible answer except bare numerical difference. The same return of the problem occurs if spacetime is not fundamental but is analysable in terms of more fundamental particulars. What can be said about the particularity of these new particulars except that they are numerically different from each other? Second, it is not at all obvious that two particulars could not exist at the same place and time. We should in this matter seek guidance from science rather than philosophy. Perhaps the *fields* of physics are real things, as contemporary physics tends to assume, and can interpenetrate. Perhaps there can even be two particulars with exactly the same properties at the same place and time. If so, difference of spatiotemporal position is not necessary for numerical difference. Third, if there are or can be particulars that remain numerically and *strictly* identical over time, then difference of spatiotemporal position is not even sufficient for numerical difference (for this see 7.22).

The doctrine of haecceity is accepted, then, in a moderate form. But the particularity of particulars is taken as fundamental and unanalysable. I speak of the particularity of particulars, rather than just of particulars, because we ought to be cautious in identifying the particularity with the particular itself. The particularity of a particular may be called the 'thin particular', the particular abstracted in thought from its non-relational properties. It must then be contrasted with the 'thick particular', already briefly introduced in 7.21. But it will be best to postpone the discussion of this part of the theory of particulars until we reach the theory of states of affairs (8.3 in particular).

The 'thin particular', the particularity of the particular, is traditionally regarded by philosophers with a certain ambivalence. If *it* is considered in abstraction from the properties it *has*, a considering of the sort that Locke called 'partial consideration' (*Essay* , bk. 2, ch. 13, sec. 13 – I am indebted to C.B. Martin for the phrase and the reference), then its emptiness of content all too easily translates itself in our thoughts into some unknowable inner constituent. This in turn invites scepticism about the existence of a specific category of particularity over and above the properties of things.

The remedy for this (as already suggested in 7.11, but the matter deserves repetition) lies in a satisfactory epistemology, and in particular a satisfactory theory of perception. Perception, not surprisingly, is adapted to the form of the world. The world is a world of states of affairs, and perception is a mental event having intentionality and the intentional object of that mental event is itself a state of affairs. The object is intentional, that is to say, the state of affairs need not actually exist. When it does not exist, we have non-veridical perception. In most cases of non-veridical perception the subject or subjects of the state of affairs will exist but some of the attributed properties or relations will not be possessed by the subject or subjects. In hallucination, even the subject or subjects fail to exist. But the perception will always take the form of an awareness or an 'awareness' that the perceiver's body and/or objects in the environment have certain properties and/or relations. Whether we think of it as a belief, as I have argued in earlier writings, is not particularly material here. Perhaps we can take over Hume's word 'impression' and say that it is an impression. But it is an impression *that* something is the case. It is propositional. (It needs to be reiterated, though, that the properties and relations that figure in perception are not likely to be what a developed science will declare to be the true properties and relations. They are but experience's first stab at the joints of reality, 'second-class' properties of particulars as we have already called such preliminary classifications in 3.9.)

Given such a theory of perception, Direct Realist and Cognitivist as it has already been characterized (4.141), the ontological doctrine of the particular just advanced seems less puzzling and less sceptical. In perception we are already aware of particulars, of things, of our body and some of the things that surround it. We are not aware of these particulars except as things that are propertied and related in certain ways. But that does not force us to conclude that what we experience is no more than properties and relations. For getting hold of the particular itself we have nothing more fundamental than the sub-verbal equivalents of such words as 'this' and 'that'. But those words do serve to pick out particular particulars, even if only 'token-reflexively'. In the same sort of way, our perceptions for the most part latch on to particular particulars and distinguish one particular from another.

It may perhaps be true that infants have to learn to latch on to *continuants* such as a toy moving out of the visual field and back again. But continuants, we have argued, have temporal parts that are themselves particulars, and some of these 'smaller' particulars are presumably perceived as particulars from the beginning of perception.

7.4 UNIFIED PARTICULARS

We have advocated what David Lewis is accustomed to call a 'sparse' theory of universals. Not every property recognized in discourse is a universal, indeed it seems that the vast majority of such properties are not universals. They lack the absolute identity in their different instances that is essential to a universal. This should make us think about particulars. It is a stock theme in contemporary discussions that particulars can be put together with the greatest freedom. Some arbitrarily chosen portion of Sirius together with my left shoe will do as a particular. It is an uninteresting particular, it is admitted, but it is there. But are we really right to combine such strictness about universals and such permissiveness about particulars?

Andrew Newman, for instance, has argued for a distinction between 'two sorts of particulars, those that have a natural principle of unity and those that do not' (1992, p. 165). But although he devotes a lot of attention to arguing that various things are 'arbitrary particulars', such things as sets and events, he has very little to say about what a 'unified particular' might be. The only suggestion to be found in his work is that the latter is 'the sort of thing with which you could interact causally' (p. 168). It is not clear to me that this even rules out the portion of Sirius taken together with my left shoe. May not this uninteresting object act and be acted upon? (Lewis suggests that, my eye caught by Sirius, I stumble and am tripped by the loose sole of the shoe.) Contrariwise, an event that involved a succession of states of affairs having as constituents property universals which are predicated of a series of *different* particulars might seem to be a unified particular, especially if the sequence was causal.

One must remain sympathetic to the attempt to find a *deep* ontological distinction between unified and arbitrary particulars. If the world can be *partitioned* into unchanging particulars that are strictly identical through time, then one could certainly see the point of describing these things as the true particulars. But although this hypothesis should not be lost sight of, and science may perhaps come to endorse it in the long run, it does not at present seem particularly attractive.

8

States of affairs

8.1 THE TRUTHMAKER ARGUMENT

8.11 The need for a truthmaker

At this point the central actors in our metaphysical drama finally take the centre of the stage: states of affairs or facts. One may well wonder why it is, if they are as central as I and some others allege, more has not been seen of them in Western philosophy. The answer, as suggested in 1.2, lies in the substance-attribute metaphysic inherited from Aristotle, together with the corrosive scepticism which later thinkers, no doubt in response to real difficulties, directed towards that model for the world.

To recapitulate this important point. One starts with substances having attributes. Relations are left hanging in limbo, or perhaps treated as attributes of particulars of a peculiar sort. What *should* be done is to interpret the substance/attribute distinction as the recognition of monadic states of affairs. That would clear the way to recognize relations as constituents of polyadic states of affairs. But at this point a failure of insight or nerve occurs. There is not sufficient understanding of relations, and the way ahead is abandoned. Instead the tradition tries to retrace its steps and to reject even monadic states of affairs, or, as the tradition puts it to itself, to reject the substance/attribute distinction.

Problems are developed about substance, about attributes, and about how the two stand to each other. Substance seems unknowable and ungraspable. Attributes tend, especially if conceived of as universals, to float up to some other realm. The way substance and attributes stand to each other is pronounced incomprehensible. The whole analysis of things in terms of subjects and attributes was a mistake. There are just the things. Relations are probably in the mind, or, more up to date, they are no more than classes of ordered classes of things. Order still smacks of relation, so perhaps ordered classes can themselves be reduced to classes of classes, either after the fashion of Wiener or of Kuratowski. So perhaps there are only things and classes in the world. Certainly there are no such entities as facts (states of affairs).

Let us turn briefly to the position of Quine, a position still enormously influential in contemporary metaphysics. Quine holds that the predicate of a true statement in canonical form either has, or at least ought to have (there seems to be some wavering here), no ontological implications. Ontology is, or at least ought to be, carried by the subject term only, the term that is subject to quantification, the only term in the statement that carries, or at least ought to carry, *reference* to what is in the world. (See, in particular, his essay 'On What There Is' in his 1961 [1953].) A disciple of Quine could admit universals. One Quinean, Jack Smart, has in recent years frequently made the point to me that he has no particular objection to my sort of universals, non-intensional ones, ones that are emphatically not identified with *meanings* of predicates, meanings being one of the objects of Quine's scorn. Suppose non-intensional universals are admitted. The Quinean attitude will be that the object *a* and the universal F both become objects of reference, with these two objects linked by a two-placed predicate 'is', the 'is' of instantiation. This predicate will then fall under the general Quinean interdiction against taking the predicate with ontological seriousness. A very *thingy* point of view. (See David Lewis, 1983b.) The world is a world of particulars, with classes somewhat reluctantly added, reluctantly because they are thought to be 'abstract'. There is no call for states of affairs.

But in this sceptical tradition's view there is further reason for being suspicious of this 'is'. If 'is' in this context stands for something in the world, then presumably it stands for a relation of some sort. But if it is a relation, then it is a funny sort of relation. Suppose that *a* stands in the relation R to *b*. R is instantiated by the pair *a* and *b*. So a special extra relation of instantiation is needed to weld the ordinary relation R to the two particulars. And if it really is needed, then why is not a still further relation needed to get the special extra relation, and R, and the two particulars together, and so *ad infinitum*? F. H. Bradley and Quineans join hands here in a rather unholy alliance.

We will not attempt to answer this difficulty at this point. Instead, let us begin by considering, *pace* the sceptical tradition, the pressures that have led so many upholders of universals to recognize the link between particulars and universals as an objective feature of the world.

We are making the venture that the world contains both particulars and universals. It would certainly seem that if this is so, then something is needed to weld them together. First, an argument from authority: It has seemed to many that such a link is needed. Plato spoke of *participation* (e.g. *Parmenides* 129–32); Duns Scotus of a *formal distinction* holding between things that were closer together than *res* and *res.* (Though his 'common natures' were not quite universals, see Boler, 1963.) W.E. Johnson (1921, ch. 1, sec. 5; ch. 13, secs. 4–5) and P.F. Strawson (1959, ch. 5, secs. 2–3) spoke of a 'tie'. Strawson actually used the phrase 'non-relational tie' which sounds like a contradiction though one can sympathize with the pressures behind the words. John Anderson, following an old tradition, spoke of the *copula*, and meant it ontologically (1962). Gustav Bergmann and many others have spoken of *exemplification* (1967). We will speak of *instantiation.*

Our argument will vindicate these thinkers, yet at the same time put their contentions in a perspective that qualifies that vindication. The perspective we want seems to have been achieved in large degree by Wittgenstein in the *Tractatus* and by Anderson. From that perspective, Bradley's regress argument can be answered.

The argument now to be given in *general* support of all these thinkers is perhaps the fundamental argument of this book. It is the *truthmaker* argument. It is an argument whose application goes well beyond the particularly important issue that at this moment engages us. Indeed, it may be thought of as a certain *style* of argument, and an appeal to truthmakers has already been made at points in this work, for instance at 5.21 when discussing dispositions.

Let it be the case that particular *a* instantiates universal F. *a* is F. Must there not be something about the world that makes it to be the case, that serves as an ontological ground, for this truth? (Making to be the case here, of course, is not *causal* making to be the case.) The truthmaker or ground cannot be *a*, at any rate if *a* is taken as the thin particular, the particular apart from its properties. Can it be the pair of *a* and F? This is getting a little warmer. But what appears to be the decisive argument against this suggestion is that it is possible that *a* and F should both exist and yet *a* not be F. F may be instantiated elsewhere.

The assumption here is that the truthmaker for a truth must necessitate that truth. In the useful if theoretically misleading terminology of possible worlds, if a certain truthmaker makes a certain truth true, then there is no alternative world where that truthmaker exists but the truth is a false proposition. Using the distinction between internal and external relations discussed in 6.2, the truthmaking relation is an internal one. This seems evident enough if we consider for a moment the idea that the relation should be external, contingent. If it is said that the truthmaker for a truth could have failed to make the truth true, then we will surely think that the alleged truthmaker was insufficient by itself and requires to be supplemented in some way. A contingently sufficient truthmaker will be true only *in circumstances that obtain in this world*. But then these circumstances, whatever they are, must be added to give the full truthmaker.

One philosopher whose thoughts have moved in this way is Kit Fine (1982). In his paper he distinguishes between two sorts of fact. There are facts that run in parallel with true propositions, and are naturally individuated by reference to these propositions. These he calls *truths*. (For myself, I would not take these sorts of fact with too much ontological seriousness, nor perhaps would he.) But he also sees the need for a more 'worldly' sort of fact that relates to true propositions by a less straightforward correspondence. He considers and discards the term 'verifier' and settles for 'circumstance'. These circumstances 'underlie' true propositions. He inclines to credit circumstances with *structure*, and this and other things that he says make his circumstances sound very like my states of affairs. But the point of particular importance at the moment is that he says that for both sorts of correspondence 'the relation will be *internal*, depending as it does, only upon the internal structure of the entities in question' (p. 53).

8.12 States of affairs as truthmakers

We are asking what in the world will ensure, make true, underlie, serve as the ontological ground for, the truth that *a* is F. The obvious candidate seems to be the state of affairs of *a's being F*. In this state of affairs (fact, circumstance) *a* and F are brought together.

It may help to illuminate this argument if it is contrasted with a different metaphysic of properties. Suppose that we take F not as a universal but as a particular, a trope. Some philosophers who take this view hold in addition that each trope *necessarily* attaches to the particular that it attaches to. (For instance, C.B. Martin, who in a personal communication speaks of tropes as *non-transferable*.) The view is not merely the contention that the property can only be *identified* as the property that attaches to that particular, a view that seems fairly uncontroversial. It is, rather, that it is of the essence of that property that it attaches to that particular. In possible world terms, in all worlds in which that property exists (it itself will be a contingent existent), it is a property of one and the same particular.

Given this view, there is no call for the introduction of states of affairs. Or, rather, there is no need to introduce states of affairs as anything additional to the particular and its property (or, given a bundle version of the trope view, to the other members of the bundle). The property will cling by necessity to its place in the world, and then states of affairs *supervene* on the tropes and their particulars, or in the bundle version just on the tropes. And if states of affairs supervene, then, it may be argued, they are not something ontologically additional to the things they supervene upon. It is the *contingency*, as I take it to be, of *a'* s instantiating the universal F that enforces the need for states of affairs in my ontology.

Is this virtual elimination of states of affairs a recommendation for this variant of the trope view? It seems doubtful. A heavy price is paid for getting rid of non-supervenient states of affairs. The price is the huge amount of necessity *in re* that this version of the trope theory has to postulate. Every property and (it would seem) every relation that exists must be instantiated where it is actually instantiated. If a relation has a direction in Grossmann's sense, perhaps because it is non-symmetrical, then, presumably, that direction must be necessitated also. The particulars that the tropes qualify or hold between need not exist. But then the corresponding properties and relations will not exist either. Given all the particulars and all the trope properties and relations, the arrangement of the world is fixed. If particulars are but bundles of tropes, then given just the individual tropes, properties and relations, the world is fixed.

This scheme of ontology requires detailed examination. But here I will only offer one criticism, internal to my own position. The tropes entail the existence of the states of affairs, so the states of affairs supervene on the existence of the tropes (in the sense I give to the term 'supervene'). But a further premiss is required: that what supervenes is no addition of being to what it supervenes upon, the doctrine of the ontological free lunch. Otherwise the states of affairs are still there, additional to the tropes that they supervene upon. Now the snag appears. If you want the ontological free lunch, you must *limit* the claims to supervenience that can plausibly be made. And is it not fairly plain that to move from the mere tropes to the states of affairs of which they are the constituents is an addition of being? The mere mereological sum of the tropes entails the states of affairs in which they are assembled. More than you should expect to get in a free lunch!

If, on the other hand, the tropes are *not* tied necessarily to the things that have them, then, once again, by the truthmaker argument, states of affairs will be required as something more in addition to the tropes. This holds both for the view that ordinary things are bundles of tropes and for the view that makes tropes attributes of ordinary particulars. The states of affairs required will, of course, have somewhat different formal characteristics from those whose constituents are particulars and universals.

It is to be hoped that the postulation of states of affairs is now sufficiently intellectually motivated. The next step is to argue, and this is the modification promised in 8.11 of the positions of the thinkers who believe in a fundamental tie between particulars and universals, that there is no relation of instantiation *over and above* the states of affairs themselves. (Already argued by Kenneth Olson, 1987, p. 61.) States of affairs hold their constituents together in a non-mereological form of composition, a form of composition that even allows the possibility of having different states of affairs with identical constituents. Suppose, for instance, that we have non-symmetrical R, particulars *a* and *b*, and that there obtain two wholly independent states of affairs: *a's having R to b* and *b's having R to a*. The difference between the two states of affairs, it is suggested, cannot be expressed better than by stating what are the two states of affairs. The 'relation' or 'tie' between the constituents, the two different 'relations' or 'ties' that in this case are associated with the two states of affairs, are not anything additional to the two states of affairs. It is often convenient to talk about instantiation, but states of affairs come first. If this is a 'fundamental tie', required by relations as much as by properties, then so be it. But it is *very* different from anything that is ordinarily spoken of as a *relation*.

Suppose, though, that it is argued, despite attempts such as that of the previous paragraph to play up the difference between the 'is' of predication and ordinary relations such as causal and spatiotemporal ones, that the predicative 'is' is sufficiently like a relation to involve a vicious regress. Constituents are gathered into states of affairs by the fundamental tie. Must we not take the constituents and the tie and then put them together by a further relation? But then we have the constituents, the tie and the 'putting together', another tie, and the old Bradleian regress proceeds. So the argument will go.

The proper response to this, I suggest, is to say that, *even if a 'relation' is conceded*, the regress is harmless. The thing to notice is that, while the step from constituents to states of affairs is a contingent one, all the further steps in the suggested regress follow necessarily. This point seems not to have been widely noticed. But once noticed, may it not be argued that the sole truthmaker required for each step in the regress *after the first* (the introduction of the fundamental tie) is nothing more than the original state of affairs? Many truths if you like, but only the one truthmaker. A natural comparison is with the truth regress. Let 'p' be some contingent truth. It will have a truthmaker. This will also serve as truthmaker for 'It is true that p', 'It is true that it is true that p' and so for ever. At some superficial level these statements are all different, even semantically different. The statements are all true. Yet, it seems, we are not forced to postulate a richness in the world to account for this potential infinity of statements. Why cannot we deal with the 'regress of instantiation' in the same way? Another way of putting the point, of course, is that after the original instantiation all the further relations postulated *supervene*. But if they supervene then the doctrine of the ontological free lunch, which can plausibly be appealed to here, tells us that here we have no increase of being.

I conclude that we can accept the truthmaker argument for states of affairs. No fatal or even unacceptable consequences flow from it. In particular, there is no call to bind together the constituents of a state of affairs by anything beyond the state of affairs itself. The instantiation of universals by particulars is just the state of affairs itself. And even if this is not so, the theory is not fatally injured because the alleged regress after the introduction of the fundamental tie is no addition of being. To accept the need for a truthmaker is not, of course, to be automatically committed to states of affairs. It is to be formally committed to no more than to finding *something* that will make a truth true. But there seems to be no acceptable candidate for a truthmaker for statements that contingently link particulars to universals other than states of affairs.

8.2 STATES OF AFFAIRS AND MEREOLOGY

In the course of the previous section we noticed, more or less by the way, that different and independent states of affairs could have exactly the same constituents. Pretending for the sake of the example that *loving* is a universal, then *a's loving b* and *b's loving a* might both be states of affairs, and states of affairs quite independent of each other. This is to be contrasted with mereology, the formal theory of the simplest sort of whole and part. If parts are summed mereologically to make a whole, then there can be no more than one whole that they make. If there is such a thing as the sum of *a*, *loving* and *b*, then it is exactly the same thing as the sum of *b*, *loving* and *a*.

It was important to say 'if there is such a thing . . . ' because, as already noted at 2.12, metaphysicians differ among themselves about the application of the mereological calculus. Some hold that we cannot put things of different categories together to make a whole. But agreeing with Lewis, who speaks of the principle of Unrestricted Composition (1991), in this essay a totally permissive attitude to the mereological summing of entities is taken. The reason for this, as has several times been indicated, is that the permissiveness appears to have no real metaphysical consequences. Mereological wholes supervene on their parts, as do the parts supervene on the wholes. Given one, the other is entailed. And on the basis of this it may be concluded that the wholes are no increase of being beyond that of their parts. This is not the case when constituents such as certain particulars and *loving* are brought together in states of affairs.

But it is the fact that independent states of affairs can have exactly the same constituents that requires attention here. Lewis actually makes this a ground of objection to states of affairs additional to his Quinean objections. He cannot see how it is possible to get different things from exactly the same constituents. His position here echoes Nelson Goodman, who defines (and accepts) what he calls Nominalism (eccentricity of terminology appears to be endemic among Harvard philosophers) in the following way:

> a system is nominalistic . . . if no two entities are generated from exactly the same atoms.
>
> (Goodman, 1958, p. 65)

(And since confession is good for the soul, I record that I myself, no nominalist in any ordinary sense, did once casually endorse Goodman's principle. See my 1978b, ch. 14, sec. 1, p. 30. It sounds attractive until you see its consequences!)

If *a* has R to *b* and *b* has R to *a*, with R non-symmetrical and the two states of affairs independent of each other, we have just the sort of situation that Lewis complains of. Another example that he himself has come up with involves only particulars and properties. Consider the molecular state of affairs *a's being F & b's being* G and then the further molecular state of affairs *a's being* G *& b's being F*. Given suitable F and G, these two will fail to entail each other, yet will involve exactly the same constituents (Lewis, 1986d).

One thing to be noticed about this second case is that, although the ultimate constituents of the two molecular states of affairs are exactly the same, nevertheless the two states of affairs contain different *complex* constituents as proper parts. Thus, the two molecular states of affairs are each made up of different atomic states of affairs, even although when we break up these atomic facts we come upon ultimate identity of constituents. So we might set up and endorse a weaker principle than the one that Goodman and Lewis endorse, and demand only that, when ultimate constituents of different states of affairs are identical, there be something in the way that they are organized inside the state of affairs that is different. At least some constituents that go together in the one state of affairs must fail to go together in another state of affairs.

But what of the *aRb* and *bRa* case, with R non-symmetrical? Does this not demand of the upholder of states of affairs that the difference be a difference solely in the states of affairs taken as a whole, without an internal difference of organization inside the state of affairs? I do not think it does, and am indebted to discussion with Reinhardt Grossmann about the matter. In 6.3 we considered his claim that all relations have what he calls a 'direction'. We rejected the general claim, instancing, in particular, symmetrical relations such as *distance*. It seems, *pace* Grossmann, that *a's being a mile from b* and *b's being a mile from a* are the very same state of affairs, or, as he would say, fact. But for non-symmetrical and asymmetrical relations, the ones that are generating our current problems, his contention seems correct. Thus, with the relation of *loving* the two places of the relation are clearly marked out from each other. One is the lover, the other the beloved. The term 'direction' is perhaps not altogether happy, although I have not got an improvement. But there is an obvious difference in the places. This shows us the *internal* difference of organization that exists between *a*'s loving *b* and *b*'s loving *a*. It is a matter of tying a term to a specific relation place. Perhaps we could use the following symbolism for the *loves* relation:

$$-_{\mathrm{L}}\,\mathrm{L}\,-_{\mathrm{B}}$$

with the subscripts (lover, beloved) explicitly showing the nature of the relation places. Filling the blanks, we would symbolize *a*'s loving *b* as:

$$a_{\mathrm{L}}\,\mathrm{L}\,b_{\mathrm{B}}$$

If the subscripts are reversed, so that:

$$a_{\mathrm{B}}\,\mathrm{L}\,b_{\mathrm{L}}$$

then this symbolizes that *a* is the beloved of *b*, that is, that *b* loves *a*. The difference in the organization of certain constituents of the two states of affairs relative to each other then becomes evident. The terms *a* and *b* are linked to different relation-places in the relation, relation-places that differ in 'direction', in the two different states of affairs. Notice how this fits with thinking of relations in a Fregean way, as state-of-affairs types with blanks ready to be 'saturated' by particulars. To get a non-symmetrical relation, such as loving, we must make the blanks a little less blank, so that it makes a difference which particular saturates which blank.

But although this concession can be, and it seems should be, made to the Goodman-Lewis position, no further concession can be made. If we have to choose between the (intuitively quite attractive) 'Nominalist' principle and the truthmaker argument that leads us toward states of affairs, then my judgment is that the truthmaker principle is by far the more attractive.

States of affairs, then, have a non-mereological mode of composition. But, of course, if states of affairs are taken as units, as atoms one might say, and one does not dive within these states of affairs, then they are susceptible of themselves being put together in a way that obeys the mereological rules. (They can be put together in other ways, of course, for instance by causal and temporal relations. But this is not our present concern.) Atomic states of affairs may be *conjoined* to form molecular states of affairs (but in this system neither disjoined nor negated) and these conjunctions obey the mereological rules. Molecular states of affairs are wholes having mereological parts. These parts are states of affairs themselves, either molecular or atomic. The atomic states of affairs are the ultimate *mereological* parts. Molecular states of affairs may also overlap mereologically. They will then have a (proper) mereological part in common. We have already tried to take advantage of the mereology of molecular states of affairs in analysing the puzzling phenomenon of the resemblance of universals, in particular the resemblance of the determinates of a determinable quantity. (See 4.13.)

Of course, these mereological relations mean little ontologically, at any rate if the doctrine of the ontological insignificance of the supervenient is accepted, as it seems reasonable to accept it for this case. If the world is a world of states of affairs, then given all the non-mereologically united states of affairs, one is given the whole world. The molecular states of affairs and their mereological relations to each other and to the non-molecular states of affairs, these all supervene. Or so we have claimed.

There is a complication here, one that we have already encountered. There is, or there appears to be, the epistemic possibility that all molecular states of affairs dissolve for ever into conjunctions of simpler but still molecular states of affairs. There would then be room for no more than *relatively* atomic states of affairs in the world. Thus, suppose that every property is a conjunctive property. Each instantiation of a property would break up into, and be identical with, two instantiations of properties by the one particular. So genuinely atomic states of affairs would never be reached. Nevertheless, one would still have, at each level, states of affairs that could be conjoined and which would stand in mereological relations to each other.

On this view one will have supervenience all the way down, and one may wonder what this will do to the ontological innocence of the supervenient. But notice that here the supervenience will be symmetrical. If P is the conjunction of Q and R, then the existence of P entails the existence of Q and R, *and vice-versa*. This is identity: P=Q & R. The only asymmetry is that the right-hand side gives a fuller analysis of the property in question. There would be no increase or decrease of being as one went down the infinite hierarchy.

8.3 THE THIN AND THE THICK PARTICULAR

We now move on to another distinction which, like the distinction between atomic and molecular states of affairs, will not add to our ontology, but which will, it is to be hoped, lead to ontological clarification. The distinction might have been introduced during the discussion of particulars, but it is convenient to draw it now, when a certain amount has been said about states of affairs.

When we have talked about particulars up to this point, the tacit assumption has usually, though not always, been that we are talking about the particular in abstraction from its properties. By 'abstraction' here all that is meant is that by a mental act of 'partial consideration' (Locke) we consider the particular only in so far as it is a particular, we consider it only in its particularity. (Remember Wittgenstein's example of attending to the colour and not the shape, or the shape and not the colour, *Investigations*, 33. Whatever the nature of the mental process is, it seems that we can do it.) It is, of course, a controversial question in metaphysics whether there is such a thing as a particular in this sense, but arguments have been given for not accepting the alternative view that particulars are but bundles of properties, whether universal or particular properties. If properties are not so much *thingy* entities, but rather are *ways* that things are (something that in no way derogates from their mind-independent reality, see 3.6), then we cannot dispense with particulars in this sense, with what can be called the *thin* particular.

Nevertheless, many find difficulty with the thin particular. Part of the trouble is epistemological, a trouble that can be traced at least back to Locke. We have tried to meet this worry by arguing that it is not implausible that perception, direct and untheoretical perception, is not confined to properties and relations but involves perception of (propertied and related) particulars (7.11).

Another useful thought, and this brings us to the point of the present section, is that, when in ordinary discourse we refer to a particular, we are not intending to exclude its properties, or some of its properties, from our consideration. The particular, strictly *qua* particular, seems to be for the contemplation of the ontologist alone. Will it not then be possible, and perhaps helpful, to introduce a notion of a particular which does *not* exclude properties?

An idea that suggests itself is to include in this new notion of a particular all the *non-relational* properties of the particular. It is this that I call the *thick* particular. (Herbert Hochberg has spoken about Socrates and 'big' Socrates and seems to have the same thin/thick distinction in mind. See his *c.* 1964. As a true son of Iowa, though, he was not speaking about a philosopher but a white square patch!)

Notice that to go beyond the non-relational properties and include all of a thing's relational properties swells the particular beyond all compass. Particulars thus conceived will, as it were, overlap with each other. In any case, relational properties, although it is often useful to refer to them, do not have the same metaphysical importance as non-relational properties. For they supervene upon those states of affairs where the particular in question has a relation to another particular. (See 6.5.)

If there is a *de re* distinction that can be drawn between the essential and the accidental properties of a particular, then there would be a case for an intermediate 'sort' of particular: the particular taken along with its essential properties only. But the distinction between essential and accidental properties of particulars seems to depend upon having *kinds* as a fundamental category, and we have, with a little hesitation, rejected kinds as a fundamental category. (See 4.3.)

So the thick particular is to be the particular taken along with all and only the particular's non-relational properties. What will this come to in terms of our scheme? The answer seems clear. The 'taken along with' should be cashed out in terms of states of affairs. We have admitted conjunctive properties as universals, provided that the conjuncts are universals and are co-instantiated. The putative conjunctive properties are supervenient upon the co-instantiation of the conjuncts. But these conjunctives are ones that run through many, and in any case there is the epistemic possibility that all properties are conjunctive (conjuncts all the way down). So let us conjoin all the non-relational properties of a certain particular, *a*, or perhaps, in order to allow for temporal parts, *a* at a certain instant. Call the resultant the property N (for nature). The thick particular *a* is now seen to be identical with the state of affairs of *a's being N*.

Once we have drawn the distinction between the thin and the thick particular, and have seen that the distinction can find its place within our states of affairs ontology, it may be easier to accept the thin particular. The thinness is the trouble. It seems so thin that we think it cannot be what we meant when we talk about particulars. But suppose there is in our non-philosophical thought the thick particular *also*, or something like the thick particular. Then we might explain our revulsion from the thin particular as no more than the mind easily sliding away from it to the full-blooded thick particular. Even if the particular be but an unimportant stone, we are not in the ordinary way interested in its bare particularity, something every particular has, but rather in what *sort* of thing it is. The thin particular is, we have argued, given in experience (7.11). But it is given in a quite unreflective, unselfconscious, way, and it takes philosophical analysis to convince us (if it does convince us!) that there is this irreducible element of particularity in experience. No wonder, then, that some philosophers deny the existence of the thin particular, thus limiting reality to properties and relations. No wonder, again, that others (Locke in particular) accept the reality of the thin particular but make it a creature of theory – the unknowable substratum that supports properties – and as a result limit *our experience* to properties and relations.

Before leaving this topic, we might note that the thick particular seems quite close to Leibniz's notion of a particular. For if a particular is taken along with all its non-relational properties, then it will have all these properties 'in every possible world'. So, in a sense, it has every such property necessarily. (And for Leibniz it will have no further properties, since he denies external relations.) Of course, at bottom, if our argument has been correct, what is involved are contingent states of affairs.

There is something else that we might note also. Quine, and those who are Quineans, although they maintain the ontological insignificance of the predicate, do have a truthmaker (if they want it!) for truths that ascribe properties to a particular. The truthmaker is the particular itself. The particular would have to be what has just been called the thick particular, and, indeed, the thick particular would be a suitable truthmaker. Perhaps this accounts, or helps to account, for the feeling among those philosophers who take the Quinean position that they have left nothing out. Their feeling is justified. But if our argument is on the right lines, then though it is true that they *have* left nothing out, their truthmaker is really a state of affairs.

8.4 THE VICTORY OF PARTICULARITY

States of affairs contain as constituents both particulars and universals. But what of the states of affairs themselves? Should they be classified as particulars, universals or neither? Confining ourselves here to *first-order* states of affairs, the only ones that have been so far considered, the answer would appear to be that they are particulars. For they lack the *repeatability* that is the special mark of universals.

There is a possible exception here. We have allowed the possibility, at least an epistemic one, that there might be particulars that had duration, but lacked temporal parts. Such particulars, it was argued (7.2), would have to be unchanging with respect to their non-relational properties. If *a* were such a particular, and F were one of its unchanging properties, then *a's being F* might be said to be a repeatable state of affairs. Such an entity partakes of the nature of both particular and universal. Particulars that persist through time but remain strictly identical during that time are particulars that are half-way to being universals ('concrete universals'?). But even here there would not be the promiscuous repeatability that is associated with universals.

In general, though, first-order states of affairs are (first-order) particulars. This is the 'victory of particularity'. For first-order states of affairs, particulars+universals=a particular. Of course, the '+' here is a non-mereological form of addition. It is the uniting of particulars and universals in a state of affairs. (Albert Kivinen has pointed out to me that this result was briefly anticipated by Russell. See his 1910–11, para 7.)

These 'state-of-affairs particulars' have some peculiarities of logical behaviour. Consider the two states of affairs of *a's being F* and *b's being F*, where F is a non-relational universal and *a* and *b* are wholly distinct particulars (they have no sort of overlap). The two states of affairs have a common constituent: F. Despite this, they are in some clear sense wholly distinct. It would be natural in the theory of possibility to hold that it is, just from the description of the case, possible that either one of the states of affairs should not have existed although the other did exist.

Again, consider the two states of affairs of *a's being F* and *a's being G*, where F and G are two wholly distinct universals (they have no sort of overlap). The two states of affairs have a common constituent: *a*. Despite this, they are in some sense wholly distinct. It would be natural in the theory of possibility to hold that it was, just from the description of the case, possible that either one of the states of affairs should not have existed although the other did exist.

8.41 Instantiation again

This phenomenon, the 'victory of particularity', may give us some further insight into the problem of the nature of instantiation. It has been argued that instantiation of a universal is not something different from the states of affairs themselves (8.1). And now that we see that the states of affairs are particulars, can we not argue that these constituents are *restricted* to the ordinary universals and ordinary particulars? There is no universal, we may assert, of *being a state of affairs* and so no universal of *instantiation*. Or at any rate there *need* not be such a universal. (A possible reason for postulating a universal of *being a state of affairs* will be mentioned in ch. 17.)

An obvious difficulty arises at this point. What about the class of these special particulars, the states of affairs? Don't we need a universal or universals to unify them, to explain why we group them all together? There seems, however, to be an easy solution to this difficulty. Classes of states of affairs are to be unified by the *universals* that they contain, together, of course, in the case of complex universals, with the pattern that they fall into (3.7). After all, what are universals? We have given a Fregean account of them. They are state-of-affairs types, understood as 'unsaturated' entities requiring to be completed by particulars in order to yield actual states of affairs. Does that not give all the unity that the classes of states of affairs require? The unity of *a's being F* and *b's being F* is given by the universal: *_'s being F*. In turn, the unity of the class of *all* the states of affairs is given by the unity of the class of all the universals. This latter, in turn, would seem to flow from the essential nature of universals: their promiscuous repeatability. This repeatability supervenes on the existence of the universal.

8.5 THEORIES OF TRUTH

8.51 Correspondence vs. Redundancy theories of truth

There are many different theories of truth, but two theories in particular have in the past competed for my allegiance, and perhaps for the allegiance of many another analytic philosopher. These are the Correspondence and the Redundancy theories. It is entirely natural to think that a proposition is true or false according as it corresponds or fails to correspond to an independent reality. But the apparent difficulty of then saying anything informative about this correspondence relation is likely to drive one to the more deflationary position that attaching the truth predicate to a proposition does not add anything to the mere assertion of that proposition, and so to the conclusion that there is really no truth relation that holds between the true proposition and the world. This, though, challenges the realistic insight that there is a world that exists independently of our thoughts and statements, making the latter true or false. One is driven back to the Correspondence theory. This author has long found himself in unstable oscillation between these two positions. In a symposium on truth some years ago (1950) Austin (Correspondence) and Strawson (Redundancy) gave us a quite memorable clash between these two positions.

The suggestion now to be put forward is that we can accept both theories. Both tell us something true about the nature of truth. The Redundancy theory gives us a true account of the semantics of the truth predicate, but it stays at the level of truths. At a deeper, ontological, level the Correspondence theory tells us that, since truths require a truthmaker, there is something in the world that corresponds to a true proposition. The correspondent and the truthmaker are the same thing.

But what are we to say about the correspondence relation that holds between truth and truthmaker? The first and fundamental thing to say is something negative. It is not a one-one relation. It is not the case that to each distinct truth there corresponds its own peculiar correspondent or truthmaker. It is not the case that to each distinct correspondent or truthmaker there corresponds its own peculiar truth. Here perhaps the Correspondence theory has in the past fallen into the gravitational field of the Redundancy theory, to their mutual confusion. If the metaphysics of this essay is correct, then the truthmakers of all truths will be states of affairs or constituents of states of affairs. But there is no one–one relation, or even an approximation to that situation, between these entities and the truths. This point is also stressed by Kit Fine about his 'circumstances' (1982).

But before considering examples, let us note again, what has been mentioned earlier in this chapter (8.1), that the relation that holds between truth and truthmaker is an internal one. Given some true statement, and given some truthmaker that makes it true, then nothing is needed but statement and truthmaker for the truth of the statement. The truth supervenes upon the existence of these terms. I have not always had a firm grip on this point. In the past I have said, for instance, that the truthmaker for the true statement that this glass is brittle is that a certain molecular state obtains in the glass. But given the contingency of the relevant laws of nature, which I uphold, this involves allowing that it is only a contingent fact that this suggested truthmaker makes the statement true. For that molecular state might have been governed by different laws 'in different possible worlds'. So what I say now is that the truthmaker is the glass being in a certain molecular state *plus* the relevant laws of nature (with 'laws of nature' taken ontologically, as whatever in the world makes the corresponding law-statements true). The correspondence relation is then, as it seems it should be, internal. Our concern, by the way, is not at this point with defending this particular account of the truthmaker for dispositional statements, but only with trying to illuminate the nature of the correspondence relation.

8.52 Correspondence of truths to truthmakers many-many

The relation is not one–one. Consider first cases where there is one truth but a plurality of truthmakers for that truth. It may be true that either *p* is true or *q* is true, with 'or' non-exclusive. In some cases both *p* and *q* will be true. The truth then has, or may have, two distinct truthmakers. A slightly less trivial case is that of existentially quantified truths. That at least one black swan exists, with existence taken to include all times, has as separate truthmakers each of the black swans that were, are or will be. That is put in *thingy* rather than states of affairs language. If one holds to the Factualist thesis, then one will wish to substitute for each swan a state of affairs where a certain thin particular has certain properties: swan-making properties. If we reject the idea that there is a kind-universal of swanhood, then there will often be *different*, if resembling, complexes of properties that make a certain particular a swan. And even bracketing difficulties about vagueness, it may be that even for just one swan alternative classes of properties of that particular swan can be chosen so that two or more different states of affairs (with overlap) will exist that are truthmakers for *this* thing being a swan.

We now want to consider cases where to the one truthmaker there corresponds many truths. Disjunction provides a simple case. If it is true that either *p* or *q* is true, and *p* is true, then the truthmaker for *p* is also a truthmaker for the disjunctive truth, and for innumerable other truths. A more sophisticated case is this. Let particular *a* have some absolutely determinate shade of colour or some absolutely determinate mass. Assume that these are universals, so that we have here states of affairs in the strict, not the second-rate, sense. Determinates entail determinables, so it is entailed that various determinable descriptions of greater and less specificity are truly predicable of *a*. These may not be states of affairs in the strict or ontological sense, but certainly they are different truths, because successively less specific. Some of the truths say more than others. All have the same truthmaker.

A more difficult case, more difficult because its description involves controversy, is this. Suppose that heat is a property of external objects. Suppose, more controversially, it is a property immediately recognizable through touch, but one for which we have none but *identifying descriptions*. By this is meant that although we can recognize heat when we feel it, and know various things about it, all our knowledge that links heat to other things is of contingent truths only. In particular, that heat causes sensations of heat in us is contingent only. It is not of the essence of heat that it causes sensations of heat in us. We do not have as a necessary truth: heat is whatever typically causes *these* sorts of sensations in us. More generally, assume, what I incline to think is true, that heat is not definable as that which plays the heat-role (heating other things up and so on). Suppose, that is, that heat is just a quality of certain objects which it happens can be felt by touch. A second controversial assumption follows: the physicalist view that heat is identical with motion of molecules, the greater degree of heat the greater degree of motion.

Now consider the truths that *a* is hot and that *a*'s molecules are in more or less violent motion. The two statements are surely not the same statement: the difference in their meaning ensures that here we have two different truths. Yet we do not have here two different states of affairs. *a*'s heat *is* the motion of *a*'s molecules and, if the assumptions of the previous paragraph are correct, no other states of affairs are implicated in the predicates. So two truths with only one truthmaker.

8.53 What are truths?

The terms of the correspondence relation are truthmakers and truths. Truthmakers entail truths. Our favoured truthmakers are states of affairs or their constituents. Something must now be said about truths, but I can only be brief, indeed dogmatic.

Truth attaches in the first place to propositions, those propositions which have a truthmaker. But no Naturalist can be happy with a realm of propositions. Consider token beliefs, token thoughts that have the same propositional structure as beliefs, and token statements. Take beliefs and thoughts first. The *intentional objects* of beliefs and thoughts provide the central, though only the central, cases of propositions. That, of course, opens up a huge topic in the philosophy of mind, which cannot be entered upon here. Token beliefs and thoughts may be grouped together into classes, where each member of the class 'expresses the same proposition', that is, has the same intentional object. Where this proposition has a truthmaker, each member of the class may be said to 'express the same truth'.

Token beliefs and thoughts are, I take it, actual states of the mind. They have intentional objects. But intentional objects are not, as I trust, to be taken with metaphysical seriousness. What exist are classes of intentionally equivalent tokens. The *fundamental* correspondence, therefore, is not between entities called truths and their truthmakers, but between the token beliefs and thoughts, on the one hand, and truthmakers on the other.

The meaning of statements (intended or conventional meaning), and so conditions for the intentional equivalence of statements, may then be analysed in terms of the intentional objects of the beliefs or thoughts that the statements are used to express.

This sketch of an account has left out the vast ocean of propositions that have never been thought on or stated, some true, some false. They are for me the non-central cases of propositions. To speak of these 'entities' is to do no more than speak of merely possible mental or statement tokens.

8.6 IDENTITY CONDITIONS

8.61 Identity conditions for states of affairs

What are the identity-conditions for states of affairs? States of affairs are a certain sort of structure, the most fundamental sort of structure that there is if the argument of this essay is correct. It is a necessary condition for their identity that they contain exactly the same constituents: exactly the same particulars, properties and relations. But we have seen that this necessary condition is not sufficient. States of affairs can contain exactly the same constituents, yet be wholly distinct states of affairs. This feature of states of affairs is made a reproach to states of affairs by some metaphysicians. We, on the contrary, advocate accepting this feature with natural piety. We must add, then, that besides containing the very same constituents, identical states of affairs must have these constituents organized in just the same way. The very same constituents must have the very same structure. But this 'organization', this sameness of constituents in the very same structure, is not anything but the states of affairs themselves.

8.62 Identity conditions for states of affairs, given tropes

If the properties and relations that are constituents of states of affairs are not universals but are tropes, properties and relations that are particulars, then exact sameness of constituents and their structure is still demanded. But the allowed structure exhibits interesting differences from that of a universals theory.

With R a non-symmetrical relation, and also a *universal*, it is possible to have two independent states of affairs: *a R b* and *b Ra*, with R=R. In a trope theory these become *aR′b* and *bR″a*, with the two relation tropes non-identical, so that the two states of affairs do not have the same constituents. A question then arises for trope theory. Can a trope-particular occur in a state of affairs except in the exact way that it actually occurs? If *aR′b*, but not *bR′a*, is it an (unfulfilled) possibility that *bR′a*, with R′=R′? Or, indeed, could R′ occur anywhere else in the universe?

A Combinatorialist about possibility will naturally be attracted to the idea that there may be fairly promiscuous recombination. To accept Combinatorialism, however, yields the (mildly) embarrassing 'Swapping problem' for *exactly resembling* tropes. It will be possible that such tropes might have been swapped around, so that *a's* trope was had by *b*, and *b's* trope had by *a*. In these circumstances, it seems a small but definite advantage for a universals theory that a swap of 'the very same property' between different particulars means nothing. You cannot swap a thing with itself. In general, a Combinatorialist version of a trope theory seems to yield too many combinations in such circumstances.

But we have already noted (8.12) that some trope theorists argue that it is of the *essence* of a trope that it is a property of that very particular that it is a property of, and similarly for relations. For them the Swapping problem does not arise. But for any version of a trope theory there may still be what may be called a Redundancy problem.

Presumably an ordinary particular could, in general, have further properties and relations than the ones it actually has. Associated with a certain particular there might have been extra tropes. And why should not these extra possible tropes include tropes exactly similar to tropes actually possessed by the particular? Indeed, is it not possible that a particular should have lacked a certain property or relation trope that it actually has, but instead have a numerically different but exactly similar trope? A universals theory automatically excludes these 'possibilities'.

I am inclined to think that this is an advantage for the universals theory. But perhaps a trope theorist can simply accept Redundancy, or even turn it to advantage. Differences in irreducibly intensive quantities, for instance, might possibly be explained by the presence in the one particular of different numbers of exactly similar tropes.

8.63 'Empirical' vs. 'Structural' Identity conditions

The identity conditions that we have proposed for our states of affairs may be said to be *structural* identity conditions. Once one has accepted the ontological reality of at least selected properties and relations, then the truthmaker argument appears to conduct one to such identity conditions, unless, indeed, one makes the properties and relations into tropes *and* makes it part of the essence of a trope that it qualifies whatever particulars it actually qualifies.

Kit Fine (1982) has considered another sort of identity condition for facts which he calls the *empirical* condition. He himself thinks of it as secondary to a structural criterion, but its claim to primacy has been argued by Kenneth Olson (1987). On this condition 'two facts will be identical when they necessarily co-exist, i.e. when it is necessary that the one exist just in case the other does' (Fine, 1982, p. 58). Given this condition, one would, for instance, rule out saying that all ravens are black and no non-black things are non-ravens are two different facts, or that if *a* has R to *b* then *b* has the converse of R to *a*. The idea in calling this the 'empirical' condition is that non-identical facts should be empirically distinguishable but that necessarily coexisting facts would not be so distinguishable.

It seems that we should accept that this is a true identity condition for states of affairs. Allegedly different facts or states of affairs that respect this condition will supervene on each other, and so according to the usual argument will be nothing more than each other. But the structural identity condition takes us nearer to the essence of states of affairs than does the empirical condition. For, after all, there are philosophers who are prepared to uphold the proposition that there can be *distinct* states of affairs that nevertheless co-exist of necessity. It is an arguable position. (See 8.61.) So, while accepting the empirical condition as a true identity condition for states of affairs, we should join with Fine in taking it to have less importance than the structural condition.

8.7 NEGATIVE AND GENERAL STATES OF AFFAIRS

States of affairs, as we have had much occasion to remark, are susceptible of conjunction. The wholes thus formed are mereological wholes, and thus are no increase of being over and above the states of affairs conjoined. Since states of affairs are always existents, there is no point in speaking of a disjunction of states of affairs. Suppose, however, that S, though a possible state of affairs, does not in fact obtain. Should we postulate a negative state of affairs, *its not being the case that S* to be the truthmaker for the true statement that S does not obtain?

Suppose a very simple world, in which *a* is F and *b* is G, with all these constituents simple, and in which no other first-order states of affairs obtain. What is the truthmaker for the true statements that *a* is not G and *b* is not F? Could the truthmaker for *a*'s not being G be provided for by the positive state of affairs that *a* is F, and similarly for *b*'s not being F? This cannot be so if the relation between truth and truthmaker is to be *internal*, as it seems it must be. The mere state of affairs that *a* is F can hardly necessitate that *a* is not G. One thing that would *ensure* that the two negative truths are true would be for the two positive states of affairs to be the *only* first-order states of affairs in this small world. What sort of state of affairs would this be? It would appear to be a second-order state of affairs: the fact that the two first-order states of affairs were *all* the first-order states of affairs. With this fact or state of affairs as truthmaker the two negative truths, and any other negative truths that obtained in this world, would supervene. (And so, incidentally, would the third-order truth that these are all the first- and second-order truths, thus dealing with the apparent regress of higher-order truths.)

Second-order facts are objectionable, though. They seem to be a major sin against economy. In the *Tractatus* vision, and in Skyrms' sketch of a reworked *Tractatus* (1981), they are banished. Might it not be better to accept negative states of affairs as truthmakers for the negative truths? Two first-order states of affairs, one might think, would be a price worth paying if it got rid of a second-order state of affairs.

The trouble is, though, that even if negative states of affairs are admitted, it will still be necessary to admit states of affairs of totality. We shall at least want to say that the four first-order states of affairs that we are now postulating for the mini-world are *all* the first-order states of affairs. The world is to contain *a*'s being F, *a*'s not being G, *b*'s being G, and *b*'s not being F. But these states of affairs could obtain in a bigger world, and there is nothing in the four states of affairs that entails that they are all the states of affairs. So it seems that we are stuck with a second-order state of affairs, the state that these four states of affairs are all the first-order states of affairs, in any case. Hence, since we are stuck with it, let it do the work all by itself, work that, as we have just seen, it can do.

The argument rests upon two pillars: (1) the need for all truths, and in particular all contingent truths, to have a truthmaker; and (2) the idea that whatever supervenes (in our defined sense, 2.1) requires no truthmaker additional to what it supervenes upon. To abandon the former, it seems, is to abandon ontological seriousness. The truthmaker demand forces an upholder of a states of affair ontology to embrace second-order states of affairs. To abandon the doctrine of the ontological innocence of supervenience is not so much of a hanging matter. It is possible, epistemically possible, to countenance both states of affairs of totality *and* negative states of affairs. The sin, as I take it to be, will be against economy only, and we have already noted that a less Occamist style of procedure than the one adopted in this work could be combined with a states of affairs theory.

Nevertheless, we shall not countenance negative states of affairs. We shall, however, accept their near relatives: states of affairs of totality, states of affairs whose content is that such and such entities are *all* the entities of some selected sort. We leave the matter for the present, until the time comes to discuss higher-order states of affairs somewhat more fully in chapter 13.

8.8 STATES OF AFFAIRS RULE

We are identifying the totality of states of affairs with the spacetime world plus anything else that there may be. (Although our *Naturalism* says that the spacetime realm is all there is.) But there are philosophers who accept the existence of facts or states of affairs, and of the properties and relations that are their constituents, who also accept the existence of the spacetime realm, yet who deny the identity of the states of affairs with spacetime.

We may consider the position of Reinhardt Grossmann, especially as set out in his 1992 book, *The Existence of the World.* Grossmann upholds the existence of properties and relations, taking them to be universals, and also upholds the reality of facts. But all these things he calls, in the unfortunate Harvard terminology, 'abstract'. They are not to be identified with, they stand apart from, that great particular, the spacetime realm. The latter he calls the *universe*. The world, total reality, is for him the abstract entities + the universe. Interestingly, but a little puzzlingly, although the abstract things stand apart from the universe, and although the instantiation relation holding between universals and portions of the universe links different realms, Grossmann sees no reason to postulate uninstantiated universals.

What arguments are given for this position? In particular, why do properties, relations and facts have to be things apart from the 'universe'? Grossmann argues that a colour shade, for instance, has no size or shape (p. 6). Things change, but properties do not change, so properties are not temporal (p. 7). If the relation of *between* is instantiated by three pencil points, the points, being particulars, will be located, but the relation is nowhere and nowhen (p. 10). If an apple is red at time t, where is the fact that this is so? It is not located (p. 10). The fact that two plus two is four is not about an individual thing and it does not involve time. It has no where and no when. It is not possible to find this fact somewhere in the spatio-temporal network (p. 30).

These arguments have a familiar, if now old-fashioned, ring to them. One heard them in the high days of linguistic philosophy, but there the object was to show that properties, relations and facts were not entities at all. You can't locate betweenness, so there is no such thing, although sentences containing the word 'between' are perfectly intelligible and can often be true.

Grossmann's position is, of course, preferable to the sceptical position of the linguistic philosophers. But it involves absurd lack of economy. We are almost invited to reject one realm or the other. Should we not, then, suspect that unfortunate infirmity, metaphysical double-vision? My suggestion is that when we say that the world is a world of states of affairs, and when we say that it is a spatiotemporal system, we are describing the one world in two different ways, ways that are linguistically and conceptually to a degree orthogonal to each other but which describe the one realm, a realm which is truthmaker for the true statements in both vocabularies. The hypothesis I advance is that the description in terms of states of affairs is, if rather abstract, ontologically more fundamental. The description in terms of a spatio-temporal system is, undoubtedly, much more accessible epistemically and conceptually. But the two descriptions are describing the same reality.

There are plenty of precedents for such a situation. Consider the languages of the 'manifest' and the 'scientific' image and, for a particular example, the way that the two languages are at odds with each other about the notion of *emptiness*. The physicist may say that the volume occupied by a table is mostly empty space. Provided that the particulate view of the entities of physics is correct, he gives us truth at a deep level. But in a more superficial way of talking, a table is to be contrasted with such a thing as an empty chest of drawers as not being full of hollows and empty spaces. The two ways of talking do not easily mesh, although, with care, rough translations can be given.

Consider again the distinction between ordinary three-dimensional language and that four-dimensional language which relativity theory in particular, and cosmological theory in general, consider closer to reality. Ordinary notions like change, coming to be and ceasing to be become somewhat inappropriate when considering things four-dimensionally. For instance, it is somewhat inappropriate to speak of the destruction of a four-dimensional particular, although we understand what is being said well enough, and can provide a translation into four-dimensional terms of what it is for a three-dimensional particular to be destroyed.

Consider further that nations are, presumably, nothing over and above nationals, and perhaps a body of land, in extremely complex relationships to each other. Yet the way we speak about the two is wildly different. Citizens may, for instance, stand in all sorts of complex family relationships to each other, relationships into which nations cannot enter. Nations can make war with each other, have various sorts of governmental systems and legal arrangements, but individuals do not enter into such relations or have such properties, although they may have some relations and properties that bear an analogy to the relations and properties of nations. Yet the truthmakers for truths about nations are no more than a subclass of truthmakers for the truths about their citizens.

That being so, can we not set aside the difficulties that would be raised by Grossmann against our identification of the totality of states of affairs with the spacetime system? Universals, and in particular relations, cannot be located. Perhaps that is like the inability of nations literally to give birth. It may still be the case that if the world is a world of propertied particulars (space-time points perhaps) variously related to each other, with the properties and relations universals, then truthmakers have been provided for truths of location in space and time.

It is true that Grossmann's facts have what one might call a rather more propositional nature than our states of affairs. He admits negative states of affairs and allows entailment relations between distinct states of affairs. But these doctrines of his were also upheld by John Anderson, who found no difficulty in identifying his proposition-like entities with spatiotemporal states of affairs. And, indeed, if it is thought that the theory of states of affairs defended in the present work carries economy too far, and that we really need to admit such things as negative states of affairs, and so on, then still there does not seem to be any special difficulty in making such an identification.

It would, of course, be worthwhile to try to work out the identification of the spacetime world with a world of our sorts of states of affairs in detail. I do not attempt this because I think that the nature of spacetime is very largely a scientific matter, and in any case a matter well beyond my competence. But the states of affairs hypothesis is so very general, as an ontology ought to be, that it would be compatible, as I conceive, with all sorts of views of space and time. So I leave the identification as a speculative, but I think plausible, hypothesis in empirical metaphysics.

We have still to consider what the truthmakers for modal truths should be. Do they require necessary and merely possible states of affairs, or are the sole truthmakers for all truths the contingent states of affairs and their constituents? I opt for the contingency hypothesis. This will be matter for the next two chapters.

9

Independence

We are arguing for a world of states of affairs, where each state of affairs is a contingent being. If *a's being F* is a state of affairs then *a* and F might have existed, but the state of affairs might not have existed. Again, the constituents *a* and F themselves might not have existed. They, too, are contingent beings. These constituents are (thin) particulars and universals. The universals may be monadic, that is properties, or polyadic, that is relations. The relations are all external. Every truth, necessary as well as contingent, so runs the hypothesis, finds its truthmaker or truthmakers here. A weaker hypothesis, which may survive even if the strong hypothesis is false, is that these contingent states of affairs are the truthmakers for all contingent truths.

The particular question now to be raised is whether these states of affairs are *independent* of each other, as Wittgenstein said his atomic facts are. Our concern is with *first-order* states of affairs alone. (For Wittgenstein, of course, there are no facts except first-order facts.) Higher-order states of affairs are (*non*-supervenient) states of affairs concerning lower-order states of affairs, facts about facts, and so automatically entail the existence of the lower-order states of affairs. Independence must, quite trivially, fail for them.

It is assumed here that there are first-order states of affairs. It could be, in some sense of 'could be', that the world is such that *every* state of affairs is a higher-order state of affairs relative to some further states of affairs. I think that Independence can then be reconstructed to cover this situation. But the matter is very difficult, and will not be discussed further here.

What is Independence? States of affairs are independent of each other if and only if: (1) no conjunction of states of affairs, including unit-conjunctions, entails the existence of any wholly distinct state of affairs; and (2) no conjunction of states of affairs, including unit-conjunctions, entails the non-existence of any wholly distinct state of affairs. The definition is given in this two-clause form because it is assumed that there are no first-order negative states of affairs.

Wittgenstein has an important formulation of Independence at 5.135 in the *Tractatus*:

> There is no possible way of making an inference from the existence of one situation to the existence of another, entirely different situation.

The point to be noticed is the phrase 'entirely different'. Wittgenstein, it appears, does not want to rule out an inference to a situation that is different, but only to one that is entirely different. He is here making use by implication (whether he is aware of it or not is a further matter) of the notion of the *partially* different, and so of the notion of the partially identical. What he says seems full of insight, although the point needs to be expressed in terms of entailment rather than inference. For instance, if one state of affairs is a proper part of another, then the two states of affairs are different but not entirely different, and the 'larger' state of affairs entails the existence of the other one. But if the two states of affairs are wholly different, then there is no entailment from one to the other.

At the same time, as has already been noted but is desirable to note again, there can be sameness, strict identity, of *constituents* of states of affairs, and yet the states of affairs be independent, wholly distinct. Let x be P and y be Q. Provided that x and y are entirely different, then it will not matter if P=Q. The two states of affairs are independent. Again, provided that P and Q are wholly different properties, then it will not matter if $x=y$. The two states of affairs are independent. We have seen, indeed, that if R is non-symmetrical, then it is possible to have *a's having R to b* and *b's having R to a* as wholly independent state of affairs, even although they have exactly the same constituents.

This, it may be hoped, suffices to *characterize* the independence of states of affairs, at any rate for the moment. But is the doctrine true? Most philosophers who have considered the matter think that it is too strong to be true. A recent commentator on the *Tractatus* speaks of the Myth of Independence, something that Wittgenstein should have excised from the book because there is no way to make it consistent with the rest of his system (Bradley, 1992).

But what are the consequences of abandoning Independence? Let us take as an example the claim that a certain relation is necessarily transitive. The temporal relation of *being before* is a good candidate. It is an external, and therefore a contingent, relation. (Remember that all the relations involved in states of affairs are contingent. The transitivity of internal relations such as *larger than* is supposed not to be a problem. See 4.13 in particular.) It seems that if *a* is before *b* and *b* is before *c*, then it is entailed that *a* is before *c*. And we have here what seem to be quite promising candidates for three *wholly* independent states of affairs.

This is disconcerting. Given our account of supervenience, the state of affairs that *a* is before *c* supervenes upon the two original states of affairs. But in that case what becomes of the ontological doctrine that supervenience thus defined involves no increase of being? Are we prepared to maintain this deflationary ontological doctrine in the light of the case being examined? Are we prepared to say that, in this situation, the entailed state of affairs is not something ontologically additional to the entailing states of affairs?

Suppose, though, that we abandon Independence at this point. If we still hold fast to the truthmaker doctrine, which should never be abandoned in ontological investigation although different sorts of truthmaker can be postulated, then what truthmaker can be proposed for the entailment? One might say, it is plausible to say, 'Just the relation of *being before*'. But what about *being before* is it that makes it suitable as a truthmaker here? Is it not the fact or law that if one has states of affairs of the form *a's being before b* together with *b's being before c* then, of necessity, one will have a further state of affairs *a's being before c*? Necessary connections between distinct existences. Necessity *in re*. Indeed, necessary connections between state-of-affairs types, between universals. That is what it looks like. The doctrine that what supervenes is never an increase in being will have to be abandoned. Furthermore, since at least some superveniences are ontologically innocent in this way, we can ask upholders of 'uninnocent' supervenience to answer a difficult but important question. Just how do we mark off the two types of supervenience? Can an answer be given to this question that is not *ad hoc*?

The consequences of denying Independence are, then, rather radical, more radical than many have perceived. I am therefore inclined instead to defend the radical *and more economical* doctrine of Independence. If the attempt fails, all will have learnt something.

What, then, is to be done? First, let us go back to *being before*. One could try maintaining that the transitivity of *being before* is nomic, and therefore contingent, rather than absolutely necessary. But although we should be prepared for surprises from the natural sciences, it does not seem very plausible to say that this particular transitivity is nothing but contingent law misunderstood as absolute necessity. The transitivity appears to be part of the essential nature of *being before*.

Here is an another suggestion, more promising I hope. We start with the simplest hypothesis about the nature of duration. Suppose that ordinary durations are made up of a *finite* number of temporal atoms, ultimate granules of duration. Between *adjacent* atoms a relation holds, a relation that may be called *before*⋆. It will not be a necessary truth, presumably it will not be true at all, that if *a* is *before*⋆ *b* and *b* is *before*⋆ *c* then *a* is *before*⋆ *c*. Transitivity fails for *before*⋆. An ordinary duration is a chain of these *before*⋆ relations. For *a* to be before *b* is for it to be linked to *b* by a chain of *before*⋆ relations. *Before* is the ancestral of *before*⋆. The identity of *before* with a chain of *befores*⋆ will have to be established *a posteriori*, like other scientific identities. But since *before* is a universal (on the face of it), the truth that it is a chain of *befores*⋆ will be a necessary one, giving the structure of the complex relation-universal *before*.

To secure Independence it will be necessary to add that although *a* is not before⋆ *c*, still this state of affairs is a *possibility*. It is possible, for instance, that *a* is linked to *c* by *before*⋆ directly while being indirectly linked by *before*⋆ to *c* via *b*. *Before*, therefore, must be a chain of *befores*⋆ along with a totality state of affairs that contingently rules out any such extra direct links. The strange hypotheses about space and time that contemporary cosmologists and quantum theorists embrace so easily, give the upholder of Independence aid and comfort here.

If all this is on the right track, then *before* states of affairs will, in general, be conjunctions of further states of affairs that are, at least relatively, atomic. The transitivity of *before* reduces to the fact that if a certain sort of chain of relations stretches from *a* to *b* and from *b* to *c* then a chain of that sort stretches from *a* to *c*. This seems to follow from our concept of a chain. There *then* seems nothing in the transitivity of *before* that challenges Independence.

Can this sort of solution be generalized to deal with other hypotheses about the nature of duration? What if durations are made up of smaller durations *ad infinitum* without any atomic durations (instants) at the end of the infinite road? Again what of the situation where there are instants but there are an infinite number of these ultimates in any finite duration, and, as a result, no *next* instants?

In the former, no instant case, it would appear necessary to argue that durations have a homogeneous structure, such that, among other things, every duration is literally made up of, is a structure, of shorter durations. As a result, the duration from *a* to *c* would actually *be* a structure involving two wholly distinct durations: say, that from *a* to *b* and that from *b* to *c*. (Of course, the longer duration would be made up of, and so would *be*, a structure that decomposed into parts in an infinite variety of ways. In David Lewis' phrase, the structure would be capable of multiple parsings.) The idea will then be to argue that the state of affairs of *a's being before c* is constituted by the conjunction of the states of affairs *a's being before b* and *b's being before c*, with *a's being before c* supervenient upon the conjunction, *and not anything ontologically additional to the conjunction.*

The *before*'s in *a's being before b* and *b's being before c* function as *before** functioned in the easier atomistic case just considered. But unlike the atomistic case, the two states of affairs will themselves supervene, redundantly, upon 'parsings' into further conjunctions of *before* states of affairs, and so *ad infinitum*.

The suggested solution involves a notion that we have already met: *supervenience all the way down*. The state of affairs of *a's being before c* will supervene upon the conjunction of *a's being before b* and *b's being before c* (with the supervenience symmetrical). The two conjuncts will also be involved in symmetrical supervenience, and so on. It has already been noted in this essay that, since symmetrical supervenience is identity, there is nothing vicious in this infinite descent. What of the (epistemic) possibility that atomic terms exist, genuine instants, but that a finite duration contains an infinite number of these particulars, and hence no adjoining instants? Presumably the same sort of solution will still apply.

The apparently necessary transitivity of certain external relations such as *before* is one of the more considerable difficulties that the upholder of Independence has to face. It is to be hoped that the preceding discussion at least points the way to a solution of the problem. The situation is not quite so difficult elsewhere.

Consider first relations that are necessarily symmetrical, such as distance, or the more general case of a relation and its converse. The obvious thing for an upholder of Independence to say is that in such cases there is only the one state of affairs. Indeed, this follows from Kit Fine's 'empirical' identity condition for states of affairs that we have already discussed (8.63).

Apparently necessarily asymmetrical relations are somewhat trickier. Given that R is external, how can *a's having R to b* exclude the state of affairs of *b's having R to a* without exclusion relations holding between wholly distinct states of affairs? Suppose that *a* is before *b*, then is it not a necessary truth that *b* is not before *a*? In fact, however, it seems to be not a necessary truth. The assumption that leads to asserting the necessity of the truth is that time must be like a straight line that extends to infinity without the two ends ever meeting. But does time *have* to be like this? We already know that in certain spaces a straight line indefinitely prolonged will meet up with itself. In a small space of the right sort it would meet up with itself quite soon. May not time be circular in the same way? This would not be 'eternal return', which is the repetition of the same *types* of events, but instead time actually coming round upon itself. Gödel apparently showed that circular time was compatible with the equations of General Relativity (1990 [1949]). This suggests that circular time may even be physically possible. Once this is allowed, then there seems to be no reason why it should not be possible that time comes round on itself in a very small circle. We know that the circle, if it exists at all, is actually quite large, so that the asymmetry of *before* is maintained for times of which we have experience. But it seems plausible that it is metaphysically possible that a given *a* can be both before and after some *b*, and it may even be physically possible.

And we might consider this. Exclusion facts or states of affairs are pretty 'big' facts or states of affairs, or so it has been argued (8.7). They demand at least all the positive states of affairs in some domain as truthmaker. Thus, if *a* is before *b*, we need as truthmaker for the truth that *b* is not before *a* at least all the states of affairs involving positive temporal relations holding between the two objects. Indeed, we need more than that, or so it was argued. We need the higher-order state of affairs or fact that these *are* all the positive states of affairs that link *a* and *b* temporally. Are we prepared to load all this onto the relation *before*?

Passing from relations to properties, the problematic cases are ones that involve exclusions. There appear to be no cases where, say, an object's having two properties seems to ensure that it has a third property wholly distinct from the two original properties. (Conjunctive properties fail to be *wholly* distinct from their conjuncts.) A scheme for dealing with property exclusion, or at least for certain cases, has already been sketched (4.1 & 4.2). If a thing has a mass of a kilogram, then it cannot have at that time the mass of a pound. The explanation given was that for something to be of mass one kilogram it must be (among many other decompositions) composed of, identical with, just two non-overlapping objects one of which has the mass of a pound and the other the mass of a kilo minus a pound. If we think of universals as state-of-affairs types then the one kilo universal is a conjunctive state-of-affairs type. It is the conjunction of the one pound state-of-affairs type and a further state-of-affairs type. In the further state-of-affairs type, some object that in no way overlaps the object in the first state of affairs has the mass that makes up the difference between a kilo and a pound. In a clear sense then, in something close to the mereological sense, the one kilo universal contains the one pound universal as proper part. The two universals, therefore, are different universals but they are not wholly different. So there is no challenge to Independence. The idea that mereology is an extension of the logic of identity, because it deals with partial identities, is important here.

This is only the beginning. The case of macroscopic masses is an extremely favourable case for us. The question remains whether such a treatment can be extended to such things as the incompatibility of shapes, where the difficulties seem technical only, to the incompatibility of very small masses – for instance, the masses of point particles such as the electron, see 4.22 – and to secondary qualities such as the colours, see 4.141. In the case of the secondary qualities, the question may well turn on the truth or otherwise of physicalistic reductions.

The case of irreducibly intensive quantities, already discussed in 4.22, deserves a little recapitulation. We saw that if there are properties of this sort, then it will not be possible to exhibit them as states of affairs types of a *conjunctive* sort. A particular with such an intensive quantity does not break up into two non-overlapping particulars where each of these particulars has 'part' of the quantity.

It is clear that if there *are* irreducibly intensive quantities, then they will violate Independence. If a certain particular has a certain degree of such a quantity, then the state of affairs of its having a different degree of this quantity will be excluded. (And, it would seem, not merely nomically.) Yet this cannot be explained away in terms of parts of the one particular, with the lesser degree strictly a property of a mere part of the particular, as it can be in the case of an extensive quantity.

Besides cases of necessary exclusion, cases of necessary co-extension demand consideration. Elliot Sober (1982), for instance, has argued that *being a three-sided plane figure* and *being a three-angled plane figure* (being trilateral and being triangular) distinct but necessarily co-extensive properties. He argues that the two properties have different causal powers. The three sides would set off a machine that counted sides, but not one that counted angles, and *vice versa*.

But it seems plausible to say that the angles in question involve as part of their being sides meeting at a point, and the sides in question meeting at a point involve as part of their being the forming of angles. So it can be argued that, given an individual triangle, what we have is just one (quite complex) property here, and just one state of affairs of a certain particular having that property. That state of affairs will be the truthmaker for what we can happily say are *two different truths*. That the truths entail each other does not mean that they are the same truth. (The absence of a one-one correlation of truths and truthmakers once again stands us in good stead.)

George Molnar has suggested to me that cases where possession of one property appears to entail another, but the reverse entailment fails to hold, will test Independence more severely. Velocity entailing (some) direction, or colour entailing extension can be instanced. Such cases are somewhat murky, and demand more discussion than can be given here. An upholder of Independence will have to argue either for partial identity, or else that, despite appearances, what we have are wholly distinct properties contingently connected only. I judge the prospects to be reasonably favourable.

But the following does look to be the situation. The truth or falsity of Independence cannot, in the end, be decided purely as a result of philosophical analysis. To a greater or less degree, it will be decided *a posteriori*, as a result of scientific investigation of the fundamental universals, the fundamental quantities, relations, etc. that are to be found instantiated in the world. This sort of investigation has always been a central part of the scientific enterprise, along with establishing laws and the large-scale history and geography of the universe. (Allowing that many have wished to substitute tropes, or even mere classes of particulars, for universals here.) The truth about the structure of these universals will be, for reasons spelt out earlier, necessary truth. But it will be a necessity established empirically. The truthmaker will be the relevant universal, but that this universal exists, i.e. is instantiated, is a contingent matter.

It remains to say, however, that Independence is a much more attractive hypothesis than the hypothesis that it fails for certain universals or ranges of universals. Kit Fine has pointed out to me the intellectual basis for this attraction. The simpler the internal relations between universals are (we are not at present concerned with the higher-order and contingent *nomic/causal* relations between universals which are not internal) the less we are asking the universal to do by way of truthmaking. If two wholly non-overlapping universals automatically satisfy the conditions for Independence their internal relations are very simple, far simpler than where they are asked to support necessary connections. And where they *do* overlap we can hope to present these overlaps, and so their entailments, in a perspicuous manner.

If instead colours, say, are simple, or relatively simple, properties, yet they also sustain internal relations with each other that determine that they exclude each other from the very same particular, the situation is much more puzzling. It is hard to take this as a mere brute incompatibility not further explicable. Independence would do something to *trivialize* the internal relations between universals, and successful trivialization is a not-to-be-despised mode of explanation. (It is to be found particularly in mathematics and philosophy. It is by no means a trivial matter to achieve it!)

It may be noted finally that even if Independence is false, as I trust that it is not, it can serve most usefully as a measuring rod or yardstick. It seems clear that it holds for many, many, cases. *In general*, for any two wholly distinct states of affairs neither will entail the other, and for possible wholly distinct states of affairs neither will exclude the other. *In general*, Independence holds. If it fails, it fails in highly particular circumstances, which we will want to discuss and catalogue. We will want to say: Independence holds, *with these exceptions*. For myself, while recognizing the difficulties in the most sweeping claim of all, I have hopes that Independence holds unrestrictedly. This hypothesis would certainly simplify the theory of modality.

10

Modality

10.1 TRUTHMAKERS FOR MODAL TRUTHS.

Knowledge that *p* entails belief that *p*, but belief that *p* does not entail knowledge that *p*. Raising the arm entails that the arm goes up, but the arm's going up does not entail that the arm was raised. In the same way, what is actual is possible, but what is possible need not be actual. As a result, just as we ask what must be added to belief to yield knowledge and what must be added to the arm's going up to yield raising the arm, so we are tempted to ask what must be added to something merely possible to yield its actuality. The parallel, however, is a dangerous one. You cannot add something to what is not there in the first place. So to pursue the parallel with knowledge and the will is to grant some ontological status to the merely possible.

Such a status is, indeed, compatible with a metaphysics of states of affairs. For one could argue that there are two sorts of states of affairs: the actual ones and those that are merely possible. The latter, one could say, have some form of reality. As a matter of fact, a recent interpreter of the *Tractatus*, the pioneer Factualist metaphysic, interprets Wittgenstein in just this way (Bradley, 1992). There would then lie open a choice between the path of Leibniz and the path of David Lewis. That is, one can in the spirit of Leibniz (or 'Leibniz') take actuality and mere possibility to be non-relational 'properties' of the states of affairs. (In contemporary philosophy there are also theories that allow only one actual, concrete, world, but have many 'abstract' worlds only one of which is actualized by its *relation* to the concrete world.) Or one can take an indexical or relational view so that world-mates, as Lewis puts it, things in the same world, are always actual relative to each other and merely possible from the standpoint of objects in other worlds.

A doctrine of merely possible states of affairs, however, is incompatible with Naturalism, in our sense of the term, the view that the world is a spacetime system and nothing more. To this an upholder of the ontological reality of the merely possible can of course reply: 'So much the worse for Naturalism'. But the merely possible entities labour under a great difficulty, the same difficulty as that already mooted for uninstantiated universals (3.8). The merely possible can stand in no causal relation to the actual. Only the actual can have effects upon the actual. Indeed, the merely possible cannot stand in any *external* relation to the actual, for instance in any spatiotemporal relation. It is true that the merely possible *lacks* causal and spatiotemporal relation to the actual, but such a lack is not a real relation. Again, the merely possible can resemble the actual to various degrees, but such resemblance is an internal relation.

Given this absence of external relation, in particular causal relation, of the merely possible to the actual, it becomes very hard to see how we could know or even have any reason to believe in the existence of merely possible entities. Our beliefs have causes. In favourable situations, a certain state of affairs in the world acts upon us, say in perception, and as a result we come to know or believe that that state of affairs obtains. A counterfactual is true. If that state of affairs had not existed, then, barring unusual circumstances, we would not have acquired that belief. Contrast the merely possible. Whether it exists or whether it does not exist, the course of thought in the actual world is exactly the same. The alternative, to allow the merely possible a link, even a counterfactual link, with the actual is to bring the two realms together in a single actuality, contradicting the hypothesis. In this respect, the postulation of merely possible entities, the giving them some sort of being, is quite unlike the postulating of entities in the natural sciences. That is why this chapter will proceed on the assumption that the merely possible is non-existent.

But, of course, it is often *true* that some state of affairs is possible, although the state of affairs does not obtain. Again, it is often true that it is possible that some object exists, although the object does not exist. What truthmakers are we going to supply for these truths?

Turning to necessity, it entails actuality, so necessary truths do not raise such a sharp dilemma as mere possibilities. But necessity seems to add something to actuality, and what can be the truthmaker for this addition? Perhaps necessary states of affairs are required? We have, indeed, a general problem: what truthmakers can our ontology supply for modal truths?

It may be suggested that truths of possibility and necessity require no truthmaker. That would be a natural way to read the *Tractatus*. This, however, is an enormous and implausible disvaluing of modal truths. I suggest, against Wittgenstein, that a modal truth, like any other truth, has a subject matter, and it gives us information about that subject matter. And this, for us at least, demands something in the world in virtue of which these truths are true.

The following compromise proposal is here advanced. All states of affairs are contingent. Their constituents, both particulars and universals, are likewise contingent existents. Since the world is a world of states of affairs, there are no other truthmakers for any truths except these contingent states of affairs and their contingently existing constituents. Modal truths, therefore, while not contingent truths, have nothing but these contingent beings as truthmakers.

Suppose, for instance, that it is true that it is possible that *a* has the relation R to *b* and also true that it is possible that *b* has R to *a*, where *a*, R, and *b* all exist and R is a dyadic universal and an external non-symmetrical relation. The truthmaker for both these different modal truths will be the same mereological sum: *a*+R+*b*. Notice that for modal truths, as for other truths, there is no assumption that the truth–truthmaker relation, the correspondence relation, is always one–one. And notice also that the *class* {*a*, R, *b*} is not required as truthmaker (though of course it exists), but the mere mereological sum.

Consider again the necessary, if unexciting, truth that if P and Q are two universals, then P is different from Q. The truthmaker for this truth is nothing but P+Q. It seems to be a necessary truth that a particular of a kilogram in mass contains a proper part that is a pound in mass. The truthmaker for this is again the two universals, assuming that is what they are, *being a kilogram* and *being a pound*.

The truthmaker or truthmakers for a particular modal truth will make that truth true in virtue of nothing more than relations of *identity* (strict identity) and *difference* holding between the constituents of the truthmaker. (Identity will be especially conspicuous in the case of necessary truths, difference in the case of truths of possibility.) Identity and difference may be merely partial (see 2.32), a matter that has not received sufficient attention in the past. These relations are, furthermore, internal relations. And whatever be the case with other internal relations, it is surely plausible that identity and difference constitute no ontological addition, no addition of being. If so, the ultimate truthmakers for modal truths are nothing more than the *terms* of these relations, terms which are all of them contingent beings.

It will emerge that this view stands in very close relation to the doctrine of Independence, which we will be coming back to shortly. A warning must be added. That identity and difference lie at the heart of modality by no means implies that the modal status of a truth can always be established by *a priori* or conceptual reasoning. For instance, our argument by no means rules out the establishment of necessities *a posteriori*, perhaps, for instance, the identity of a water molecule with an H_2O molecule.

Although Wittgensteinian extremism about modality has been rejected, it must be conceded that what is being put forward is still a *deflationary* doctrine of modal truth. The non-deflationary view is that, over and above the contingent states of affairs (automatically, *actual* states of affairs) there are both merely possible states of affairs and necessary states of affairs. (And such a non-deflationary view is, of course, a rival worthy of the most serious consideration.) But although deflationary, the view here defended may be said to be an *intensional* account of modality, intensional as opposed to the extensional view proposed by those who put metaphysical faith in possible worlds. For it is the individual constituents and states of affairs themselves, *in the actual world*, that serve, in their various ways, as the sole truthmakers for the modal truths. By contrast, a metaphysics of possible worlds takes necessity to be a universal quantification, and possibility an existential quantification, over a plurality of worlds.

It may help to explicate further the position being upheld if we consider another fairly trivial necessary truth: that *being a frictionless plane* is a property different from *being a body not acted upon by some force*. Assuming that there are no frictionless planes or bodies not acted upon by a force, what are the truthmakers for this truth? Are we forced towards uninstantiated universals?

The problem can be resolved without much difficulty. Assuming for simplicity's sake that the two properties under discussion are possible universals (which does not of course make them universals), it is clear that they are *complex* possible universals. The truthmaker for the necessary truth that they are different possible properties is then fairly plain. Actual plane surfaces exhibit friction in greater or lesser degree, actual bodies are acted upon by forces in greater or lesser degree. These instantiated universals provide sufficient truthmakers for the difference between the two merely possible universals.

This brings out the point that different modal truths may have to be provided with truthmakers in different ways. (And I have no general taxonomy of these ways to offer.) But it also brings us face to face with a more serious problem. What of the (apparent) possibility of universals that could be but are not in fact instantiated and which are *not* complexes of universals that are instantiated somewhere and somewhen? These are what David Lewis calls 'alien' universals (1986b). By hypothesis, they are not instantiated in our world, although Lewis, if he were to accept universals, could instantiate them in other worlds. That option is not available for us one-world chauvinists. Yet is it not possible that *this* world might have contained instantiations of such universals, universals alien relative to the actually instantiated universals? But what is the truthmaker for this apparent modal truth?

We shall, however, postpone the consideration of this important matter, and turn for the present to questions about more ordinary possibilities.

10.2 POSSIBILITY IN A LOGICAL ATOMIST WORLD

10.21 Logical Atomism

Logical Atomism is the hypothesis that at the bottom of the world there are nothing but simple particulars, simple properties and simple relations (the relations being all external) which are the constituents of atomic states of affairs (facts). It is a hypothesis only. It may be that the progress of science will in time make it seem a plausible hypothesis. Its upholders may even take some hope from the *quantization* that is so conspicuous a feature of contemporary fundamental physics, although yet to be applied to spacetime. Max Planck may yet point the way in metaphysics! And even if spacetime is an *infinite* assemblage of spacetime points, that will still be compatible with Logical Atomism. But although only an hypothesis, Logical Atomism is a valuable simplification. Problems can be posed, and perhaps solved, within this framework, and only then need we abstract from Atomism and consider whether we can advance from a special to a more general theory of possibility. Take the easier problem first!

10.22 Emergence and Logical Atomism

Before proceeding further, though, it is desirable to take note of the following (epistemic) possibility. If all particulars dissolve into assemblages of simple particulars, and all universals into assemblages of simple universals, then it is easy to fall into thinking that simple universals, whether properties or relations, are instantiated by simple particulars alone. Perhaps that was in the thoughts of the original Logical Atomists, and in particular Russell. But we can rather easily conceive of there being particulars which are not atomic but which have atomic properties and/or relations. Thus, suppose that atomic particular *a* has atomic F, and stands in the atomic relation R to the atomic particular *b*, which has atomic G. It may be that the non-atomic particular *a*+*b* has the further *atomic* property H, although neither *a* nor *b* (nor, indeed, any sum of proper parts of *a* and *b*) has property H. It might further be that, for *a*+*b* to instantiate atomic H, one of the two particulars nomically had to have atomic property F while the other had to have atomic property G. In this situation, perhaps, the molecular state of affairs *a's being F*+*b's being G*+*a's having R to G* nomically ensures [*a*+*b*]'*s having H*. We might call H an 'ontologically *Gestalt*' property. Other, more complex, scenarios could be devised. But it will be seen that Logical Atomism could in this way be made compatible with *emergent* laws, as the above law might well be.

It might be objected that in this case the purity of the Atomism is sullied because the H state of affairs cannot be the only state of affairs in which *a* and *b* appear as constituents. The particulars *a* and *b* must have properties of their own and so the H state of affairs involves the existence of two further states of affairs. However, (a) if a Strong principle of the Rejection of Bare Particulars is accepted, i.e. if each atomic particular has to have some non-relational property, then the instantiation of H would not seem to falsify the spirit of Logical Atomism, because *a* and *b* would have had to have non-relational properties in any case. Furthermore, (b) if it is wished to jettison this Principle, we have already canvassed (without endorsing) the possibility that there are ultimate particulars that have nothing but relations (see 6.1). We could then amend our case by stripping *a* and *b* of their non-relational properties, yet still have *a*+*b* instantiate H.

We might call a Logical Atomism that did *not* allow 'emergence' of this sort *micro-reductive* Atomism. The discussion here may be linked with the point made at 3.9 that a Physicalism is not necessarily a micro-reductive Physicalism. We may also note that, although non-atomic particulars are thus permitted as constituents of atomic states of affairs, there seems to be no such dispensation available for non-atomic universals. That this is so follows from our account of complex universals as conjunctions of state-of-affairs types (3.72).

10.23 Independence and Logical Atomism

Consider, now, a Logical Atomist world. Stipulate further that we consider only first-order states of affairs. It has already been suggested, with

Russell, that we will require at least one *totality* state of affairs, and that is the state of affairs of the lower-order states of affairs being the totality of states of affairs (8.7). But for the present we ignore this and any other higher-order states of affairs that there may be.

We are interested in the possibilities for this world, in particular we are interested in the *mere* possibilities, the ones 'over and above' the actualities. These possibilities are all of them (merely possible) states of affairs. Given our general approach, the only other candidates for possibilities, it appears, are particulars without any properties or relations (totally bare particulars) and properties and relations that are not instantiated. Are such things possible? It has already been argued, against more substantialist conceptions, that properties are *ways* that things are and relations *ways* things stand to each other (3.6). If this is correct, then uninstantiated properties and relations are very strange beings indeed. For they will be ways that are ways that nothing is. Can we take such ways with ontological seriousness? Similarly, totally bare particulars would seem to be strange entities. What would a thing be that had no vestige of a nature and no relation to anything else? (See 7.3. Just as uninstantiated universals might have been instantiated, so presumably bare particulars might have had properties and relations.)

We appear to have no reason to assert the existence of such entities, perhaps the strongest consideration being the difficulty of seeing how such things could have any causal relation to a world of propertied and interrelated particulars. But I am a bit reluctant to claim that it is *impossible* that there are such entities as uninstantiated ways and bare particulars. The categories of possibility and necessity have entered deep into the thinking of many philosophers. It has become a reflex to ask of any proposition at all whether it is a contingent or a necessary truth. This may be taking things too far. Without abandoning the whole necessary/contingent distinction as some have done, we might ask whether at the bottom, the bottom where the theory of modality gets stated, we want to do more than claim *truth*. If, in particular, we hope, as I do, for a *reductive* theory of modality, then it would seem to make things very much harder to have to maintain that the theory itself has some modal status. It may be, then, that it is *true*, as I maintain, that there are no uninstantiated universals and no bare particulars, but that this is neither a necessary nor a contingent truth. That some truths are necessary, some contingent, but that there are further truths that are neither necessary nor contingent may seem a hard saying. But I believe that the suggestion ought at least to be seriously considered.

At any rate, it is among states of affairs that do not obtain that we will look for the paradigms of possibility. For the present, let us consider only possible *atomic*, strictly atomic, states of affairs. Given this restriction, no two (thin) particulars overlap. They are not merely 'distinct existences', they are '*wholly* distinct existences'. They do not even have partial identity. They are wholly *different*. It is a natural thought, at least within the Humean tradition of thinking about possibility, that the existence of one of these thin particulars never entails and never excludes the existence of any other. What about the simple properties and simple relations? They too will be wholly different from each other. The simplest hypothesis about them, attractive if only because of its simplicity, is the parallel idea that, first, every simple property is compossible with every other, and, second, that all simple relations are compossible also, so that any *n*-place relation may hold between or fail to hold between any *n* particulars. The internal relation of mere difference of particulars, of properties, of relations, automatically yields possibilities in these cases.

It will be seen that the above is the hypothesis of Independence applied to the first-order Logical Atomist world that we are at present considering. We see also, what has perhaps not always been realized, that the mere Atomism of Logical Atomism does not *automatically* involve Independence. You could hold that the world is a huge conjunction of atomic states of affairs, states of affairs that have none but simple particulars having none but simple properties and relations, yet maintain that entailments and exclusions hold between these atomic states of affairs. You would not then be able to hold a *purely* Combinatorial theory of possibility.

The hypothesis of Independence faces real difficulties and it was suggested in the previous chapter that it may be the task of total science to decide, to the extent that the question can be decided, whether or not it is true. For it is science, after all, that can best inform us about the nature of fundamental properties, quantities and relations. But let us consider for a moment the problems faced by an hypothetical Atomist who denies Independence. (Whether such a one should be called a *Logical* Atomist is perhaps a merely verbal question.) As we have just noted, what such an Atomist would have to hold is that there are certain simple properties and/or relations which necessitate the presence of certain wholly distinct and simple universals or else exclude them. These necessitations and exclusions will follow certain rules, presumably. What might these rules be?

In the case of properties we have the distinction between determinables and determinates, with determinates falling under the same determinable excluding each other from the very same particular. Presumably these exclusions are among the cases that a Logical Atomist who opposes Independence should appeal to. It is to be noted, however, that this distinction between determinables and determinates fits *quantities* most naturally and transparently, and quantities, with the possible exception of *minima*, are not simple. Colours do appear to have but little structure, and the opponent of Independence will presumably make play with this apparent lack of structure. But if a physicalist account of colours is correct (4.141) colours have structure, even if structure we are unable to perceive, and so colours are not simple.

Transitivity is perhaps more hopeful for the opponent of Independence. If *a* is before *b* and *b* before *c*, then it may be argued that it is a supervenient but *additional* state of affairs that *a* is before *c*. However, in the previous chapter it was suggested that the supervenient state of affairs is not in fact an ontological addition. Given a finite number of atoms of duration the situation is like a linked chain. Adjoining links are linked to each other. That is the fundamental relation. There is a relation between non-adjoining links, but it is not something ontologically additional. It is no more than the iteration of the relation holding between the adjoining links. It is true that, as we have noticed in chapter 9, the case where durations subdivide *ad infinitum* is rather more tricky. But perhaps it, too, can be dealt with.

10.24 Necessary states of affairs?

Suppose, though, that Independence must be given up. Continuing to assume the truth of Atomism, then the falsity of Independence will mean that certain state-of-affairs types involving nothing but simple universals either entail or exclude states of affairs involving further simple universals. This is not a matter of contingent laws of nature. If it were the latter then Independence would not be threatened. These entailments we are at present considering supervene on the existence of the particular universals involved. But it can hardly be a supervenience that involves no increase of being, no ontological addition, the doctrine of the ontological free lunch that we have supported in this work. It would seem that we require necessary states of affairs, much like laws of nature but not contingent. These states of affairs would seem to be higher-order states of affairs involving connections between simple universals, that is, connections between simple state-of-affairs types.

I submit that this is a fairly puzzling situation. Various difficulties may be proposed for necessary states of affairs. (1) Postulating such entities is less economical. I do not want to put *too* much weight on this. The Necessitarian Factualist, as we may call an upholder of this position ('Necessitarian' for short in this context), may not be very impressed by economy, and will in any case argue that in this situation the economy is a false one.

(2) The necessary states of affairs involve epistemological problems. How do we come to know, or have rational grounds for believing in, such states of affairs? The answer that a necessary states of affairs acts upon our intellect, producing knowledge or rational belief in the existence of the state of affairs, is perhaps not very plausible. It would certainly be difficult to integrate this account into cognitive psychology. But perhaps it can be said that such a state of affairs is a plausible postulation, a postulation that explains (by providing a special sort of truthmaker) the peculiar nature of certain entailments and exclusions?

(3) But now for more serious difficulties. The simplicity of the universals involved creates a problem. What foundation can there be in these simple entities for the entailments and exclusions? It would seem that these relationships must forever be opaque to the intellect, inexplicable in the same way that ultimate contingent truths are opaque. They are truly brute necessities.

The point to be emphasized is this. By contrast with the 'brute necessities' Independence is a *transparent* doctrine. It is a simpler and more economical idea than the alternative conception or conceptions, which indeed are still to be worked out. As Kit Fine has pointed out to this author (see also ch. 9), with Independence we are asking the universals to do less, indeed a minimum, in the way of truthmaking. That must yield a gain in plausibility. But still more than this, we seem to be able to see *why* Independence should hold. Leibniz seems to have thought it *evident* that simple properties are all compossible. Let us be the last to claim that the intuitions of even the greatest philosophers on such matters are sacrosanct! But they have some weight.

(4) A problem that the Necessitarian must face is how to deal with various infinite regresses that face *any* Factualist philosophy, and in particular how to deal with the Bradleyan regress, where the argument is that the constituents of a state of affairs have to be held together by an organizing relation, but that this relation itself becomes a further constituent, equally requiring a new organizing relation that welds the original

organizing relation to the original constituents, so that the problem is not solved. We dealt with this problem by pointing out that, once given the *contingent* 'relation' that organizes the constituents into a state of affairs (this 'relation' is just the state of affairs itself on our view), then all the further alleged relations are necessitated, and so supervene upon the state of affairs. Then, it was argued, these relations are no increase of being. Their truthmaker is the original state of affairs.

But once necessary states of affairs are admitted alongside and additional to contingent states of affairs, then this way of dealing with the Bradleyan regress and other such regresses becomes suspect. What supervenes is not, for the Necessitarian, automatically no ontological addition. Yet if every necessary truth demands its own, extra, necessary state of affairs, then the Necessitarian's world becomes very full indeed.

It is true that the Necessitarian might distinguish between necessities that are ontologically innocent and those that demand necessary states of affairs for truthmakers. Indeed, this would seem to be the best line for a Necessitarian. The further claim might then be made that the necessities involved in the regresses under discussion are innocent ones, and so do not involve an increase in being. It would greatly strengthen the Necessitarian position here if a principled distinction could be drawn between those necessities which do, and those which do not, require necessary states of affairs as truthmakers, between the ontologically loaded and ontologically innocent superveniences. Such a principled distinction seems, at present at least, lacking.

So much in criticism of Factualist Necessitarianism. But these considerations in no way constitute a disproof of Necessitarianism, and so perhaps a proof of Independence, by *reductio ad absurdum*. It is conceded, indeed insisted, that, like most other and perhaps all propositions in metaphysics, deductive disproof or proof of Independence is not to be had. Indeed, we have suggested that the last word on the proposition, if there can be a last word, is more likely to be said by science than by philosophy. But it is to be hoped that the spelling out of the Necessitarian alternative has done something to show the attractions of Independence, or, at least, its attractions given the metaphysics of states of affairs involving particulars and universals that this essay is trying to work out.

10.25 Does Independence give us the essence of modality?

We have been confining ourselves so far to atomic states of affairs. First-order molecular states of affairs are all, according to the theory being advanced, mere conjunctions of atomic states of affairs and not an ontological addition. 'Second-class' states of affairs, with their properties and relations that in general are not universals, are equally no ontological addition (see 3.9). Their truthmakers are the first-class states of affairs. They are merely semantically askew to the atomic states of affairs.

With molecular states of affairs and with second-class states of affairs we leave simplicity behind. We do not have the exclusive and exhaustive disjunction of absolute identity or absolute non-identity. Partial identity enters the scene, overlap, with overlap understood to include part-whole relations. Molecular states of affairs may overlap with states of affairs, molecular or atomic, that they are not identical with. Particulars with parts may overlap with other particulars. Complex universals, properties and relations, may overlap with other universals. All these overlaps will, in certain circumstances, generate counter-instances to unrestricted Independence. The situation becomes still more complex with second-class properties, relations and states of affairs.

If, then, we wish to defend the principle of Independence we shall have to restrict it to the strictly atomic states of affairs. Each one of them is independent of any other atomic state of affairs. It is important to remember, though, that these independent states of affairs may still have, in a certain sense, partial identity. For instance, the two states of affairs *a's being F* and *a's being G* can be independent despite the fact that they involve one and the same particular. Indeed, as we have seen (8.2 in particular), states of affairs can be independent when containing exactly the same constituents.

Given the truth of Logical Atomism, which we are assuming for the present, and abstracting from anything but first-order states of affairs, the world is a vast conjunction of atomic states of affairs. The particulars which are the constituents of these atomic states of affairs may not in every case be atomic, as we have seen in the discussion of emergent properties (10.22). But the universals involved, that is, the state-of-affairs types, will be atomic.

What we want for Independence to be true is, first, that all simple properties be compossible. It must be possible that any particular have any of these properties, or any combination of these properties. Similarly, of any pair of particulars it must be possible that these be related by any simple dyadic relation or by any combination of these relations. If the relation has a 'direction' in Grossmann's sense (see 6.4), then it must be possible for the relation to hold in either or both directions. *Mutatis mutandis*, this holds for simple relations of higher polyadicity. For all *n*, for all *n*-tuples of simple particulars, it will be possible for an *n*-termed relation to hold between them.

The idea for possibility, then, is that all the combinations of simple particulars, properties and relations that respect the form of atomic states of affairs constitute the possibilities for first-order states of affairs. Notice that I am not saying 'all the possible combinations', which would be trivial, but 'all the combinations'. The hypothesis is that these combinations are all of them possibilities.

It is, as we have seen, controversial whether *all* these combinations are really possibilities. *Perhaps* there are entailments and logical exclusions holding between simple universals, that is between simple state-of-affairs types. Granted the need for truthmakers, this seems to involve Necessitarian Factualism. But an interesting thing to see about unrestricted combination is that, in the language of computer programmes, it is a *default setting*. Even if there are certain exceptions, even, that is, if Independence is not true for all cases, it is combination that yields us the possibilities *in general*.

Suppose, then, that Independence has no exceptions. This should make us wonder whether such a notion of combination may not (epistemic may!) constitute the very essence of possibility. One can say, more cautiously, that Independence is no more than a theory about *what possibilities there are*. But one can be more ambitious. One can argue that the promiscuous recombination allowed by Independence is *what possibility IS*, at least for the case of simple constituents. This is the line taken in Armstrong 1989b, and I still want to maintain it. But it is a very ambitious thesis, and it may be involved in some hidden circularity. (For argument that this is so, see Shalkowski, 1994.) If that turns out to be so, then one can retreat to the more modest thesis, and claim no more than this: Independence provides us with an ultimate modal principle, an irreducible modal truth whose truthmaker is the modal structure of reality. (It would be a minimal Necessitarian Factualism. I am not clear how the details would be filled in.) Empiricists have, historically, shied away from a modal structure of reality, but it seems that it would be compatible with Naturalism and Factualism, though the latter will have to be augmented with necessary as well as contingent states of affairs. Independence will then be no more than the *simplest* thesis about the modal structure of reality.

Suppose, however, that Independence is false. Then we have a mixed theory. Certain entailments and exclusions flow from the nature of the simple universals involved. For the rest there is combinatorial freedom.

This does not augur at all well for a reductive account of modality. The disjunction makes it implausible to say that this is what possibility *is*. The idea that there are certain entailments and exclusions that to a degree limit combinatorial freedom, would appear to be no more than a modal principle that *governs* possibility. It would not be the very essence of possibility.

One way that one might tackle the situation would be to see the entailments and exclusions as a species of *law*, but laws that are of greater modal strength than the 'laws of nature'. (Assuming that the ordinary laws are contingent, as I wish to maintain.) Independence, so far as it holds, would be freedom from, absence of, modal constraint just as the empirically possible is the realm of freedom from, absence of, constraint by the ordinary laws of nature. Certain state-of-affairs types would entail or exclude certain further state-of-affairs types. Assume what I take to be false, that the colours are simple or relatively simple universals. The state-of-affairs type of something's being a surface of a certain colour would exclude that same something's being a surface of another colour. In virtue of this exclusion between state-of-affairs types, a universally quantified generalization about the relevant first-order particulars would hold. (This, it may be noted, will serve as a model for the contingent connections of universals which, it will be argued in ch. 15, constitute the laws of nature. The only difference would be the substitution of necessity for contingency.)

In working this out, one could perhaps still think of Independence as a modal law, but it would be a *defeasible* law, one that did not hold in certain special circumstances. The contrast would be with an *iron* law, that is not so modified. See 15.21, to come, for this distinction between defeasible and iron laws.

But for purposes of exposition, at least, let us assume that Independence holds quite generally. We can then rather easily start to construct 'possible worlds'. We begin with all and only those worlds that can be constructed – they are, of course, worlds of states of affairs – using in *each* world all and no more than all the simple particulars and simple universals *of our world*. (It is to be remembered that we are still going along with Logical Atomism.) For obvious reasons, these worlds were called in Armstrong 1989b, 3.iii, the Wittgenstein worlds.

Various matters then call for our attention. (1) What account should we give of the distinction between the possible and the conceivable? (2) There are quite pressing problems concerning 'expanded worlds', possible worlds which involve simple particulars or simple universals ('aliens') that are not to be found in this world. (3) Certain not quite so pressing problems arise in connection with 'contracted' worlds, worlds that omit certain particulars and/or universals. (4) There is the question how, on a Combinatorial approach, we can deal with 'complexity all the way down', that is, with worlds that are not Atomist worlds. (5) There is the question of what we should say about (merely) possible worlds. Can we treat them as useful fictions? All these matters were considered in 1989b but it is hoped that in each case something of value can be added here to that discussion.

10.3 THE POSSIBLE AND THE CONCEIVABLE

Since Descartes, at least, our tradition has tended to blur the distinction between the possible and the conceivable. They are, nevertheless, two quite different things. What is conceivable may not be possible. It is conceivable that every even number other than 2 is the sum of two primes (Goldbach's conjecture). It is also conceivable that there is an even number that is not the sum of two primes. Yet, given that mathematics is a body of necessary truths, one of these propositions is a necessary truth and the other is a necessary falsehood. So what is conceivable may be impossible. Escher has even shown, by means of certain of his drawings, that what can be pictured may be impossible. Again, if Kripke is right, it is a necessary truth that water is H_20. Yet it is conceivable, and was conceived by many, that water is an element. For all these reasons, conceivability is not sufficient for possibility.

Conceivability is not necessary for possibility either. It must no doubt be granted that conceivability is a relative matter, but that granted, we can have truth without conceivability. Thus, in the past the notion that our space be finite but unbounded would have been inconceivable for many thinkers.

So the conceivable and the possible are not identical. What is conceivability? There seems to be no clear answer to this question. The concept is something of a mess. Under these circumstances it seems appropriate to introduce a clearer notion of conceivability in a more or less stipulative way. What follows is a *Combinatorial* theory of the conceivable. In Armstrong 1989b such a theory was put forward as a theory of *doxastically possible* worlds (5.ii & iii).

In constructing possible worlds, the Combinatorialist wants to use in the possible states of affairs nothing but simple or relatively simple particulars and universals, the 'atoms'. Using simple particulars and universals in all the combinations yields possible states of affairs which, if Independence holds, are automatically compossible. If Independence fails at certain points, free combination must be suspended for certain particular cases. If what are used as atoms are relatively simple only, then it must be stipulated that the atoms are *wholly* non-identical.

To get doxastically possible worlds we substitute atoms that *seem* simple or *seem* wholly non-identical. The 'seem' here could have various forces. It is obviously person-relative. It could have the force of belief. But it might have a lesser force, a force familiar from perception as when we say that the stick seems bent ('looks' is more natural, but does little more than indicate that it is vision that is involved) although we know quite well that it is straight. Thus, heat is motion of molecules, but it does not *seem* to be motion of molecules, that is, there is nothing in tactual and proprioceptive perception to indicate that it is motion of molecules. Furthermore, the 'Headless woman effect' (see 4.141) will actually tend to make it seem that it is *not* motion of molecules. This is nicely consilient with the fact that, even after the march of science, we are prepared to say that we can *conceive* of heat not being the motion of molecules.

A doxastically possible world may be an impossible world. There are worlds that are conceivable but are not possible. A world where heat is not motion of molecules is such a world, if Kripke is right. Again, there are conceivable but impossible worlds where a particular has both of two properties, each complex, but where one of these properties involves a concealed negation of a certain further property while the other involves having that further property. (The first of the two properties could not be a universal.) For more detail see 1989b, 5.ii.

From time to time in this book, we have talked about certain things as epistemically or doxastically possible. One value of a theory of the conceivable is to assist with an analysis of these notions. I make no claim to have carried the matter very far here. But we have reminded ourselves to distinguish conceivability from possibility, or, we can instead say, we have reminded ourselves to distinguish two sorts of possibility.

A final point. At various points in this book I have talked about possibility, and have not meant a restricted sort of possibility, such as empirical (nomic) possibility. But I have tried not to call this unrestricted possibility *logical* possibility. The reason for this should now be fairly obvious. It is too easy to assimilate logical possibility to conceivability. Suppose that one has a statement, and that no manipulation of that statement using nothing more than logical laws, plus nominal definitions and true conceptual analysis, reveals a contradiction. Then, it is easy to say, what this statement says is a logical possibility. But this is no guarantee of anything more than conceivability. There may be an impossibility there all the same.

10.31 Analytic truth

It seems desirable to insert here something about analytic truth. The notion of analytic truth presupposes the intelligibility of the notion of synonymy, that is, sameness of meaning, and, presumably, meaning. These notions have been criticized by Quine, on the grounds that no satisfactory definition or theory of these notions is available. For myself, I think that the work of Grice, and the further work of Jonathan Bennett, goes far to meet Quine's criticism, showing promise of developing a thoroughly naturalistic theory of meaning. Given meanings, we can go on to form the notion of those meaningful linguistic units that are capable of truth and falsity, linguistic propositions. Where true, they will be first terms of the correspondence relation, the relation whose second term is the truthmaker. This correspondence relation, we have insisted, is not a one–one relation. And if, as it seems, we can think and believe without using language, then there will be meaningful mental units that are capable of truth also.

We do not have to reify meanings. For the basic units of meaning, whatever they are, equivalence classes of synonymous expressions will do justice, much as equivalence classes of exactly resembling tropes can do much of the work that universals do. It is true that one wants to allow that there are true statements that have not and will not be expressed in any way. But I suppose that they can be covered by adding to the central cases merely possible cases of synonymous statements.

If we have the notion of meaning, then we can have the notion of analytic truth. The definition that I prefer to use is the wide one: a truth is analytic if and only if it is true *solely* in virtue of the words or symbols (or mental contents) in which it is stated. Given the doctrine of the truthmaker, these facts of meaning constitute the truthmakers for analytic truths.

But I believe that Kit Fine (1994), has made an important contribution to the theory of the analytic. He points out (p. 10) that analyticity can regularly be relativized to certain terms rather than others in the analytic truth. Thus, 'all bachelors are unmarried men' follows from the definition of 'bachelor', but there are no legitimate definitions of 'unmarried' and 'man' from which it follows. Given what he calls a 'thick' conception of a word, one that includes its meaning instead of just taking it as a mere sequence of sounds or letters, we can then see the definition of 'bachelor' as giving the essence of the word's meaning. Essence here, as I understand Fine, is identity, what the meaning *is*. The analytic truth then emerges as assimilable to other truths of identity. Chemists tell us what water *is*, lexicographers tell us what the meaning of 'bachelor' *is*.

10.4 THE INNER AND OUTER SPHERES OF POSSIBILITY

Combinatorial possibility does not appear to exhaust the sphere of the possible. It seems possible that there should have existed particulars additional to the particulars that have existed or will exist, and that these additional particulars are not 'made up' of particulars that have existed or will exist. In Armstrong 1989b, the example is given in 4.ii of a mouse in the study that is an addition to the world's mice and the world's matter. Bill Tarrant has pointed out that this case is not very happily chosen. If, for instance, the mouse is some very particular configuration or warping of spacetime at that place, then there is nothing in the case that would defeat a Combinatorialist approach. The study is there, so the space is there, though unmoused. All that is needed is that universals sufficient for mousehood be instantiated at that place, yielding a mouselike state of affairs. But though the example was badly chosen, genuinely extra possible particulars seem possible, for instance, an *addition* to actual spacetime.

Again, it seems that there might have been more universals, both properties and relations, than actually exist or will ever exist, universals that are not 'combinatorially accessible' from the actual, instantiated, universals. The simplest cases are those of additional *simple* properties and relations.

In this work, these merely possible additional particulars and universals are called aliens. The term is taken from Lewis (1986b), although he has no particular use for the term 'alien particular'. All non-actual particulars are automatically alien in his system, because they are no more than *counterparts* of actual particulars. For us, however, both sorts of alien are a problem. They appear to be possible, though by definition they are *merely* possible. But what truthmaker can we provide for this apparent truth? We do not want to reify such possibilities.

The first step, as was clearly seen by Skyrms in his 1981, is to relegate the aliens to what we can call an outer realm of possibility, a sort of second-grade possibility. As he has pointed out to me, this setting up of class distinctions is justified by the fact that, in talking about these alien possibilities, *haecceitism*, thisness, even the very moderate haecceitism that he and I favour (I some time after him, see 7.3), is not involved. In talking about alien particulars we are not talking about any particular particular. Our talk involves nothing but an existential quantifier.

To illustrate this point a little more concretely. Suppose that it is claimed, as seems possible, that the world might have contained two extra, atomic, particulars in addition to the world's actual particulars. Let them have exactly the same properties. Call them *a* and *b*. Now suppose we back-track and say that the world might have contained only one of these extra particulars. In considering this amended suggestion there cannot be *two* possibilities, one that just *a* was added, the other that just *b* was added. There is just the one possibility: that the world is increased by just one of this sort of particular.

The same goes for alien universals. What we might call *quidditas*, whatness, seems (perhaps no more than seems, see 10.41 to come) to be involved in talking about actual universals or non-actual universals constructed combinatorially from actual universals. But when we talk about *alien* universals, then a mere existential quantifier is all that is required and all that we can supply.

One good way of bringing out this point is in terms of Carnap's distinction between state-descriptions and structure-descriptions (see his 1962, ch. III, secs. 18, 27). We saw (7.3) that state-descriptions, descriptions involving particular particulars, are required to do justice to actual states of affairs and combinatorially reached possible states of affairs. But for the outer sphere of possibility, the sphere of aliens, we need only structure-descriptions, indeed structure-descriptions that use existential quantifiers alone, for both particulars and universals. 'It is possible that a certain number of extra particulars might have existed. They might have had certain extra properties and certain relations of a certain polyadicity. The distribution of these properties and relations over the particulars might have had such and such a (topic-neutral) pattern.' The outer sphere of possibility seems a rather abstract and dilute sort of possibility.

Nevertheless, superseding what I said about the aliens in my 1989b, I now offer an account of this sphere which makes this possibility a metaphysical, as opposed to a merely conceptual, possibility, and which is even, after a fashion and to a degree, a combinatorial possibility.

Consider a certain number of simple universals and simple (thin) particulars. (To make them simple is not really necessary, but does make exposition easier.) Between each of these entities the internal (and so ontologically costless) relation of *difference* holds. We can go on to form the notion of a further such entity which is different from, other than, *each* of these original entities. We can specify further whether this entity is a particular or a universal, and if the latter the number of 'places' this universal has. Relative to the original assemblage, this new entity is an alien. Our conception of it is in a way combinatorially formed: using the original assemblage and the relation of difference. If this is legitimate, it is easy to see that further relative aliens can be introduced, each alien different from each other alien as well as different from anything in the original assemblage. These aliens constitute an outer sphere with respect to the original assemblage.

Suppose now that the simple entities that we are considering are *all* the simple constituents, particulars and universals, that reality contains. If we are given, besides the entities themselves, the higher-order totality state of affairs that these *are* all the constituents, then the existence of any further simple constituents is ruled out. But if we are allowed to 'bracket' the higher-order state of affairs (which, like any state of affairs, is a contingent existent), then it seems that we can say that these further constituents are possible (and not merely epistemically or conceptually possible). The truthmaker proposed for this modal truth is the actual constituents and their relations of mutual difference. The situation (with the totality condition thought away) is no different from the situation already envisaged using a sub-class of the simple constituents. And since the relations of difference are internal, the ultimate truthmaker is no more than the plurality of the actually existing constituents. Though given a very reduced truthmaker, aliens thus find their place in an outer sphere of possibility.

This solution does leave me uneasy. The situation has been well summed up by Evan Fales (private communication). The reason for thinking the suggestion satisfactory is that we are given a recipe, stated in terms of existing items, for specifying what it would be for there to be an alien. At the same time, though, there is reason for thinking the solution unsatisfactory. For some violence is done to combinatorial intuitions, because the being of the alien is not to be understood in terms of reshuffling the existing items. Nevertheless, I am inclined to stretch my Combinatorialism here, because aliens do seem to be more than conceptually possible.

10.41 A difference between particulars and universals?

Before leaving the question of the metaphysical status of the aliens, it may be worth inquiring whether there is any difference in ontological status between alien particulars and alien universals. In Armstrong 1989b, 4.i & ii, it was argued that there was such a difference, and that alien particulars were admissible to the outer sphere while alien universals were totally inadmissible. The ground for this discrimination was that, taken simply as particulars, apart from properties and relations, particulars did not, as it were, differ in nature. Grasp the concept of one particular and, as far as their bare particularity goes, you had grasped the nature of all. Contrast universals with particulars, it was said there. Each of them has its own nature, its whatness or *quidditas*, so that to have encountered one is emphatically not to have encountered all.

But does this distinction hold? Here is a way, some may think it an implausible way, in which one might avoid having to postulate quiddities. One would say that every universal that had the same -adicity, that is, each property, dyadic relation, triadic relation, . . . was, if simple, merely numerically different from every other universal of that same -adicity. The -adicity could not be conjured away. It would be essential to the universal, and the possession of -adicity would continue to set a divide between what a particular is *qua* particular and a universal *qua* universal. But within an -adicity equivalence class (a class containing all and only the universals of a certain -adicity) the difference between different members would be no more than the difference between different particulars considered merely as particulars. One could think of this difference as a difference in another 'dimension', orthogonal to the dimensions of spacetime. Each different universal within an -adicity equivalence class would presumably be *identified*, though not constituted, by the different causal powers that they bestow.

Complex universals would be a little trickier, because they could contain as constituents simpler universals of different -adicity, and because their constituents might overlap, that is, be partially identical. The account would become more complicated. But there do not seem to be difficulties of principle in applying the suggestion to complex universals.

This deflationary account of the quiddity of universals restores the parallel with the (somewhat deflationary) account of haecceity that Skyrms, and now I, advocate. That seems all to the good. A stronger account of quiddity, like strong accounts of haecceity, seems to involve ontological embarrassment. In both cases the strong accounts give to the two sorts of entity an inner nature that seems to elude the resources of natural science to deal with. The phenomenologically minded may think that, in selected cases, we have a direct acquaintance with this inner nature. But it is notoriously difficult to integrate such acquaintance into a scientific psychology. So much the worse for science, some may argue. My own inclination is to say so much the worse for strong haecceity and strong quiddity.

10.42 Possibilities for actual entities

Every actual thing is what it is, and not another thing. This entails that when we say that some actual thing, such as Descartes, might have been, in his own nature, different from what he actually was (for instance, by dying earlier than he did), it is not *strictly* Descartes that we are envisaging. It can only be one of Descartes' 'counterparts', and this for us must be an *alien* particular. If the counterpart is to be said to be the very same entity as Descartes, it can only be the same in some loose sense.

This argument might be evaded for certain cases by distinguishing between Descartes as thick particular, with all his non-relational properties upon him, and Descartes as thin particular (see 8.3). But if Descartes has temporal parts, as I maintain, dying earlier will make him a lesser *thin* particular. That can be no more than a counterpart of the thin Descartes. (It could perhaps be maintained that the thin Descartes is strictly identical at all times, even if his properties change. But from a Naturalist standpoint, there seems to be no reason to accept such an hypothesis.)

Fortunately, there does seem to be a loose sense of the word 'same', as was argued in chapter 2. Given that Descartes has temporal parts, there is still *a* (loose) sense in which he is the very same person even although he does not live as long as he actually did, or else lives longer. There are combinatorially constructed Descartes counterparts, and these can properly be *said* to be Descartes himself.

In chapter 2.31 it was suggested that things identical in this loose sense form equivalence classes, or at least some rough and ready approximation to equivalence classes, where the equivalence relation is salient in situations where this loose use of 'same' is naturally used. I hypothesize, therefore, that when we speak of (mere) possibilities for some actual entity, but are envisaging what can be no more than counterparts of that entity, what we will accept as counterparts will fall inside an equivalence class of this sort.

10.5 CONTRACTED WORLDS

If all particulars and all universals are contingent beings, then there will be possible worlds in which both some or all particulars that exist in the actual world and some or all universals which are instantiated in the actual world, are not to be found. Some of the universals that are abolished in thought will be such that, in a world in which they are not instantiated, they will be aliens relative to that world. They will be relegated to the 'outer sphere' of possibility of the world in question.

In my 1989b, 4.iii, I argued that alien universals were no more than conceptually possible, and as a result of this said that worlds containing such aliens were *combinatorially inaccessible* from the contracted world. With accessibility not symmetrical, for the class of all possible worlds it was necessary to embrace a S4 rather than the attractive S5 logic. With aliens now adjudged metaphysically possible, can a return be made to S5?

I think it probably can be, which, if so, is a distinct advantage for the new view. But since aliens must still be relegated to an outer sphere of possibility, it may be argued that some important sort of inaccessibility remains.

10.6 ABSTRACTING FROM ATOMISM

A Combinatorial theory of what possibilities there are is greatly simplified by the assumption of Atomism. Given Independence, or Independence modified by certain relatively minor rules of exception, then the constituents of the atomic states of affairs rearranged in a way that respects the general form of an atomic state of affairs, yields the totality of all possible states of affairs. This is itself a possible world, an extremely dense world where all that is possible is actual. The rest of the possible worlds, including the actual world, can be thought of as constituted by all the different contractions of the densest world. If negative atomic states of affairs are admitted, as they are *not* in this essay (8.7), then replace each contraction by the corresponding negative state of affairs.

There is a minor question here, whether we should admit the ultimate contraction, the empty world or totally negative state of affairs. In Armstrong 1989b, this is rejected as a possibility, except as the ideal and unreachable limit of contraction. But it would not be a hanging matter to go the other way on this. (As was strenuously urged on the author by Elliot Sober in a seminar at Madison, Wisconsin, in 1985.

Peter Anstey, however, has asked what can be the truthmaker for this alleged possibility.)

But suppose that, as is conceptually possible, that is, free from contradiction at the level of our mere concepts, and in any case not a matter to be settled *a priori*, that at least some particulars or universals are complex and, in addition, are not composed of simple constituents, even an infinite number of simple constituents. Suppose that there is complexity all the way down. How is the Combinatorialist to proceed?

The matter seems not too difficult. Consider some state of affairs having the form of a particular instantiating a property or two or more particulars instantiating a relation, but abstract for the present from whether the particulars and universals are or are not complex. Given Independence (it is simplest though not essential to assume this thesis) there will exist some partition of the rest of the world into further, independent, states of affairs of the same general form whose constituents also may or may not be complex. 'The world divides into facts' as Wittgenstein puts it so memorably at 1.2 in the *Tractatus*. Call this the original division.

A set of possible worlds can then be formed from these states of affairs in the way adumbrated at the beginning of this section. Now we turn back to the state of affairs that we began the previous paragraph with. If it is genuinely atomic, that is, has nothing but genuinely atomic constituents, then there is nothing further to be done concerning it, and we pass on to consider one of the other states of affairs in the original division. Suppose, though, that one of the particulars or else one of the universals involved in the first state of affairs is complex. If our arguments about complex constituents in this work, e.g. 4.7, are correct, then in general the state of affairs will turn out to be analysable into some molecular state of affairs, where the two or more states of affairs (call them relatively atomic states of affairs) involved in this molecular state of affairs may be themselves covertly molecular. (For the exception, see the emergence cases discussed in 10.22.) These relatively atomic states of affairs will then be available for constructing new possible worlds in addition to the set of worlds contemplated at the beginning of this paragraph. Perhaps new, simpler, particulars or new, simpler, universals will now be available for recombinations. In any case, there will be new worlds where at least one, but not all, of the original relatively atomic states of affairs have been eliminated because they have been broken up into simpler states of affairs. One would go on in this way adding more and more worlds, and if some particulars or universals were such as not to resolve in the end into simple elements, then the process would go on *ad infinitum*. Repeat this exhausting process with all the other states of affairs in the original division.

10.7 POSSIBLE WORLDS AS FICTIONS

In *A Combinatorial Theory of Possibility* (1989b) I tried to use possible worlds in my account of modal truths, but at the same time to treat these worlds as (useful) fictions. An attempt to transform David Lewis' theory of possible worlds into a useful fiction is to be found in Gideon Rosen's 'Modal Fictionalism' (1990). For a difficulty for his and my own fictionalism (and an excellent account of the latter) see Rosen 1993.

My attempt was misguided, as I now see it, and in the present chapter it is suggested that it is contingent states of affairs and constituents of states of affairs that are the suitable truthmakers for modal truths. The theory of modality put forward is deflationary because, at least if the thesis of Independence holds, necessary and merely possible states of affairs are not required. The contingent states of affairs are to provide truthmakers enough. But modal discourse does not have to be accounted a species of fictional discourse.

But given that the theory now put forward does not go *through* fictional possible worlds, may they not still be admitted as useful fictions? They do seem to have proved their worth as tools in philosophical analysis. The comparison here is with the useful, indeed well-nigh essential, fictions of natural science, fictions that even the stoutest defenders of scientific realism (among whom the author accounts himself) cannot in practice dispense with. See, for instance, Keith Campbell's 'Selective Realism in the Philosophy of Physics' (1994). Another Factualist, and Combinatorialist about possibility, who thinks of possible worlds as useful fictions is Brian Skyrms (private communication).

The physicist's phase-spaces are a particularly good parallel. Such a space is given by an n-tuple of numbers associated with the position and other states of particles, with the 'space' representing physical possibilities of an important sort for these particles. Nobody thinks that to the *n*-tuple of numbers corresponds a real *n*-dimensional space. But it is convenient to think of it as a space. One can then consider e.g. in what part of the 'space' values tend to cluster. The restrictions on possible values in a phase-space are much stricter than the restrictions on possible worlds. The laws of nature restrict in a phase-space, but laws being (as I hold) contingent, do not restrict the possible worlds. Restrictions remain, however, even with the possible worlds, which indeed would have no value if there were no restrictions. These restrictions or constraints are, according to the present work, restrictions to the general form of a state of affairs (Fa, Rab, . . .) along with the restrictions that even that very permissive doctrine, Independence, imposes, together with whatever further restrictions need to be imposed upon Independence (none, I hope!). These restrictions in place, philosophers can use possible worlds to cast light upon the actual in the same sort of way that phase-spaces are used to cast light on actuality. And if somewhat less light is cast on philosophical problems by the philosopher using possible worlds than the physicist casts on his concerns by using phase-spaces, that reflects no more than the low epistemic credit-rating of philosophy as compared to physics. It is far harder to reach agreed truth in philosophy than in physics. But even in philosophy, light can be cast by using the fiction of possible worlds.

We require, therefore, some theory of fiction, some theory that makes the fictional object or state of affairs non-existent and, I would add, one that does not allow the sometimes proposed Meinongian compromise of *reference* or other relation to the non-existent. There can for us be no more than pseudo-reference, a sort of play-reference, to what does not exist. It would seem unnecessary here to pursue the general theory of fictions in detail. But surely a satisfactory one is available?

But perhaps we do not even need to think of the possible worlds as fictions. We have seen that second-class states of affairs can be admitted alongside second-class properties and relations, because they are no ontological addition (3.9). Among the second-class states of affairs, there seems no objection to admitting disjunctive states of affairs. Soa_1 v Soa_2, for instance, where the disjuncts are first-class states of affairs, could be a second-class state of affairs in good standing even if one of these states of affairs did not exist. Now consider all the possible worlds. Each of them can be represented as states of affairs, most of them conjunctive states of affairs, with a closure or totality state of affairs in each case. Assemble all the possible worlds as a disjunction of all these totalities. Since the disjunction includes the actual world, this should count as a second-class state of affairs. The merely possible worlds, the other ways that the world can be, are the other disjuncts. Does this dodge avoid treating possible worlds as fictions?

To conclude. A central thought has underlain the discussion of possibility in this chapter. It is that the actual determines the possible. There is a picture in Leibniz, in Lewis, and in other metaphysicians that the actual swims in a wider sea, the sea of the possible. The actual is just one case of the possible. What is true about this, if our account has been on the right lines, is that *truths* about the actual are a sub-class of the truths about the possible. But at the metaphysical level, at the level of the *truthmaker*, the sphere of the possible is determined by the actual. Indeed, if Independence can be upheld, and if Independence is of the very essence of possibility, possibility is determined purely by the contingent states of affairs that make up the world.

10.8 NECESSITY

After this extensive discussion of possibility, the topic of necessary truth can be very briefly handled. Recapitulation only is required. It is to be emphasized again that necessary truth is not to be defined 'extensionally', as truth in all possible worlds. It is, it would seem, a necessary truth that an object that is a kilo in mass has proper parts that are a pound in mass. The truthmaker for this truth is not to be found in any world but this. The truthmaker is no more than the two universals (and if they are not universals they are at least properties) that are involved. In this particular case it is a matter of the *merely partial identity* of the two properties. *Being a kilo in mass* is a structural property that, among its multiple parsings, is the having of just two non-overlapping parts, the one a pound in mass, the other a kilo minus a pound in mass (see the more extended discussion at 4.13). Again, if it is a necessary truth that being a water molecule is being an H_2O molecule, then the property of being this sort of molecule is the truthmaker for this truth. Some necessary truths involve difference rather than identity. It is a necessary truth that mass is not velocity. The two properties are the truthmaker for this truth.

If, however, something more than identity and difference of constituents of truthmakers is involved, then it seems that the metaphysician of states of affairs must countenance necessary states of affairs.

11

Number

11.1 THE NATURAL NUMBERS

Mathematical truths, such as the proposition that 7+5=12, involve nothing but mathematical entities. These entities, however, are also to be found, as some sort of constituent, in contingent and empirical truths. Thus, it may be observably true that there are just seven black swans on the lake. Let us begin by considering what would be the truthmaker for a truth such as this one.

Given a Factualist metaphysics as starting point, we will be looking for a state of affairs to be the truthmaker. It is clear that it will be, in part at least, a molecular state of affairs. This molecular state of affairs will be a conjunction of seven states of affairs, each involving a particular, where the particulars are wholly distinct from each other (Siamese swans we will bar) and each particular has properties sufficient to make it a swan. The black-swan-making properties, of course, may differ from particular to particular. Presumably there is no universal of black-swanhood. To get the force of 'just' we shall need in addition the higher-order state of affairs that this is the *totality* of black-swan-presently-on-this-lake states of affairs. Here we shall not concern ourselves further with this totality-fact.

Each of the seven states of affairs is truthmaker for the truth that there is at least one black swan on the lake. At this point one begins to see the attraction of Reinhardt Grossmann's view that numbers should join a group of entities that he calls 'quantifiers', meaning by the word not certain expressions such as 'some' and 'all', but rather the features of the world that these expressions pick out (1983, 137–42). We, however, will take a different tack, one that may be more ontologically economical.

Instead of considering the class of the seven black swans on the lake, or the molecular state of affairs that is the conjunction of seven relatively atomic black-swan-presently-on-the-lake states of affairs (two entities that are not all that different from each other if our theory of classes to be advanced in ch. 12 is on the right track) let us take the bigger particular that is the mereological sum of the seven swans. And let us take each swan, each part of the bigger particular, as thick, not thin, particulars, that is, as particulars with all their (non-relational) properties upon them. What number does this bigger object have? As we know, as Frege (1884, sec. 22) in particular insisted, that question has no clear answer. It has just about any number you choose, perhaps up to the number of the continuum. But now consider the (second-class) property of *being a swan currently on the lake*. It is available in the situation, it is instantiated there. It is also a unit-determining property; it picks out just one swan among those now on the lake. (For more on the notion of a unit-determining property see the next chapter, on classes.) Now further consider the relation that this property has to the mereological object. What relation? The salient relation, the one where the property carves the object up and so yields a class of seven swans. *That relation*, it is suggested, *is the number seven*. The ontological economy now appears. The relation is an internal relation, one that supervenes upon, is entailed by, its terms. (Though if you were to take the mereological object as a *thin* particular, the relation would be external.)

To this account Reinhardt Grossmann has objected (1992, p. 69) that what we would have here is the relation of *having seven parts each with the property of being a swan now on the lake* (he uses a different example), of which seven is a mere ingredient. This 'relation' though, despite what he says, seems to be a property, a structural property of the mereological object. (See the next paragraph.) By contrast, the relation that we are pointing to really is a relation, though it is internal, and it holds between *being a black swan now on the lake* (a genuine, if second-class property) and the object, the aggregate. One might put the matter by saying that this property *sevens* this object. Suppose that there are also just seven pelicans on the lake. The property of *being a pelican now on the lake* stands in the same relation to the aggregate of the pelicans that *being a black swan now on the lake* stands to the aggregate of the swans. Both properties seven their corresponding aggregates. Incidentally, they carve out a class of just seven things. (If the aggregate was a round cake, and the property was *being a quarter-portion of the cake*, the property would carve out indefinitely many classes of just four things.)

Associated with relations, superveniently and trivially, are relational properties (see 6.4). If *a* has R to *b* then *a* has the relational property of *having R to b*. If *b* is an F, then *a* has the relational property of *having R to an F*. So if *being a black swan now on the lake* sevens a certain aggregate, then this aggregate has the relational property of *being sevened by (being a black swan now on the lake)*. In other words, the aggregate has the property of *being made up of just seven black swans now on the lake*. This appears to be the property that Grossmann wrongly thinks I am identifying with the number seven.

The numbers 1 and 0 require only a little further consideration. 1 reduces to the internal relation holding between a (unit-determining) property and any particular which has that property. The nought relation holds between any unit-determining property and aggregates which lacks any part that instantiates the property even once. This is the negation of the numerical relationship rather than itself being a numerical relation. But since the relation is an internal one, dictated by its terms, we do not need to ban it in the way we have banned negative universals. There is a special case where the property is not instantiated anywhere or anytime. This, for us, can be no better than a merely possible property. But we can, I think, allow an internal relation between this possible property and some aggregate, with a combinatorial account of what it is to be a possible property. Strictly, perhaps, as Peter Forrest has suggested to me, it is a merely possible internal relation.

The cases that we have considered so far are the favourable cases, where the unit-determining property cleanly divides the whole aggregate into instances that do not overlap. But there are other cases where the property fails to respect this last condition, for instance, the case proposed by Peter Simons (1982) of two delineated squares that overlap on a plane surface but where the overlap is itself a square. How many squares do we have? The most natural answers are 'two' and 'three', depending upon exactly what one takes as the unit-determining property.

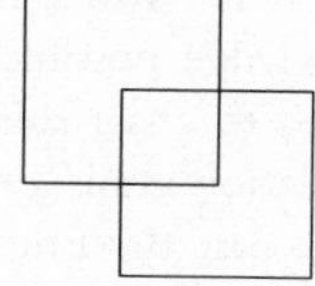

This sort of case does not, however, seem to be a counter-example, provided that we are prepared to have the cookie-cutting unit-determining property cut cookies that overlap within the aggregate, and to note further that in certain situations it may be necessary to disambiguate exactly what is to count as the property. For a little more discussion of these issues, see Armstrong, 1989b, 9.iii.

11.2 MATHEMATICAL EXISTENCE

This account just given of the nature of the natural numbers raises the question of what we are to do about very large natural numbers. Perhaps there will be no aggregate to be the second term of the internal relation that we are identifying the number with. We have already anticipated in places the modification of our account that this objection forces us to make. It is a general point, applying to all mathematics. Mathematical 'existence', it seems, is not really existence. For a mathematical object to 'exist' it need only be possible. We need only require that corresponding to each cardinal number, including the infinite cardinals, it be *possible* that an aggregate having that number of parts should exist, where that aggregate has no parts that are mere mathematical objects.

Following up a suggestion by Peter Forrest this view of mathematical existence may be formulated thus: mathematical entity X 'exists' if and only if there is a (large enough) possible world where X is instantiated. The definition would be available both for realists about possible worlds and anti-realists like myself who nevertheless find talk of possible worlds acceptable and useful.

This account of mathematical existence is not motivated simply by a desire to defend the account of number given in this chapter. It also addresses and helps to solve the very difficult problem that mathematics poses for empiricism. The natural sciences, however beholden to mathematics, must in the end appeal in the testing of hypotheses to observation and experiment. Mathematics, however, proceeds in an almost purely *a priori* manner, with proof the termination of the enterprise. We Empiricists have a problem here. How is mathematics possible? (More generally, how is *a priori* knowledge possible?) What was Cantor doing when he discovered and started to chart the realm of the infinite using nothing but thought and calculation as his guide?

It seems to do a great deal to ease the Empiricist's problem here to say that Cantor did not literally discover new entities, in the way that Hubble discovered the galaxies, but instead only discovered possibilities that had not been previously grasped. It goes without saying that these discoveries are important and may require genius to make. But the force of the word 'discovery' does then require qualification! I am not saying that the

Empiricist problem is completely solved. Mathematics is still a surprising affair even if all it does is to chart logical space or a portion thereof. But the problem begins to wear a more hopeful aspect. A bit more will be said at 11.4.

11.3 RATIONAL AND REAL NUMBERS

We now come to what seems a significant recommendation for this account of natural number, something brought to my attention by Peter Forrest. (See Forrest and Armstrong, 1987, where the whole theory was first set forth. A considerable debt is also owed to an earlier paper by Glen Kessler, 1980.) It enables us to give a *univocal* account of the natural, rational, and real numbers. The unit-determining property functions in the same way for the rationals and the reals as it does for the naturals, but now it is a property that acts as a unit of *quantity* and the aggregate that is the other term of the relation is, as it were, measured by the unit. The unit-determining property and the aggregate stand in a relation to each other that is a relation of *proportion*. Thus, the aggregate, say a partially eaten cake, may be two-thirds of the quantity of the unit, say a complete cake of this sort. This proportion can be identified with the rational number 2/3. The aggregate, say the area enclosed by a circle, may be πr^2 times the unit-quantity, here r, the length of the radius. That proportion is the real number πr^2. The special feature of the natural numbers, which differentiates them from the rationals and the reals, is that they carve up the aggregate into units, into ones. (In the simplest cases these units or ones are non-overlapping.) This gives the natural numbers a special link with classes. But just as in the case of the natural numbers, for the rationals and the reals the relations are internal.

This view is actually an old one to which Forrest and I returned to, partly as a result of dissatisfaction with the Frege-Russell account of natural numbers, which, if taken as a starting point, does not permit a unified account of the three sorts of number. This old view was beautifully summed up by Isaac Newton in his *Universal Arithmetic* (1769), and I am indebted to John Bigelow for drawing my attention to the quotation:

> By *Number* we understand not so much a Multitude of Unities, as the abstracted Ratio of any *Quantity*, to another Quantity of the same kind, which we take for Unity.
>
> (p. 2)

'A multitude of unities' is actually a wonderfully good description of a many-membered class. But, as Newton intimates, a natural number (if greater than one) is not a multitude of unities, but rather it is a ratio of a multitude of units to a unit. A number (natural, rational and real) is always a ratio, a certain sort of relation.

(Although Newton puts the view so concisely, it goes right back to the Greeks. I am indebted to Jim Franklin for the following passage from Aristotle (1941):

> 'the one' means the measure of some plurality, and 'number' means a measured plurality and a plurality of measures. . . . The measure must always be some identical thing predicable of all the things it measures, e.g. if the things are horses, the measure is 'horse', . . .

Metaphysics, 1088a4–9, trans. W. D. Ross.)

Joel Michell (1993), though sympathetic to our general view, holds that it needs to be modified. (For Michell's important work, see also his 1994.) The trouble arises with continuous quantity. He argues, giving examples, that:

> [f]or continuous quantities, relative magnitudes are themselves relative to additive relations. A magnitude of any quantity together with an additive relation defines an infinite series of multiples of that magnitude. . . . Numbers may then be understood as binary relations between infinite series of multiples, where the multiples are based upon the same additive relation. In the special case of discrete quantities these binary relations reduce to relative magnitudes between quantitative properties. In the case of continuous quantities they do not.
>
> (p. 332).

But while granting the importance of Michell's qualification, it seems that even in the continuous case there is a simplest sort of additivity, additivity where the sum of two quantities is nothing more than their mereological sum. This would seem to have strong claims to *be* their sum. If this is correct, then Forrest's idea can still be upheld.

11.4 MATHEMATICAL AND LOGICAL TRUTH

We have suggested that the mathematical truth that some mathematical entity exists has as its truthmaker the possibility of the existence of certain states of affairs. These states of affairs are the contingent ones involving particulars and universals, from which we are proposing to build the world. Thus, the number aleph$_0$, the number of the class of the natural numbers, exists. One sufficient condition for this truth of mathematics is the possibility that the class of electrons is an infinite class, a class which can be correlated one–one with the natural numbers. The infinity of the class can be explained in a non-circular manner by saying that it is possible that, for every class of electrons that has a (finite) number, there exists a class of electrons having greater finite number.

But unless one thinks that possibilities, including mere possibilities, are real entities, an actual truthmaker has not yet been provided. Consider, however, the actual class of electrons, past, present and future. Assume, to take the most difficult case for us here, that this class is finite. Each member of the class has the properties necessary and sufficient for being an electron, and *being an electron* is a unit-determining property. Given the combinatorial ways of arriving at possibilities, and provided that the indefinite reduplication of particulars is one of these ways, then we have the possibility of $aleph_0$ electrons. That this is a genuine possibility is sufficient, I suggest, for the 'existence' of the mathematical object $aleph_0$. So the finite class of electrons (we are supposing it to be finite) will be the truthmaker for the possibility that this class is infinite.

What sort of possibility is it that is involved? The supposed extra electrons would be *alien* electrons. It is important for our argument, therefore, as argued in 10.4 contrary to an earlier view of mine, that alien electrons be possible and not merely conceivable. If there is an actual infinity somewhere else in the world, for instance, if space is genuinely continuous, respectable combinatorial principles give us the possibility of an infinite class of electrons. But suppose the world is finite in every respect. Then clearly there will be need for aliens. If alien electrons are thought of as electrons that are *different* (numerically different) from the electrons that happen to be the totality of the electrons, then, it was argued with a little trepidation, we have genuine possibilities. So it is genuinely possible, in a world that contains only a finite number of electrons, for there to be $aleph_0$ electrons. And that, it seems, will suffice for mathematics.

The question of what the existence of the infinite numbers comes to, is a very special question. What of more ordinary mathematical truths? What, for instance, of $7+5=12$? Given that such truths are necessary, then it is necessary that the conjunction of any seven objects and any further five objects is twelve objects. But this is a supervenience, an entailment. So, according to our usual argument, there is no increase of being in this conclusion. Furthermore, the supervenience is symmetrical. It is necessary that twelve objects divide into a conjunction of seven objects and five further objects. But symmetrical supervenience can be nothing but identity (see 2.12). We thus reach by a new route an old conclusion that mathematician and logician mean the same thing by their sign '='. The truth that 7+5=12 is an identity. (The numbers 7 and 5 will each be partially identical with 12. Mathematical addition, +, is identical with the mereological +.)

The metaphysician has options here, though. One could accept that such truths are necessary and so, given our definition of supervenience, that the two sides of the equation do supervene on each other, yet at the same time hold that there is no identity involved. What we would have, on this view, is necessity with increase of being. Note that this is a rejection of Independence in this situation. Two distinct states of affairs are each entailed by the other. It would be natural, if one took this line, to see this as a connection between distinct universals. The connection will take the following form. Something being of the 7+5 state-of-affairs type entails and is entailed by the same something being of the 12 state-of-affairs type. The inference from this to the universally quantified truths about the tokens of these types then seems perspicuous.

Another option is to deny that mathematical truths are necessary. Presumably this will be done on the radical ground that the whole necessary/contingent distinction is a mistake. The difficulty with this position is that it cannot explain the huge difference between the way of proceeding in the rational sciences of mathematics and logic, on the one hand, and the way of proceeding found in the natural sciences, on the other. Mathematics proceeds through calculations and proofs, that is to say it proceeds *a priori*, and achieves, not certainty in every case, but a very high degree of rational assurance. The natural sciences proceed by observation and experiment, and though the certainty achieved can be very great, the obtainable degree of rational assurance often falls short of that achieved by the rational sciences.

This difference is in some degree obscured in contemporary theoretical work in the natural sciences, particularly in such disciplines as theoretical physics. Chains of formal reasoning, proof of theorems and so on, are found in such work just as they are found in mathematics and logic. Nevertheless, a difference remains, one that sets an uncrossable gulf between the rational and the natural sciences. In mathematics a proof terminates the enterprise. The proof may be controversial and require checking. Absolute certainty may not be achievable. But proof is the natural termination of the enterprise. In the natural sciences, however, the mathematical derivation of consequences of assumptions is only a beginning. An essential and empirical step remains. Are these proved consequences borne out by observation and experiment? That the conclusions drawn from observation and experiment are themselves to greater or lesser degree 'theory-laden' does not remove the distinction drawn here between mathematics and natural science.

It seems, then, that we should reject the rejection of the necessary/contingent distinction. In mathematics and logic, at least, we have *a priori* knowledge of necessary truths. But, as already noted in 11.2, this raises a Kantian question. How is such *a priori* knowledge possible? (It is, of course, an Empiricist question. A Rationalist, postulating necessities *in re* and a faculty of Reason to know these necessities, will have no problem.) Kant's answer for the case of synthetic *a priori* knowledge, that the mind imposes such forms upon the world, and so knows what these forms are, has little to recommend it. Why, for instance, even if ordinary physical reality is a construction by the mind, should the mind know so exactly what it has done? But Kant's *question* remains even if his own answer is wrong and a better answer has to be found.

The question is answered, partially at least, if we suppose that these necessary truths, though certainly not trivial, do not involve any increase of being. This is the justification for the doctrine of the younger Wittgenstein that all necessary truths say the same thing, viz. nothing. We should not accept it in this form, but we can see its force. Different necessary truths have different truthmakers. 7+5=12 has as preliminary truthmaker the number 12, while the preliminary truthmaker for 7+6 is 13. These numbers, in turn, we have suggested should be analysed as (internal) relations. Hence the truth that such numbers exist have as truthmakers their terms. In general, these terms will exist. But in special cases the terms will be no more than possibilities.

This doctrine of the truthmakers for mathematical truths does to a degree trivialize the latter, even if not in the radical way that they are trivialized in the *Tractatus*. By comparison with contingent truths their truthmakers are reduced. It takes less to make them true. The Empiricist can therefore live more easily with the idea that we can have *a priori* knowledge of them. That, to a degree, answers Kant's question.

If what has been said in this section about mathematical truth is along the right lines, the same general account can be given of the truths of logic. They, too, are necessary and are discovered *a priori* by thought and calculation, with the usual qualification that what comes to be accepted *a priori* is not, because of that, certain. And the truths of logic will not involve any increase of being. This by no means entails the *Tractatus* doctrine that the logical constants, which are among the *terms* of these truths, do not signify. At least one such constant, the universal quantifier, allness, does pick out an objective feature of the world. Allness facts, higher-order states of affairs of totality, are the subject of our next but one chapter.

12

Classes

12.1 CLASSES AND AGGREGATES

If we want to bring classes down to earth, down to spacetime, out of the clutches of those who call them abstract (meaning apparently by this that classes stand above and beyond particulars, even when their members are all ordinary particulars!), nothing is more helpful than to attend to the close relations between a class and its corresponding aggregate. The aggregate is what David Lewis calls the fusion of the members of the class, and an excellent account of the class/fusion distinction can be found in Lewis' 1991, 1.1. Peter Simons (1987) calls aggregates 'sums'. I retain the word aggregate because it is the term I have used in earlier writings.

It will be assumed here, as Lewis also assumes but Simons denies, that to *every* class there corresponds its aggregate. Indeed, still in agreement with Lewis, it will be assumed that wherever there are some things, there is an aggregate of them, whether or not there is a class of these things. This is the principle of Unrestricted Mereological Composition. As has been emphasized a number of times already, this 'permissive mereology' is an ontologically uncostly assumption because the aggregate supervenes on the sum of its parts, a supervenience that seems an excellent candidate for an ontological free lunch.

Considering the more restricted principle, that for every class there exists the aggregate of their members, it is interesting to ask whether something near to its converse is true. Is it the case that for every aggregate there exists classes of which it is a member? More particularly, is it the case that for every aggregate there exists its *singleton* class, the class which has that aggregate as sole member? I think that this is an attractive principle, but we shall see that Lewis, for reasons internal to his particular system, is forced to deny it for certain special cases. More of this at the end of the chapter.

It is convenient, though not more than convenient, to concentrate in the first place upon aggregates that themselves contain no classes as parts.

Consider one of these aggregates. We can operate upon the aggregate by distinguishing parts within it in all sorts of ways. This 'division', as we may call it, is to be an exhaustive division, leaving nothing over. I picture the aggregate as a rather big thing, and the division as a matter of drawing lines that mark out smaller portions of the thing, so dividing the aggregate into parts. It does not matter if the portions overlap, or if some portions are proper parts of other portions, though it is nice and neat if neither of these things is so. There is even the limiting case where the line is drawn round the aggregate as a whole, the improper part of the aggregate. Indeed, a+A, where a is a proper part of aggregate A, counts as a 'division' of A.

This gives our first fix on classes. Given permissive mereology, Unrestricted Mereological Composition, to every class there corresponds an aggregate which is the mereological sum of the members of that class. The class is, in a way, the aggregate, but it is the aggregate with something added, viz. a certain particular division of the aggregate, *with that particular division as essential to making it that class*. Suppose, for instance, we have:

$$\text{A (the aggregate)} = b + c + d + e$$
$$\text{C (associated class)} = \{b, c, d, e\}.$$

The aggregate could have been divided in all sorts of different ways, say:

$$\text{A} = f + g + h$$

yet still be the same aggregate. That the *sum* is the same, is all that matters. This would be so even if b, c, d, and e are all atoms. Not so the class. It has to have just the same members, the same division, if it is to retain its identity. So the class C is the aggregate A *plus a strict way of dividing A into parts*.

But what is this division? It is not literal physical division. But it is not mere thought either. There must be some *point d'appui* in the aggregate that makes that division real. What is it? But before answering this question, we turn to an important contribution to the ontology of classes made by David Lewis.

12.2 CLASSES AS MEREOLOGICAL WHOLES

Lewis (1991) has pointed out that classes can be represented as mereological sums of the singletons (unit classes) of their members. Thus:

$$\{a, b, c, d, \ldots\}$$

is equivalent to, identical with:

$$\{a\}+\{b\}+\{c\}+\{d\}+\ldots$$

What Lewis perceived, and then took to this limit, is that the relation of a class to its (non-null) sub-classes is a whole/part relation and that this relation is governed by nothing but the rules of the mereological calculus. By presenting a class as the fusion or aggregate, the mere mereological sum, of the singletons of its members, the mereological element in classes is laid fully bare. Mereology, it seems, we understand. Furthermore, we have the plausible thesis that mereological sums are no increase of being over and above their parts. We can then focus more clearly on the non-mereological element in classes, the singletons, and ask '*What are they?*'.

It is at this point that Lewis gives us a very dusty answer. He finds the relation of singleton to its member utterly puzzling, a puzzle well brought out by Gideon Rosen in his 1995 (sec. 2, 'Mysterious Singletons'). About the only positive conclusion Lewis comes to is that singleton and member are 'entirely distinct' (p. 41). Yet if philosophical commonsense is worth anything, that should be false. In some way, the singleton must contain its member. (Not that I want to place philosophical commonsense on the same high epistemic pedestal as Moorean commonsense. But it has its value.) Nor is Lewis, quite rightly, willing to solve his problem by jettisoning classes. To impugn the mathematical discipline of set theory on the strength of a philosophical argument would be, one supposes, rather like impugning motion on the strength of Zeno's paradoxes.

The reason for Lewis' difficulty is the point that we have already touched upon (3.721 & 8.2). Lewis holds that mereological composition is the *only* form of composition that there is. Hence he concludes that a singleton class, which is not a mereological complex, cannot be a complex entity. We ourselves part company with Lewis here. The moral drawn in the present work is that there has to be at least one other form of composition in the world. We have already found non-mereological composition in states of affairs. Perhaps, then, states of affairs will help us with our present problem.

Consider a molecular state of affairs:

a's being F & b's being G & c's being H & . . .

We have already argued that the & here can be replaced by, is identical with, the mereological +, giving us a mereological whole of 'mereological atoms'. (So-styled because they are impenetrable by mereology.) But now consider the mereological whole of singletons:

$$\{a\}+\{b\}+\{c\}+\ldots$$

If & is no other than +, then the mereology involved in many-membered classes must remind us of molecular states of affairs. The simplest hypothesis will then be that a singleton is an atomic state of affairs. The embedding of member in its singleton will be the embedding of a particular, or more generally some entity, in a state of affairs. To put the hypothesis in more neutral language, which may recommend it more generally, it is giving the entity some property. (I will suggest shortly that the property should be one that marks the entity out as *one* thing, as a unit.) This, *subject to a weakening amendment still to be introduced*, is the hypothesis that will be defended in this chapter.

12.21 Resemblances between classes and states of affairs

The fact that many-membered classes, when analysed as mereological sums of the singletons of their members, model conjunctions of monadic states of affairs when analysed as mereological sums of their conjuncts, is an important resemblance. There are two others. This, of course, does not prove that classes are states of affairs, but it does give aid and comfort to the thesis.

It has already been pointed out that first-order states of affairs, despite having universals among their constituents, are particulars. This is the 'victory of particularity' (8.4). The same goes for classes of *first-order* particulars. Such a class, whether or not it is a singleton, is not a repeatable, it is not 'predicable of many'. So it seems to be a first-order particular. This, incidentally, is one reason why it is potentially so misleading to call classes a species of universal. (It would seem, however, that classes of universals *are* repeatables.)

The third point of resemblance is that the location of classes and the location of states of affairs are rather obscure matters. In the case of classes this has encouraged the silly idea that classes are not located at all. As has been pointed out, just thinking about the way that classes stand to their aggregates should dispel this idea, at least for the case of ordinary particulars. Some have suggested that states of affairs (facts) are not located either (Grossmann, 1992, ch. 2, sec. 2 -*The localization problem*). And, indeed, it is true that some features of our discourse encourage the idea that states of affairs are not located. If we are asked where we would locate the fact that Brisbane is to the north of Sydney, we are a bit stumped. At the same time, states of affairs involving first-order particulars, and in particular monadic states of affairs involving such particulars, do seem to be located *in a way*, viz. where these particulars are located. In 8.8 we tried to explain this somewhat confusing situation by pointing out that it is in spacetime that things are said to have locations, but that if a Factualist ontology is correct then spacetime consists of (is identical with) an assemblage of states of affairs. It may therefore be *strictly* incorrect, but all the same reasonably intelligible, to locate states of affairs within the thing that they are supposed to constitute.

12.3 UNIT-DETERMINING PROPERTIES AND UNITHOOD

We are seeking (for the present) to interpret $\{a\}$ as a state of affairs, where *a* has a certain property. The braces will stand in for a property of *a*. What property? The following constraint, it is now suggested, must be put on any candidate for the property. The property must be such that it *determines a unit*. A class is one or more units, one or more ones, a mereological whole of these ones, and the property required must be such that it picks out the particular *a* as a one. Barry Miller has pointed out the link between such properties and count-nouns. Roughly, these properties are the ontological correlates of count-nouns. (In Armstrong, 1978a, such properties are called, not very happily, 'particularizing' properties.) Thus, *being extended* is not a unit-determining property. The particular *a* may be extended. But it is not one as opposed to many extended things. The same goes for a property such as *being red*. But the property of *being a (delineated) square* is a unit-determining property. The property must be a property that makes the object *a* just one instantiation of the property. Under these conditions it will play its part, where *a* is a member of a many-membered class, in dividing up the associated aggregate in such a way as to yield that class (see sec. 1). For singleton classes there is no division involved. But there is still a distinction between the singleton and its member. On the present theory, this will be taking the member as a single thing, a one, a unit. And a many-membered class will be just a mereological whole of these ones, each member taken as a one.

These unit-determining properties need not be universals, and in most cases they will not be universals. If the member of a singleton is a first-order particular, then it is plausible to think that there will always be *some* unit-determining property-universal which it instantiates. (And it is an interesting speculation, which I do not however know how to support further, that every first-order property-universal is unit-determining.) But our theory is meant to deal with all classes, and so unit-determining properties will be required for *classes* when they are members of classes. It is unlikely that there are many classes which have property-universals among their unit-determining properties. The higher up the class hierarchy, the more unlikely that this is so. In general, even when the member is not a class, unit-determining properties will be *second-class* properties, *being a delineated square*, *being a cat* and so on. That means that the states of affairs involved will be second-class states of affairs (3.9). Such properties and states of affairs exist, though, even if they are supervenient upon the first-class states of affairs, and are available to us to use in our analysis of what a singleton is.

In the discussion of second-class properties at 3.9, it was emphasized that second-class properties attach to their subjects *contingently*. All states of affairs, even second-class states of affairs, are contingent. If then, a singleton is to be analysed as the embedding of the member in a state of affairs, the unit-determining property will have to attach to the member contingently. I believe that this condition makes intuitive sense. A singleton is its member *plus* something more. The image of drawing lines on an aggregate to carve it up in a certain way, a carving up that transforms a mere aggregate into a class, certainly suggests something more. It suggests an addition of being to the mere member. I should add that in earlier expositions of my theory (in particular my 1991) I failed to make this important point explicit.

The condition of contingent attachment is rather strong though, and it will soon be seen that it leads to trouble, trouble that will force us to modify the theory of what a singleton is.

For the present, though, we consider another less troubling difficulty. A particular is as it were put into a singleton by a unit-determining property. But we do not really want that unit-determining property appearing in the analysis of being a singleton. We want something much more abstract. We want the member to be *one* of something, and that requires a unit-determining property. But we don't want that unit-determining property actually appearing. After all, the member might have many other unit-determining properties that would do. We don't want them all.

The problem does not seem particularly difficult. There is a second-order property of the member that will do the job admirably. It is *the prop-*

erty of having some first-order unit-determining property. David Lewis has suggested to me the excellent name of 'unithood' for this property. It comes with no ontological cost. It supervenes upon each of the unit-determining properties that, contingently, the member of the singleton happens to have. The unit-determining properties of the member are each one of them truthmakers for the having of unithood by that member. But that is the limit of their role. Unithood itself has the right abstractness for the abstract notion of a class. ('Abstract' here in Locke's sense, not Quine's.)

So as our theory of singletons stands at present, the theory presented in my 1991 paper, it is a matter of the member having unithood, of its having *some* property, first or second class, contingently attaching to the member.

12.4 PROBLEMS FOR THE 1991 THEORY

But the theory of singletons presented in that paper faces great difficulties.

(1) One immediate worry is whether unit-determining properties can always be found. Consider the singleton $\{a\}$. There must be a unit-determining property for *a* so that we get a state of affairs. If all states of affairs are to be contingent, even second-class states of affairs, the property must attach to *a* contingently. Suppose such a property found. But then we face $\{\{a\}\}$. We want a property for this further state of affairs. It will probably have to be a second-class property. But then there is $\{\{\{a\}\}\}$ and so on *ad infinitum*. A lot of contingently attaching unit-determining properties are going to be needed. Have we any assurance that they exist? Do we need a special axiom to say that they exist? And if we did provide such an axiom, what would be its truthmaker?

(2) This leads on to a second worry, drawn from Nelson Goodman's protests about set theory in 'A World of Individuals' (1958). Goodman refuses to accept the classes of the set theorist. His protest is an Empiricist one. Set theorists, proceeding by purely *a priori* reasoning, populate the world with the set theoretical hierarchy. There are all these classes *in addition to* their members. How can this be reconciled with our intellectual conscience as Empiricists? It is as if we are being asked to give countenance to the Ontological Argument!

It seems that this second worry would be removed if it could be argued that the set theorist's classes are not something ontologically additional to the aggregates that they are associated with. That in turn may seem quite plausible. Given the members, is it not entailed that the class is there? That is to say, the existence of the class seems to supervene on the existence of the members. It is true that there are certain entities that cannot all be put together in the one class, or at least, if 'proper classes' are admitted, cannot be put together in the one set. There is no class of all singletons, or at least no set of all singletons. But if the proposed members, put all together, are suitable, the class must automatically be there. Such supervenience, one might then argue, is no ontological addition.

This attempt to rescue classes from the strictures of Goodman seems quite hopeful in itself. Unfortunately, however, it appears to be fatal to the view that singletons are states of affairs! Solving Goodman's difficulty in this way makes our own theory untenable. Singletons are said to be a certain sort of state of affairs: an entity having unithood, where, behind the second-order property of unithood, there must be some unit-determining property. These states of affairs, though they will regularly be second-class states of affairs, must themselves, like the first-class states of affairs, be contingent (see 3.9). But if they are contingent, then they might not obtain. The entity would then not have any unit-determining property. But if so, we must say farewell to any ontologically innocent supervenience of a singleton on its member.

(3) These difficulties may seem to pall beside a difficulty raised by Gideon Rosen (1995). (For other, I think less damaging, criticism see Alex Oliver, 1992.) Rosen has shown that the 1991 theory of singletons together with unrestricted mereological composition (which I am committed to) produces a contradiction. Indeed, as he points out, the contradiction has really nothing particularly to do with classes. The desire to give an account of the nature of singletons led me to suggest that every object is embedded in its own unique state of affairs (the unithood fact). The latter is, mereologically, an atom. So a one–one correspondence between objects and atoms is required. But given unrestricted mereological composition, this is impossible. Given *n* atoms in the universe, there are at least 2^n–1 objects, because for each non-empty class of atoms there exists the mereological sum of their members. And it is a familiar fact, since Cantor, that for all $n > 1$, 2^n–1 is a greater number than *n*, even if *n* is an infinite cardinal. The full detail of Rosen's paper is greatly worth studying, but space forbids this here.

I suppose that one could object to Rosen that there may be objects (some special states of affairs?) that do not have singletons, and so do not require unit-determining properties. But unless much more can be said, the move seems desperately *ad hoc*.

(4) There is yet another difficulty for the theory. Consider the world,

pleonastically for me the actual world. To be *the world*, the totality of being, it must be the world as thick rather than thin particular. It must be the world with all its properties upon it, a huge molecular state of affairs. The world so taken appears to be an object, a particular. As such, it should presumably have its singleton. But can it have a singleton, given the theory being defended? To embed the world into a contingent state of affairs, say F(W), is to set up a *further* state of affairs in addition to the states of affairs that constitute the world. Another contradiction.

12.5 THE THEORY MODIFIED

Formidable objections indeed! But I suggest that they can all be met by a relatively simple modification of the theory. (Set out briefly in my reply to Rosen, 1995.) The key to the modification is to accept that the set-theoretical hierarchy is a mathematical structure. For me it is not *the* fundamental mathematical structure, as some philosophies of mathematics will have it, but it is a mathematical structure. (And one in which other mathematical structures can be modelled.) Now it was argued in the previous chapter, on independent grounds independently arrived at, that mathematical structures may or may not be instantiated. The proper reaction to this, it was further suggested, is not to embrace a Platonist theory of mathematics. Rather we should accept that the 'existence' of such a structure is no more than the *possibility* of the existence of *objects* that instantiate the structure, with the *mere* possibilities non-existents. This changes our view of set theory. It describes certain mathematical structures which are not necessarily instantiated, and so do not necessarily exist in the full ontological sense. Accepting this, then the pressure of Goodman's case against taking all classes with ontological seriousness is greatly relieved. (Though, of course, weight is thrown on the theory of possibility.)

We now introduce a distinction between 'empirical' and 'non-empirical' singletons. In an empirical singleton the member is embedded in an actual state of affairs, a unithood fact. In a non-empirical singleton there is a mere (unrealized) possibility that the member is so embedded. Rosen's result shows that not all singletons can be empirical. Somewhere in the set theoretical hierarchy empirical singletons must give out. (And the case of W, the world, seems to give us an actual case where an empirical singleton is impossible.) But that does not matter for set theory, which describes a possible, not necessarily actual, structure. For the *a priori* discipline of set theory, no more is required for a singleton than the possibility that the member has a unit-determining property.

So we may now re-define unithood, oneness, as demanding no more than the *possibility* of a unit-determining property. And the truthmaker for the modal truth that a certain object might have had a unit-determining property, though it actually lacked such a property, will be the object itself. To have a singleton, the object need only be such that a unit-determining property *could* attach to it contingently.

A helpful way of grasping this modification involves using the notion of possible worlds. When the set-theorist says that a certain class, C, exists, we are to think of this statement as prefaced by 'In some (large enough) possible world . . .' (See Peter Forrest's remark about my view of mathematical existence at 11.2.) Take a C some of whose members – perhaps classes themselves – lack unit-determining properties. There will still be a world, a merely possible world, where these members (or their suitable counterparts) exist and do have a unit-determining property. These states of affairs do not exist from the standpoint of the actual world. They add nothing to the sum of actuality. But *inside* the merely possible world they are empirical classes and add to the sum of that 'reality'.

For me, of course, the possible worlds, taken realistically, are a fiction. So this theory of classes depends on there being a satisfactory Actualist theory of modality.

12.6 HAS THE WORLD A SINGLETON?

The case of W, the world, is very illuminating, at least for the grasping of the present theory. So we finish this chapter by giving it some attention.

It can be seen *a priori* that the world, the totality of being, cannot have an *actual*, contingently attaching, unit-determining property. For that would demand that the world be a mere constituent of some contingent state of affairs, and then it would not be the world. Yet can we not form a class of which W is the sole member, indeed can we not go on to erect the whole set-theoretical hierarchy on top of W? It certainly seems so.

But suppose that all that is necessary for something to have a singleton is that it be *possible* that it have a unit-determining property. Then we can provide W with its singleton. For is it not the case that the world might have been a mere part or constituent of a larger object? For instance, if the world is a spacetime, it might have had a twin attached to it, Siamese fashion, at a single spacetime point. Then the 'original' world would have been related to its twin in a state of affairs, and so would have had certain actually instantiated unit-determining properties. It would have had an *empirical* singleton. Of course, the *new* W, call it W′, would lack an empirical singleton. But we can allow W′ to have a singleton, because it would again be possible that W′ was embedded in a still larger W″.

If, *pace* Lewis, the actual is all that there is, then no aggregate, no fusion, can be larger than W. The fusion of all *empirical* singletons, for instance, would seem to be W, and certainly cannot be anything more. W, we have argued, has a singleton, though a non-empirical singleton. Any aggregate less than W presumably has a singleton of some sort. It would seem, then, that every aggregate has its singleton.

We may contrast this with Lewis's position. Consider, in particular, all the set-theoretical singletons. Set-theory tells us that there can be no *set* of these singletons. Perhaps, however, they form a 'proper class'. Or perhaps the word 'all' here is no more than the universal quantifier, here used to make plural reference to each singleton. Or perhaps these two positions are really the same position. However this may be, Lewis, holding like myself to Unrestricted Mereological Composition, thinks that there is a fusion, an aggregate, of all the singletons. But on pain of contradiction, he is forced to say that this fusion of all the singletons lacks a singleton. Yet there seems something anomalous about a fusion without its singleton.

My theory avoids the anomaly. 'All the singletons' is a set-theoretical notion, a mathematician's notion, and if the actual is all that exists only some of these singletons will be *empirical* classes. The non-empirical singletons will be states of affairs that do not exist. As such they cannot swell a fusion. The states of affairs will be possible, and so may be said to swell a fusion in some possible world that is larger than the actual world. But such worlds are fictions, even if useful fictions.

To sum up, the empirical classes are given when the world is given. They supervene on certain aspects of the structure of the world. The set-theoretical hierarchy is not so given. It, as it were, stretches out and beyond the empirical classes. But it can do this because it does no more than chart a *possible* mathematical structure.

13

Totality states of affairs

13.1 HIGHER-ORDER STATES OF AFFAIRS

The main object of this chapter is to discuss a particular sort of higher-order state of affairs: totality facts. But it will be useful to begin by saying some things about higher-order states of affairs generally.

If it is true that what supervenes is no increase of being beyond its subvenient base, no increase beyond that which it supervenes upon, then our only concern here is with *non-supervenient* higher-order states of affairs. 'Higher-order' here, of course, has no reference to any higher realm, to anything cut off from the world of first-order states of affairs, the space-time world if the thesis of Naturalism is true. It simply picks out those states of affairs which themselves have one or more (lower-order) states of affairs as constituents or else it picks out states of affairs that involve only universals: relations between state-of-affairs types.

Thus, suppose there is, as I maintain, singular causation involving one state of affairs bringing about another state of affairs, as it may be *a's being F* bringing about *b's being* G. Suppose this to be a genuine dyadic relation, external and not involving any further entities. Because the terms of the relation are states of affairs, this will be a higher-order state of affairs. But it is not otherworldly! Again, if one state-of-affairs type brings about a further state-of-affairs type, this is a higher-order state of affairs because it is a causal relation between universals. It exists only in its instantiations. So it, too, is not otherworldly.

It was contended in chapter 10 that, in considering what possibilities there are, one should think combinatorially. Consider first-order states of affairs only, abstracting from the existence of any higher-order states of affairs that there may be. Complete combinatorial freedom for these states of affairs exists if and only if all wholly distinct states of affairs are *independent*, that is, they fail in every case to entail or exclude each other. (This, of course, is the *Tractatus* vision. It also owes something to Hume.) Such Independence may not indeed obtain, but we can at least hope!

Higher-order states of affairs, however, because they have lower-order states of affairs as constituents, presuppose the existence of the latter. Furthermore, higher-order states of affairs, once in place, set certain limits to what further lower-order states of affairs there can be or not be. This sounds mysterious, but is not really so. If a relation of singular causation really holds between two first-order states of affairs, then this rules out the cause, say, existing in the absence of the effect. If a certain aggregate of states of affairs really is the totality of states of affairs, then further states of affairs are excluded. And if a certain deterministic nomic relation really holds between universals, say that something's being an F causes that same thing to be a G, then Fs that are not Gs are excluded at the first-order level.

But because the higher-order states of affairs are not supervenient upon these lower-order states of affairs, the latter never entail the presence of the higher-order states. Thus, suppose that laws of nature are higher-order states of affairs involving (contingent) relations between universals. Then a world exactly like our world, but with these higher-order states absent, is a possible world. It would be a specimen of what Frank Jackson has called a Hume world, a cosmic coincidence world whose regularity mimics (miraculously!) the regularity imposed by the higher-order relations of universals.

13.2 STATES OF AFFAIRS OF TOTALITY

Consider the conjunction of all the states of affairs, lower- and higher-order, that there are. If the hypothesis of this essay is correct, then this conjunction is everything that there is, but we are not concerned with that point for the moment. Now consider the truth that this conjunction is all the states of affairs. What is its truthmaker? Could its truthmaker be just the conjunction itself? The conjunction certainly is an essential part of the truthmaker. But is it sufficient? It would be nice and economical if it were sufficient. There would be no need to introduce a higher-order fact. It seems, however, that, as Russell argued (1918, V), we cannot get away from recognizing 'general facts'.

The point to appreciate is that it is a *contingent* fact that this conjunction is the totality of states of affairs. It is surely possible that the actual totality of states of affairs might have been increased by other states of affairs, say by the addition of just one extra state of affairs. (In order to steer clear of the question of aliens, let the extra state of affairs be that of one already existing thing having just one more property, where that property is also instantiated elsewhere. A Combinatorial view of possibility clearly allows such an extra possibility.) Is it enough for a truthmaker to be no more than *contingently* sufficient for the truth of some truth?

The following consideration seems weighty. If it is true that a certain conjunction of states of affairs is all the states of affairs, then this is only true because there are no more of them. If there are more, then the proposition is not true. That there are no more of them must then somehow be brought into the truthmaker. But to say that there are no more of them is to say that they are *all* the states of affairs. This, then, must be brought within the truthmaker. The truthmaker must be the fact or state of affairs that the great conjunction *is* all the states of affairs.

More generally, the relation of truth to truthmaker is an internal relation, one necessitated by and supervenient upon, its terms. If this is denied, are we prepared to say, echoing and parodying Hume, that to consider the matter *a priori* anything may be truthmaker for any truth? Surely not. But if not, how are we to limit what the truthmaker for a truth can be without making the relation internal? Hume thought that, at bottom, all external relations, all 'matters of fact', reduce to spatiotemporal and causal ones. It is a plausible hypothesis, though one that we will shortly have to modify. Do we wish to add the relation of true proposition to its correspondent (its truthmaker) to the external relations? If we do, it would seem that philosophers ought to turn the question of the nature of the truthmaking *relation* over to empirical science!

There is one awkward little difficulty that ought to be confronted at this point. It is the threat of an infinite regress. If we say that a certain conjunction of states of affairs is all the states of affairs, and that the latter is a state of affairs, then it appears that the original conjunction is not the totality of states of affairs. The original conjunction is no more than the totality minus the totality fact. To get that latter state of affairs into the collection we need to go to a higher totality fact and so *ad infinitum*. At the very best, we will require an infinity of such facts, which is rather unattractive.

This difficulty, however, can receive what has become a stock answer of ours. The regress becomes unthreatening at the point that supervenience occurs. The first totality of states of affairs fact is a contingent state of affairs. But the further alleged totality states of affairs after that point are all entailed by the first totality fact. That is why we are able to see that the regress 'must' go to infinity. That being so, we are able to say that the further states of affairs supervene and further involve no increase of being.

Different truths, if you like. But all the truths have the very same truth-maker. The world is not bigger for them.

So we will take it that we do require non-supervenient states of affairs or facts of totality. This is one logical constant that, *pace* Wittgenstein, does signify. It has already been noted in the previous section (it is fairly obvious but had to be pointed out to me by David Lewis), that this state of affairs constrains the states of affairs 'below' it. Given this state of affairs, there cannot be any further states of affairs in the totality. Independence only goes one way. Given just the great conjunction of lower-order states of affairs, the totality fact is not entailed. But given the totality fact, the great conjunction is given because, trivially, it is a constituent of that fact. It was this that alerted me to the truth that higher-order facts *always* constrain the states of affairs that fall under them. This is important, for instance, in considering the way that non-supervenient nomic relations between *universals* constrain lower-order states of affairs that involve these universals.

But let us now try to delve a little more deeply into the structure or form of states of affairs of totality. This will by no means be a matter of saying what totality or allness is, still less a matter of saying what the word 'all' means. But it does seem possible to get a more perspicuous philosophical view of the form of totality facts (totality states of affairs).

We saw that numbers (natural, rational and real) could all be treated as relations holding between a unit-property or unit-quantity and the thing that is numbered. We have a similar situation with totality, although the natural way of thinking of the relation is reversed, going in the totality case from aggregate to unit. Suppose the unit-property to be *being a state of affairs*. A certain aggregate, a vast conjunction of states of affairs, stands in a certain relation to this property. We may call it the *alling* or *totalling* relation, and will symbolize it as T. This aggregate *totals* this property. The property of *being an electron* stands in the converse of the T relation to that aggregate that happens to be the totality of electrons. The 'property' of *being something* stands in the converse of the T relation to the world, the world which, if our argument is correct, is identical with the aggregate of all states of affairs. The world totals what there is.

Unlike the numerical relations, however, the T relation is not dictated by the nature of the terms of the relation. It is not an internal but an external relation. (It needs to be added to Hume's list of relations of matters of fact.) As such, it is a universal, a real entity, a constituent of the world. It does not seem quite correct, however, to say that T is what we pick out when we use the word 'all'. Allness, if one may so speak, appears in discourse to be a relational property of aggregates, one that supervenes upon the holding of the T relation between the aggregate in question and some unit-property. It is the 'monadic reduction' of the T relation, rather than the T relation itself (see 6.4 for the notion of a monadic reduction).

Given totality facts, and in particular the all-embracing state of affairs of totality, then it is easy to see that all negative states of affairs supervene. So we do not need negative states of affairs in the basic ontology in addition to totality states of affairs. We can have, as obviously we must have, negative *truths*, but their truthmakers are always positive states of affairs plus some state of affairs of totality.

We could consider taking negative states of affairs as ontologically primitive, and then trying to exhibit totality states of affairs as supervenient. Each first-order thin particular would be a constituent of innumerable negative as well as positive states of affairs. But even then we would need some sort of closure condition to eliminate further particulars and universals, and that condition looks to be a totality fact. It is true, of course, that totality facts themselves partake of the nature of negation. They are 'no more' facts. They set a boundary, beyond which nothing, or nothing relevant, exists. All determination is negation, as Spinoza said. All the more reason, though, to work with these totality states of affairs only, and not admit negative states of affairs into our ontology in a more promiscuous manner.

C.B. Martin has objected in discussion that this T relation cannot be the right answer to the problem of totality facts. The relation is supposed to hold between a property or relation (second-class properties and relations being, of course, allowable) and an aggregate that *totals* that particular property or relation. Suppose that the property is that of *being a state of affairs* and that the aggregate is a certain aggregate of states of affairs. How, Martin asks, can this relation, holding as it does between just these two things, embrace the *lack* of any state of affairs that lies beyond the aggregate?

I believe that this penetrating objection says nothing that I cannot concede. Because all determination is limitation, it can be freely admitted that totality states of affairs are a species of negative states of affairs. They exclude anything further. They 'say' that there are not more Fs. But we do not need *in addition* negative states of affairs having the form that certain particulars lack certain properties, or that certain *n*-tuples of particulars lack certain relations. These latter negatives supervene upon positive states of affairs plus the totality or 'no more' states of affairs. The 'no more' states of affairs, these 'general facts' as Russell calls them, are required in any case, or at least one is required, the all-embracing totality fact (which entails all the lesser totality facts).

It is important to realize that allness is an empirical or at least quasi-empirical notion. We can surely observe that there are just two persons in the room, that these two are all the persons here. It is true that there is something theoretical about the knowledge acquired. The absence of further persons is, I take it, not a cause of the acquiring of the knowledge. Some *reasoning* is implicit: here is a certain number of persons, and if there had been more persons, then they too would have been observed. That prompted the phrase 'quasi-empirical'. But it is a very low level of theory. Our understanding of allness or totality begins with such simple cases, and can then be extended to such grand matters as the totality of states of affairs and the totality of all being.

There is one final point about totality states of affairs. If our reasoning has been correct, then there must be a totality state of affairs for the world. Of a certain something, it is true that this is all that there is. That it is true of this something is contingent. The totality might have been more, it might have been less. But that a totality fact exists appears to be necessary. So something, the fact that there must be a totality-fact for the world, supervenes. Contrast this with the contingent relations between universals, which, it will be argued, constitute the laws of nature. There is no supervenience at all with them. A 'Hume world', where the first-order states of affairs are exactly the same as those found in a law-governed world but which merely mimic what happens in the law-governed world, a cosmic coincidence world, is a possibility. (Some philosophers, I am sorry to say, think that this possibility is actual.)

But even in the case of the totality state of affairs, there is no *one* state of affairs that supervenes. The actual totality state of affairs might have not obtained. *It* does not supervene. So I can perhaps argue that what supervenes here, viz. that there must be *some* totality fact, is a trivial truth that involves no increase in being.

14

Singular causation

14.1 INTRODUCTORY

The hypothesis now to be defended is that in a token causal sequence, *this* causing *that*, the causal relation that holds between cause and effect is a *non-relational* attribute of the sequence. The existence of the relation, furthermore, is independent, in the sense spelt out in our discussions of the hypothesis of Independence, of anything that is the case elsewhere. The concept of singular causation is, moreover, *conceptually* primitive. It is not to be further analysed conceptually. All this is matter for the present chapter.

At the same time, in opposition to those such as Anscombe (1971) for whom causation is *essentially* singular, singular causation is not ontologically primitive. It can be given an ontological analysis, or so it will be argued, as the instantiation of a law of nature. Laws of nature, the truthmakers of true law statements, the truthmakers of nomic truths, are not to be conceived of as mere regularities. Indeed, amazing as it may seem, the *nomic* nature of a singular causal sequence is itself a non-relational property of the sequence. This turns out to be a happy consequence of the idea that laws are relations of universals, where these universals are conceived of in a Fregean-Aristotelian manner as state-of-affairs types. But the nature of law is largely a matter for the two chapters that succeed this one.

One of the many unfortunate results of a Humean account of causation is that confusion is engendered between causes and laws. For a Humean, cause is no more than a regularity or, in the singular case, the instantiation of a regularity. A law, also, is no more than a regularity. The distinction, if any, between a causal regularity and a nomic regularity then arouses little interest or enthusiasm in Humeans, and it is easy for them to pass from one to the other without noting the difference. And, indeed, the Humeans are right to this extent. There really are deep connections between causes and laws. Nevertheless, the *beginning* of wisdom is to distinguish the two quite sharply. We shall find that they are only to be brought together as the result of some hard argument and with the aid of plausible assumptions, assumptions that can be questioned despite their plausibility.

14.2 AN ARGUMENT FOR SINGULAR CAUSATION

A striking case has been worked out independently by Michael Tooley (see my 1983, p. 133) and John Foster (1979, pp. 169–70). Suppose that we have two particles of the same type which are at a certain distance from each other in a two-dimensional world (to simplify matters). Each is governed by the same law to the effect that there is a certain probability (<1) that in a certain time it will create a further particle of the same type at a certain fixed distance. (To make things even simpler, let this creation involve no intermediate causal chain. The creation of the particle is *directly* caused.) So each is surrounded by a circle of positions where a further particle may or may not appear at some point. In this particular case, the two circles intersect, and so have two points in common. Furthermore, a particle is created exactly at just one of these intersection points. See the diagram:

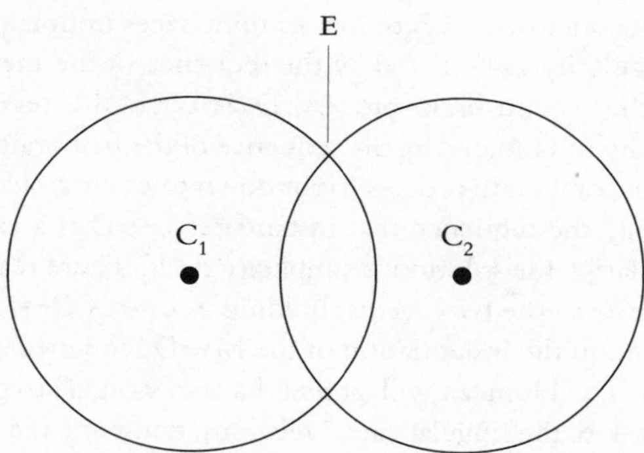

There seems to be an objective question which it was of the two particles that brought about the creation of the third particle. (There would also be the unlikely possibility of causal overdetermination with the new particle created by *both* original particles.) In one case there would be an instantiation of the causal law by the pair $\{C_1, E\}$. In the other case there would be the instantiation of the very same law but by the $\{C_2, E\}$ pair. These instantiations are different states of affairs, even if we might have a hard time determining which one (or perhaps both – the overdetermination case) actually occurred.

Tooley and Foster think of themselves as *arguing* for singular causation. And despite the merely possible nature of the case, it does, with its ease and naturalness, constitute some argument for the real, non-relational, existence of singular causation. But perhaps the chief value of the case is simply to give us a sharp realization of what singular causation involves if it exists: a direct relationship between one token state of affairs and another such.

That singular causation does exist, and that the world's work is done by such causing, is the natural assumption of all those who have not fallen under the Humean spell. Anybody who thinks about the mechanism of a thing or process, arguably even the physicist working at the level of quantum physics, is trying to determine the causal pattern of operation in the thing or process, and thinks of it as a causal pattern that exists at the singular level.

A simple example that brings out the point is a problem that exists for an Epiphenomenalist Dualism about the mind. Suppose that on a certain occasion, a token brain-process of type C produces both a mental state of type M, which latter is epiphenomenal, and also a brain-process of type D. We have two causal sequences: C→M and C→D, with M epiphenomenal, impotent. The Humean about causation who wants to hold this (admittedly unsatisfactory) theory of mind faces trouble. For, perhaps, the M→D regularity instantiated by the sequence of the mental event M followed by the second brain-process, D, is as good a regularity as the C→D regularity instantiated by the sequence of the first brain-process followed by the second brain process (right down to counterfactuals). Yet, by hypothesis, only the sequence that instantiates C→D is a causal process. For the Singularist, the solution is simplicity itself. There really is a causal relation, intrinsic to the two events, holding in case of C→D, but there is no such relation in the instantiation of the M→D sequence. The problem is no problem. The Humean will, at best, have to struggle to get this result.

We may think of the singular causal relations, transeunt and immanent, as linking together their terms, the causes and the effects, together into a huge net. (C. B. Martin has spoken of the power-net. My net, though, is the net of actual singular causings.) At the level of first-order states of affairs, does anything escape this net? I see no reason to believe so. The laws that govern the net may be probabilistic only. But the net may still be all-embracing.

14.3 THE TERMS OF THE RELATION

What are the terms of the (singular) causal relation? The obvious hypothesis for us is that both cause and effect are states of affairs. Such a view seems quite plausible in itself as well as dictated by our general thesis. It is particulars that act, this stone or this lightning flash. At the same time, the particulars act in virtue of their properties, the mass or the momentum of the stone, the electrical properties of the flash. These two considerations cry out to be brought together by holding that the true cause and true effect are always certain token states of affairs. *a being F* brings it about that *b is G*. (Too simple a schematic example, of course. Both cause and effect may in practice be complex conjunctions of states of affairs.) Notice that this has the formal consequence that, given that causation is contingent, singular causation is a *non-supervenient* second-order relation, holding between first-order states of affairs. It is an external relation.

Various points require to be considered here. First, should we say, instead of *b* being G, that *b becomes* G? That complicates matters, because the *becomes* entails that up to that time *b* was not G. The truthmaker for *b not being* G will, given our account of negative truths, have to be *b*'s having, at the time of the appearance of the effect, the positive properties that it has plus the totality fact that these *are* all the properties it has at that time. We may note, however, that it is not necessary for causal sequence that *b* should *become* G. It could be the case that *b* was G before the cause operated, but that in the absence of the cause it would not have continued to be G. *a* being F could still be the cause of the later time slice of *b being* G.

But speaking of *b* before and after the operation of the cause brings us to a more important point. It has already been argued (7.2) that if a particular exists for a time, then it has temporal parts, and further that, for a particular to continue to exist, earlier temporal parts must be ('immanent') causes of the coming to be of later temporal parts. So really we need to say that it was *b′* that was not G and a later *b″* that was G. If the causation is immanent, then it will regularly take a quite monotonous form, say *b′ being F* bringing about *b″ being F*.

Even in the case of singular *transeunt* causation, paradigm causation, it will in general be a necessary condition that there be a particular on which the external particular *a* operates, a particular that exists before and after the cause operates. In this way, immanent causation is involved in transeunt causation. Furthermore, *a* will have to be in some particular relation, R, to the second particular. So the states of affairs involved in the transeunt cause will be at least *a′ being F* and *a′ having R to b′* (the particular acted upon). The effect will be *b″ being* G with *b′* and *b″* successive temporal parts of *b*. Thus, an object might have a certain mass, and come to be in the relation of resting upon the balance-pan of a balance. That this object is on the balance-pan will be the cause. The effect will be that the whole balance, continuing to exist (immanent causation), will nevertheless give a new reading. The situation is at least as complicated as this. But it does seem that we can render this complexity as a relation between states of affairs.

It may be noted that, if we think of the succession of states of affairs just described as an *event*, it is an event in a 'thin' sense, rather than the 'thick' sense advocated by Donald Davidson in his 1967.

14.4 SINGULAR CAUSATION AND INDEPENDENCE

What are the formal properties of the causal relation, this relation between states of affairs? Does the principle of Independence (ch. 9) hold for this relation? We have seen that if this principle can be upheld for all external relations then our metaphysical scheme is greatly simplified. At the same time, we have seen that Independence is, with some show of reason, accounted by many a rather improbable doctrine. Finally, we have conceded that the final verdict on Independence may have to be given, in some hypothetical future, in the light of total science. (If true it would seem to be necessarily true, but it would be a necessary truth that can be established or overthrown empirically.)

Singular causation is a dyadic relation. For Independence to hold, it must not be *necessarily* a transitive or an asymmetrical relation. If the relation had either of these properties necessarily, then one state of affairs would entail or necessarily exclude a wholly distinct state of affairs, which is what Independence denies. There would be no objection to the relation being governed by contingent laws of nature that happen to ensure transitivity or asymmetry, but it cannot be part of the essence of the relation. We begin by considering whether causality must be transitive.

It is clear that singular causality is normally *spoken of* as transitive, at any rate in suitable circumstances. We do *a* in order to bring about *b*, and bring about *b* because it brings about *c*. We then think of *a* as bringing about *c*. If immanent causality is admitted, then the transitivity seems particularly clear. If a continuing thing is a causal line, as Russell averred in his later thinking (1948, pt VI, sec. V), then the transitivity might seem compulsory. It is possible, though, to argue that our ordinary concept of causality is the *ancestral* of the ontological relation of causation.

We have already discussed this sort of problem in connection with the relation of being temporally before. *Being before* is transitive, but it seems possible and reasonably plausible to argue that it is the ancestral of a relation that we can call *before*★ which is not transitive at all. The same manoeuvre is available, indeed seems even more plausible, in the case of causality. State of affairs S_1 causes★ state of affairs S_2 which in turn causes★ S_3. The state of affairs S_1 causes S_3 but does not cause★ S_3. The situation may be made more graspable by considering that it is at least conceivable, and I would argue possible, although presumably false, that S_3 be overdetermined so that not only does S_2 cause★ S_3 but so also does S_1 the latter acting directly, without any intermediary. Causing, of course, supervenes upon causing★.

The situation becomes more complex if causal chains subdivide for ever. But this is only to reopen the question that has already been discussed (10.6 especially) of what happens to supervenience if there are 'structures all the way down'. What we would then have is *relative* supervenience, where each level supervenes upon levels that are below it, a supervenience that is symmetrical because the lower levels also supervene on the higher level, thus yielding identity. (There is asymmetry, but it consists only in the degree to which the one situation is analysed.) Under these circumstances, macroscopic causality would be analysable in terms of ever more finely structured, but shorter, causal processes.

What of the apparent asymmetry of causation? (And of causation★ to which the remarks to follow are intended to apply.) It will be recalled that we dealt with the same problem in connection with *before* taken temporally by suggesting that there was no objection to the *possibility* of circular time. The laws of nature may rule this out, but it may be a possibility for all that. And then *before* will not be asymmetrical. Cannot causality ride piggy-back on this suggestion? Why cannot this time-circle (different from the eternal repetition of events of the same sort in a 'straight-line time') contain a circle of causes?

Humeans about causes could have no objection, it seems, provided that they accepted the possibility of circular time. We, however, are not Humeans. It seems there is one doctrine about time, a not unattractive one, that *would* rule out a causal circle. This is the view that, before the operation of the cause, its effect does not exist. Not just does not exist now, but does not exist, period. It does seem that to uphold the possibility of a causal circle we need the view that the future exists, the so-called 'four-dimensional' view of the world. This is the view favoured by modern cosmology, the one that fits in best with Special Relativity and the resulting relativity of simultaneity that makes what is future relative to the particular inertial system that is in question.

That the future does not exist is, however, a view that has considerable attractions. The idea that the past also does not exist seems almost ridiculous, though it has been held by some good philosophers. Without the future *and* the past, nothing would exist except the present instant, which seems a truly parochial view. But if we think of the past as real, then we can think of being as continuously increasing in bulk, with the present as it were the moving edge of being. A difficulty that arises is that no truthmaker is provided for truths about the future. Perhaps the difficulty can be met by arguing that there *will be* truthmakers for these truths, but that the states of affairs that will constitute the truthmakers (if the Factualist metaphysic is correct) do not exist before they become present. But what is the truthmaker for the truth that there will be these truthmakers?

As already mentioned, Special Relativity poses a difficulty for this view. If two spacetime points have a space-like separation, and if a state of affairs S is present relative to one of the points, then S may be future relative to the other. S then exists relative to the first point but does not exist relative to the other, which seems absurd. It appears that this view would have to make simultaneity a non-relative matter and then accommodate the facts on which Special Relativity is based within this non-relativist framework. Perhaps this can be done. But certainly neither circular time, nor, *a fortiori*, circular time plus circular causation, can be accepted. If the future does not exist, then causes bring their subsequent effects into existence in the most thoroughgoing sense of 'bringing into existence'. The non-existent cannot cause, so singular causation must be an asymmetrical relation. Independence must then be given up. And it is not a possibility that state of affairs S_1 should be, directly or indirectly, cause of a later S_2, *and* that S_1 should be, directly or indirectly, cause of S_1.

It is not clear just how far all this constitutes an argument for adopting the four-dimensional view of the world, with the future an existent. But it does seem that friends of Independence should lean to this view. We will so lean. Tentatively, at any rate, and with the usual proviso that this matter may have to be settled, if it can be settled at all, by total science and not by mere philosophers, we accept the possibility of a circle of causes.

How small could the circle be? As small as two, presumably, with the relation causation*. We can draw the line at a state of affairs being *causa sui*: The cause and the effect must always be (wholly) distinct states of affairs. Causation cannot be reflexive. This seems mandated by Instantial

Invariance (see 6.1), at any rate if *causes* is a universal. Causation would not be identical with itself if it linked a different number of terms in different instantiations. But there seems to be no objection to S_1 causing★ S_2 together with S_2 causing★ S_1.

In pursuit of Independence, we have given a charter to the possibility of backward causation. (From liberty to licence!?) For there seems no reason why the circle of causes has to embrace the whole world, as it may do if time is circular. Within a linear time, there might be causal circles (causal loops) that reached back to the past and came forward again, like whirlpools or eddies in this otherwise linear progression.

But notice that besides backwards causation, there is also a possibility of causal circles whose constituent states of affairs all exist at the same time. There is no reason to reject the possibility (we are talking possibilities the whole time, of course, possibilities that may well be *mere* possibilities) that co-existent states of affairs should exist in a mutually sustaining circle, causes of each other, and such that if any member of the circle had been absent, the other members would have been non-existent also. We are given a phenomenological picture of this when we have, say, two tiles propped up against each other in such a fashion that if either were not where it was the other would not be where *it* was. Physics tells us that the situation is not quite as it seems: there is actually a propagation of forces in both directions such that one tile at t_1 is responsible for the other tile being where it is at t_{1+}, where the time difference is very small. But it is certainly conceivable, and would seem to be possible, that each tile provides the other with *instantaneous* support.

It may be concluded, or at any rate surmised, that the ontological relation of (singular) causation is not transitive or asymmetrical. If S_1 causes★ S_2, then this higher-order state of affairs neither entails nor excludes the existence of any other state of affairs except for entailing the existence of S_1 and S_2.

14.5 SINGULAR CAUSATION AND COUNTERFACTUALS

Singular or token-token causation 'supports counterfactuals'. If the striking broke the glass, we are generally prepared to say that *if* the striking of the glass had not happened at that time, then it would not have broken at that time. Such counterfactuals are often true. It is very important to realize, however, that singular causation never actually *entails* a counterfactual of this simple sort.

For consider. Is it *necessary*, given that the striking broke the glass, that in the absence of that striking, then the glass would not have broken? Clearly, it is not. For it is certainly possible that there should have been another striking of the glass at that time, which would have done the job instead. It is even possible that the situation was such that if the one striking had failed to occur, the other would have occurred. The two strikings would have been back-ups for each other. There may have been no such alternative singular cause in the actual situation, but the operation of a singular cause does not exclude such alternatives. So the ordinary counterfactual is not entailed. Another, weirder, case would have been an absence of striking followed by the glass breaking, but the breaking of the glass having no cause at all. How can we rule this out as a possibility?

Putting the point in general terms, if token event C causes E, then if C had not happened, E would not have happened, provided that (i) no other event C′ had caused E and (ii) E had not happened without a cause. That, but only that, seems to be an entailment.

It may seem not very important that the original counterfactual, if not-C, then not-E, although often true for many values of C and E, is not actually entailed by C's causing E. But it *is* very important because the additions necessary to get the entailment involve reference to (singular) causation. Once we notice this, we realize that there is little prospect of rendering the essence of singular causation in terms of conditionals. A conditional analysis is likely to be involved in circularity.

A further important thing about the conditionals that are actually entailed is that they remain obstinately singular. No reference to laws or generalizations is involved. Our identification of causation as a relation that holds between states of affairs means that in singular causation *properties* are always involved in both cause and effect. But even where we have identified the properties involved in a singular causal process, which is by no means always the case, there still seems no way of writing into the entailment that the same sort of total cause will bring about or has a certain probability of bringing about the same sort of effect. That belief, it seems, can be no more than warranted by experience. (This may suggest, at this stage in the argument, that the 'same cause→same effect' principle is at best a contingent truth. But bear in mind, though, that some necessities are discovered by experience!)

All we have in our concept of singular causation, I suggest, besides the rather weak entailment that has been spelt out, is that something (plausibly a state of affairs) *makes something happen* (another state of affairs). At the conceptual level this making something happen, this singular causation, is a primitive. We can walk round it, but we cannot analyse it conceptually.

14.6 THE EPISTEMOLOGY OF SINGULAR CAUSATION

We begin with a quotation from Alvin Goldman, who has the bad luck here to stand for whole generations of analytical philosophers:

> As we have known since Hume (1748), causal connections between events cannot be directly observed; nor can they be introspected.
>
> (1993, sec. 11)

There is in fact very little argument in Hume against 'impressions of causality' from which we might derive the idea (concept) of singular causality directly from experience. What Hume constantly assumes is that experience of causality would involve a perception of necessary connection between cause and effect. (He often uses the word 'connexion' in this context, but he always means *necessity* by this.) Hume's target, in other words, was the old rationalist conception of causation where causation was assumed to be necessary in the way that, say, Euclidean geometrical theorems were assumed to be necessary. He was certainly right to argue that we perceive no such necessity in causal sequences.

But here is a position that Hume does not consider. It is the position that, in favourable situations, singular causal relations are perceived without any perception of the *necessity* of the relation. We can perceive visually that one object is to the left of another, or above it. Such a perception can be as little theory-laden as any perception we have. It involves the perception of relations. It involves no perception of necessity, and there is no necessity there. Why might there not be certain perceptions of singular causation (perhaps not visual) of the same sort? They need involve no perception of necessity, nor need there *be* any necessity.

It should go without saying in contemporary philosophy, though it would not have so gone in Hume's day, that these perceptions of singular causation, though direct or non-inferential, can yet be erroneous.

In fairness to Hume we should remark that the perception of relations, as opposed to qualities, was something that the tradition was very confused about at the time that he wrote. Hume shared in the confusion. This epistemological confusion no doubt sprang from the ontological confusion about relations to be found in the whole Western philosophical tradition until quite recently. I have already suggested (ch. 1) that this ontological confusion was a major factor in holding back the development of Factualist ontologies until this century.

But with the ontological confusion removed, the epistemological confusion can be tackled. William James' Radical Empiricism called for the recognition that relations (for us, states of affairs involving relations) are given in experience (1943 [1912]). It was an important epistemological contribution. In Essays II and III he argued that relations are as much experienced as qualities are (that was the radical aspect of his Radical Empiricism) and in Essay VI, 'The Experience of Activity', that even causality is experienced.

If there are perceptions, sense-impressions, of causality, from what sense, or from which of our senses, are these perceptions derived? In our ordinary talk we do, of course, constantly speak of visual perception of causal sequence. We say that we *see* that one billiard ball makes the second ball move when it hits it. In *The Perception of Causality* (1963 [1946]), the Louvain psychologist A. Michotte argued, on the basis of experimental evidence, that there are in fact impressions of causality involved in such cases. But the matter is difficult, and it is certainly possible to argue against Michotte that visual perceptions of causality have a considerable admixture of theory in a way that most visual perceptions of, say, spatial relation do not. It is probably better to turn elsewhere. In chapter 1 of *Causation and Universals* Evan Fales argues for impressions of causality in two cases: (i) the perception of pressure on our own body; and (ii) introspective awareness of the operation of our own will.

Fales' candidates are rather natural ones to nominate, and have been appealed to by previous thinkers. It is introspective awareness of the operation of the will, when we go to move a limb or set ourselves some mental task, that has in the past been the really popular choice. Fales does not go into details, but in a footnote mentions the names of Reid, Whitehead, Keynes, Stout, William James, Searle and the psychologists Maine de Biran and Piaget. As Keith Campbell has pointed out to me he might have mentioned Locke (*Essay*, II, XXI, 4), although Locke does a bit of hedging. Berkeley would seem to be a candidate also.

It is, however, perception of pressure on our own body that Fales sets greatest store by, and I rather briefly anticipated him in my 1968. I suspect that it was the influence of the Representative theory of perception, so ubiquitous in the past, that made it hard to focus clearly on the pressure case. A sense-datum of causation seems a strange idea. By contrast, nobody holds a Representative theory of introspective awareness! If we are directly aware of (some) of our own current mental processes, then direct awareness of singular causal relations between such processes becomes something that we can at least consider. (Direct introspective awareness should not, of course, be construed as indubitable or incorrigible awareness.)

So let us consider the case of pressure on our body. (Hume, by the way, does discuss this topic very briefly, and unsatisfactorily, but only in two footnotes to the *Inquiry*, Section VII, which was published long after the *Treatise*, long after he had put forward his denial of an impression of causality.) Fales suggests that to have a sensation of pressure is to be aware (it could be non-veridical awareness) of a *force vector*. Here is his evidence. (1) The pressure is felt as having a location, a point or area on our own body. (2) It is felt as having a magnitude. (3) It is felt as having a direction in space. (4) Where there is more than one force applied to more or less the same part of the body, these forces can sometimes be distinguished from each other, for example, by direction. (5) Felt forces can be felt to add together in a way that depends on their respective magnitudes and directions (1990, p. 16). I think that these claims are all phenomenologically quite plausible. And, as Fales says, '. . . they are exactly those which have been taken over into physics and given a precise representation there by means of the vector calculus'. He points out further that we can add to (3) that the force is felt as repulsive rather than attractive.

I suggest that this is a most impressive correlation between the properties of the force vectors and the properties encountered in the perception of pressure. Such a correlation must suggest identity. Of course, it does not *compel* us to accept the identity. It might be that sensations of pressure have certain features that are correlated, but no more than correlated, with the properties of the vector forces acting on our body. Experience, or some innate programming, might then take us from the properties of the sensation (whatever they are) to the properties of the force that is acting. But is this a plausible alternative?

In any case, is not the onus upon those who assert that tactual/proprioceptive perceptions of pressure on and by the body are not what they appear to be: direct, immediate, perceptions of forces acting upon the body or the body acting with force upon other things?

Three remarks need to be made here. Suppose, *first*, that one starts, as many today start, from the *premiss* that singular causes are no more than instantiations of cosmic, or at least very widespread, uniformities. Then of course it *must* be the case that recognition of singular causation is a more or less sophisticated inference triggered off in us by the perception of the current sequence plus memory of the outcome of other such sequences. Suppose, however, that one is convinced that a philosophy of causation which takes it to be no more than certain sorts of regularity is wrong, and that there is something *intrinsic to the sequence itself* that makes a token sequence a case of causation. Then one can be open to the idea that singular causation can be perceived, and perceived directly. A further great question here is whether a Regularity theory of *laws* can be sustained. If the latter collapses, a Regularity theory of causes can hardly be kept going. In Armstrong, 1983, it is argued in the course of five chapters, for the most part using traditional difficulties for a Regularity theory of laws, that this account of laws is untenable for many different reasons.

A *second* matter, or perhaps the same matter approached from a different angle, is what one thinks that forces are. Until relatively recently, empiricist philosophers were not disposed to grant ontological reality to forces. *Talk* of forces was all very well, but it was not literally true that when, say, two hands pull at the one piece of cloth, producing a temporary stalemate where nothing much moves, there are entities in the world called forces with each hand exerting one of them. The truthmakers for truths about forces, it was thought, were to be construed in a far more operationalist or instrumentalist way. This, however, involved a suspicious number of appeals to counterfactual truths with an unwillingness to consider very deeply what the further truthmakers for these counterfactuals might be. But once one becomes a Realist about forces in token situations, then one will naturally begin to wonder whether, in favourable circumstances, forces cannot be perceived. (We argued in ch. 5 that they are categorical properties of the things exerting the force, properties instantiated at the time the force is being exerted, but categorical properties *described* in terms of what they tend to bring about.)

Biologically, nothing could be more valuable to an animal than an unmediated awareness of forces acting upon its body. This suggests that, if it is at all nomically possible, nature will produce such an awareness. It cannot produce an infallible awareness, of course, and it cannot produce an all-embracing awareness of forces, or indeed of anything else. But it might be able to give us a relatively narrow window onto singular causation, and that window might give us inductive or hypothetico-deductive grounds for attributing singular causation to the processes of nature generally.

A *third* point. There are those who are suspicious of using, as I have been using, a distinction between direct perception and perception that involves inference. I do not share their suspicion, although I accept that past theorizing has often set up too sharp a gap between perception and inference. But those who do not like the distinction must come to terms with the point that ordinary thought and language continually assumes that singular causation is observed. We are surely entitled to say that we can see that this knife is now cutting, not simply moving through, the butter. It is quite plausible, I think, to go on to say that this perception is not direct perception, but is perception involving inference. But one who does not accept the distinction between direct perception and inferential perception can hardly say that. They ought, it seems, just accept that the knife/butter case and innumerable others show that singular causation is perceived all over the place, and perceived as singular causation. The sceptic about the observation of singular causation actually *needs* some distinction between direct and non-direct perception in order to rule out these 'ordinary language' cases.

I will not take up still more space by arguing at length about the will. But I think it is plausible to suppose that we have similar non-inferential awareness of the successful operation of our will, both in the physical and the mental realm. (Hume, amazingly, takes the topic up first only in the *Appendix* to the *Treatise*, and there briefly, although he does deal with the matter at some length in the *Inquiry*.) Like our awareness of forces acting on our body, introspective awareness of the operation of our will has considerable biological value. It is very important, in our dealings with the world, to have direct information as to what we *did*, as opposed to what merely happened. It may enable us to empathize with others, giving us a sense of when they do and do not *act*. The importance of this for the profoundly social beings that we are can hardly be overestimated.

Such desk-chair evolutionary speculation is all very well! But we now need to consider two arguments designed to show that, desirable as it may be, it is just not possible that there should be any awareness of singular causation parallel, say, to our awareness of spatial and temporal relationships.

Peter Menzies (1993, pp. 202–3) has suggested that the counterfactuals involved in singular causation make it a relation that 'cannot plausibly be claimed to be an object of direct awareness'. His main argument is that, although counterfactuals are entailed by truths of singular causation, the truth of a counterfactual can hardly be perceived.

We have seen that the counterfactuals associated with singular causation are themselves purely singular, and that to get an entailment they must be weakened by adding clauses that exclude the operation of such things as back-up causes (14.5). It is far from clear that if we have not grasped this entailment as it applies to the particular case, then we have not got perceptual awareness of the causality involved in that case. I can perceive that something is square or circular without grasping many of even the simpler entailments that squareness and circularity involve. The counterfactual is not part of the central essence of the causal situation, as was argued in 14.5. It is a sophisticated entailment, grasped only with intellectual difficulty. We come to it late in coming to understand what singular causation is. So its existence is no argument against the direct perception of causes.

There is another difficulty for the direct perception of singular causation that is perhaps a bit more worrying. When something presses upon our body, are we really aware directly, non-inferentially, of the whole situation of some object acting upon our flesh? Is not the situation rather that we have access to no more than *one term* of the causal relation, that is, the effect? The other term, the cause, can be no more than inferred or at best perceived by another sense. If so, we do not perceive causality directly, non-inferentially.

My reply to this is that the effect might be non-inferentially perceived, and it might be further non-inferentially perceived that this state of affairs had the relational property (a 'monadic reduction') of being an effect of some cause, but the nature of that cause, otherwise than it was exerting a certain vectorial force, might not be given non-inferentially. The cause would have to have its own nature. That is good ontology. But why do we have to be in any way non-inferentially aware of this nature? That is *a priori* epistemology. The recognition that, considered as a mental event, perception is always a perception or misperception *that* (it is a mental event with an intentional object) rather than the awareness of some external or internal *thing*, a recognition which appears central to a satisfactory theory of perception, should allow us to live with perceiving effects *as effects* without perceiving any non-relational properties of the cause.

It is to be hoped, therefore, that a reasonably strong case has been made out for saying that *in certain favourable cases* we perceive singular causation in as untheoretical a manner as anything else that we perceive. *Causation is part of our experience*. This premiss will be very important (though perhaps not quite essential) in developing further our theory of cause and of law.

14.7 FROM CAUSES TO LAWS

If the argument of the previous section has been correct, we have – in certain favourable cases – perception of forces acting on our bodies or our body exerting force on things, and perhaps also introspective awareness of the successful application of the will – direct or non-inferential, awareness of singular, that is, token-token, causation. In Humean terms, there is an impression from which we derive the idea of causality. The way is then at least open to postulate singular causation in cases where it is not directly perceived, for instance, the will of others and forces in inanimate nature.

We also learn by experience that the world proceeds in a more or less regular way. And Hume is right to think that this experience of regularity in particular instances generates within us, in a quite unreflective way, the assumption that that regularity will continue. Even a general expectation of regularity arises. This gives us a first, undeveloped, concept of law. But at a certain point, it seems, we *bring together* our experience of singular causation and our experience of regularity. We come to think that singular causation brings forth its effects in such a way that, roughly, the same type of cause brings forth the same type of effect. Indeed, we come to think that the regularities of the world are, in general, the effects of singular causes.

I am not clear just how it is that we arrive at this correlation between type of singular causes and the type of effects that they produce. All that is clear is that it turns out to be a very fruitful way of systematizing and, eventually, explaining the workings of the world. A couple of suggestions about how we do it. In the case of the successful operation of the will there is a very good correlation, for a wide range of cases, between the thing attempted and its implementation. Same cause→same effect can be observed to obtain with a minimum of theory.

(A speculative suggestion. The prevalence of *anthropomorphic* modes of explanation in early theorizing may gain part of its psychological attractiveness from our direct awareness of the causal action of the will, which we then 'project' upon the world. That, of course, turned out to be a scientific dead end which we had to work beyond.)

In the case of the perception of the action of forces upon our body, it is less clear that we have direct confirmation of the same cause→same effect principle. Suppose we accept the idea, mooted in 14.6, that our direct awareness of such action on our body is confined to our body being acted upon by a force, without awareness of the nature of that which acts. As Jim Franklin has pointed out to me, this seems to make direct confirmation of the principle difficult. Perhaps, however, indirect confirmation is available. We also have the interesting suggestion by Roy Sorensen (1992) that natural selection might have programmed us with some intuitive grasp of physical possibility in an Earth-like environment. This would, in effect, link the directly perceived forces with physical law.

It is at this point that the following hypothesis becomes empirically attractive. The world moves, and endures, through causation, understanding by causation the sort of thing that we actually experience in some of our perceptions and introspections. It is a matter of certain particulars, states of affairs if the hypothesis of this work is accepted, bringing about an effect, a further state of affairs. This is *strong* causation, something in the singular case that is more than the mere instantiation of a regularity. And these causes are regular in their operation.

Should we leave the matter at this point? Is it just a brute matter of fact, added to the fact of singular causation, that singular causation is regular in its operation so that, at the level of types, the maxim 'same cause, same effect' holds good, at least in general? This view, a strong view of causation plus a regularity account of laws, is one that can be held. It contrasts with a regularity account of causation plus a strong theory of laws, which we have already mentioned only to dismiss as unworkable.

But the regularity theory of laws has grave weaknesses of its own, as argued, for instance, in Armstrong 1983. The natural companion of a strong theory of causation is a strong theory of laws. But then the question is how to combine the two. How is the relation of causation related to lawhood? A natural way to do this is to argue that singular causation *is identical with* the instantiation of some strong law or laws. But how is this contention to be made good?

Not *a priori*. Not by analysing the concept of a cause. Elizabeth Anscombe has protested vigorously, and it seems to me successfully, against Donald Davidson's assumption that given a true statement of singular causation then it *follows a priori* that the sequence falls under some law, although the content of this law is not given (1971). She simply points out that no argument is given for this alleged following and asks what the argument could be. Nothing comes to mind, and, moved by this, I was for some years unable to see how cause and law were to be brought together except by a mere *de facto* correlation.

A simple solution to the difficulty was proposed to me by Adrian Heathcote (Heathcote and Armstrong, 1991). Why should it not be the case that the identification of a singular causal sequence with the instantiation of a law (singular causal sequence=instantiation of some particular law) is not conceptual, but is rather an empirical, *a posteriori*, matter? The model is such identifications as heat=motion of molecules or water=H_2O. If one holds, with Kripke, that these identifications are necessary truths then these are empirically justified necessities. But the vital point is that they are discovered empirically. And it is easy to *conceive* that they are false. The empirical evidence for the suggested identity is just that the *patterns* of singular causation exhibit regularity, regularity that is evidence for a law.

The law will have to be a strong law, something better than a regularity. In particular, it will have to postulate a nomic connection that manifests itself in each individual instantiation of the law. Only so will it do justice to the making it happen, the producing, the bringing about, that is involved in singular causation.

But a loose end remains. We distinguish between laws that are causal from those that are not. If singular causes are nothing but instantiations of (strong) laws, then what makes law into a *causal* law? After all, some laws are causal, some are not. It may seem that the special nature of causality is still eluding us. A suggestion for answering this important difficulty will be proposed in the next chapter. In brief, the suggestion is that all *fundamental* laws are causal.

15

Laws I

15.1 REGULARITY THEORIES OF LAW

One obvious attraction of regularity theories of laws is the ontological economy that they promise. A Factualist, however, cannot say, as it is tempting to say, that laws will then supervene on first-order states of affairs. For true statements of instantiated law will be true universally quantified propositions, and such truths, according to our argument in chapter 13, demand, over and above first-order states of affairs, the higher-order state of affairs that these are all the relevant first-order states of affairs. Not only do we require a collection of first-order states of affairs where, say, each F is a G, we require the further state of affairs that these are *all* the Fs. But granted this totality fact, a type of fact required quite independently of the existence of laws, then Humean laws do supervene. What is more, provided it has been conceded that laws are nothing but regularities, the supervenience is a supervenience which can be said fairly uncontroversially to involve no increase of being.

A Regularity theorist will find properties and relations very useful in formulating the theory. What is to be done about the 'grue' problem? What are we going to say about predicate expressions in a true unrestricted universally quantified statement that are mere disjunctions of more respectable predicates? Such statements do not really assert regularities. (A 'disjunctive regularity' is a falling away from a regularity. The more disjunction, the more falling away.) There had better be some ontological way that respectable predicates, ones that yield real regularities, earn their respectability. The most complete respectability, on my view, is achieved by predicates that apply in virtue of universals, while predicates approximate to respectability to the degree that they approximate to applying in virtue of universals. Of course, there needs to be some way in which we can determine what are the true universals. But it is surely quite a good answer to the question of how to discover them, even if not a Deceitful-Demon-proof answer, that this is done, so far as it can be done, by our best science.

A trope theory is not too far behind. Using the transitive and symmetrical relation of exact resemblance, equivalence classes of tropes (properties and relations taken as particulars) can be formed. Predicates that apply in virtue of equivalence classes of tropes, using the equivalence relation of exact resemblance, function in the same general way as do predicates that apply in virtue of the instantiation of the one universal. And a trope theory can be science-based as much as a universals theory can be.

But if an extreme Nominalism is embraced, one that denies that there are properties and relations *in re*, whether these properties and relations are universals or particulars, then it is extremely hard to construct classes that will yield genuine regularities. If all that one has in hand are classes and predicates, with the addition perhaps of *in re* resemblances and degrees of resemblance, then it becomes very hard to give any content to the notion of an objective regularity. No wonder that among Nominalist thinkers, positions such as that held by van Fraassen emerge, positions denying that there are any such things as laws.

So properties and relations, whether universals or tropes, seem necessary, or at least highly desirable, for laws, even a Regularity theory of laws. It should be the Regularity theorist's hope that universals (or tropes), together with suitable totality facts, are sufficient. My own view, of course, is that they are not sufficient. Reference may be made once again to Armstrong, 1983, for detailed arguments against Regularity accounts of laws. But there is an interesting argument that has recently been developed by Peter Forrest (1993, pp. 48–9) with the aim of showing that, provided these properties and relations are universals rather than tropes, then the generality of laws can be explained simply by considering what a universal is.

Suppose that something on a particular occasion causes there to be a G, causing it to be a G solely in virtue of property F. F and G are both universals, no doubt complex ones. It can then be said that *in this instance* the F produced a G because of something about F-ness. Call whatever it was about F-ness that did this Ω. 'Ω' is a predicate that must be referentially transparent, but whose analysis need not be entered into any further. Now consider another instance of an F. Since we are dealing with universals, we are dealing with strictly the same thing. By the Indiscernibility of Identicals, therefore, it will be true of F-ness in this new instantiation that Ω(F-ness). This, Forrest then claims, 'explains the way in which causal regularities hold at all times and places'. Identical properties should play an identical causal role in identical circumstances.

Forrest points out that this style of argument is not available to one who takes properties and relations to be particulars. The best that a trope theorist can do is to adopt as a meta-law the principle that *like causes like*. Exactly resembling tropes will play an exactly resembling causal role in exactly resembling circumstances. Intuitively, this is a somewhat less compelling principle than the principle that the identical cause gives rise to identical effects.

Returning to universals, it is to be noticed that Forrest's argument, as he is surely well aware, cannot be regarded as a *proof*, using the Indiscernibility of Identicals, of the same cause → same effect principle. Consider an attempt to *disprove* the existence of universals by appealing to the Indiscernibility of Identicals. A multiply instantiated universal will be a constituent of numerically and, often, generically different states of affairs. As a result, the universal will have a series of different sorts of immediate 'environments'. After all, the particulars that instantiate the universal are overwhelmingly likely to have unlike relational properties. So, it might be argued, having these different environments, the putative universals cannot be identical. To this argument, the upholder of universals will reply by saying that there is no contradiction in saying that the universal has *all* these environments. It is multiply instantiated and so multiply environed. A problem would arise only if the universal's own nature, its intrinsic nature, were different in different instantiations.

But sauce for the goose is sauce for the gander. A thing's effects would seem to be *not* part of its own nature. If so, is there not a possibility that different instantiations of a universal should give rise to different effects, even in an environment otherwise identical in nature? A Dispositionalist theory of properties would reject this possibility, except for the case where the causality is merely probabilistic. But we argued against this theory in chapter 5.

The question must arise, therefore, what is the truthmaker for the (admittedly natural) claim that the one universal will operate in the same way in different instantiations. The truthmaker provided by contingent higher-order relations holding between universals has been rejected by Forrest. So it is hard to see what truthmaker he can appeal to except the nature of universality, what it is to be a universal, perhaps following this up with the claim that the identical universals→identical effects principle supervenes upon what it is to be a universal. But this supervenience can hardly be the ontologically innocent sort of supervenience that we have upheld in this essay.

Forrest's suggestion is attractive for the economy of means which it proposes for the linking of universals and laws. And if one thinks that laws are constituted by the truth of universally quantified propositions, that is, if one holds a Regularity theory of law, then to make all the constituents of the states of affairs involved universals, and further to point to the intuitive attractiveness of the principle of same universals→same effects, is perhaps the best that can be done. My judgment is that it is not enough.

15.2 LAWS AS RELATIONS BETWEEN UNIVERSALS

The Regularity theory of law faces many difficulties. But its fundamental weakness is its inability to come up with a sufficiently strong distinction between law-like and non-law-like regularities. To rehearse once more the old well-tried case. If a quantity of uranium 235 reaches critical mass, then it *has* to disintegrate violently, or at least there is an overwhelming probability of it so disintegrating. That is why there is no very large continuous mass of this element, no sphere of the stuff that has, say, a diameter of a hundred yards. Such a sphere is not nomically possible. Equally, in all likelihood there is and will be no such sphere of gold. But the sphere of gold is nomically possible. The Regularity theory can, in my judgment, give no convincing account of this distinction. The best chance appears to be the Mill–Ramsey–Lewis suggestion that the fact that the uranium sphere fails to exist belongs to a systematic and organized set of regularities (which we dignify as the laws of nature) while the non-existence of the gold sphere is not, nor does it follow from, a regularity of this special sort.

My objection (which I re-emphasize is a matter for judgment rather than proof) is that this difference is relatively trivial, that it fails to do justice to the point that uranium 235 cannot be organized into such a sphere while (we have good reason to think) there is no such truth about gold. Some 'strong' theory of laws seems required, although we may still deny that the laws involved are *necessary*.

Once one has decided that even a sophisticated Regularity theory must be abandoned, and one has universals in one's ontological system, then it is natural to look to the universals to give an account of the difference between uranium and gold here, in particular in the form of a *connection* of universals. Some of the universals instantiated by critical masses of uranium nomically ensure, or practically ensure, violent disintegration. The same or greater masses of gold nomically ensure no such result.

It may perhaps be conceded that once the idea of a connection of universals has been accepted, it at least appears to have a good deal of *explanatory* force, a force conspicuously greater than the Regularity theory, even at the latter's best. But it has been argued powerfully by some contemporary philosophers, for instance, David Lewis and Bas van Fraassen, that when examined this alleged connection of universals turns out be an incoherent conception. It fails, in particular, to set up any intelligible link between the postulated relationship of the universals and the regularities that must flow from the relation if we are to speak of *laws*. (Laws of nature have to be *obeyed*.)

So, conscious that this is by no means the first time I have made the attempt, and trusting that patience is not wearing too thin, I devote this section to a defence of the *intelligibility* of the idea of a nomic connection of universals. If the mere intelligibility can be made good, then perhaps the theory is in quite a good way, perhaps even, as the horse-racing commentators say, 'home and hosed'. The situation may be a bit like the situation in the fifties of this century when the Identity theory of mind was being canvassed. People like Place and Smart thought that if only they could meet the *a priori* objections to the identifying of sensations with brain-processes, then the scientific plausibilities were in their favour. I think that many opponents were prepared to concede this hypothetical while denying the truth of its antecedent. In the end, though, it was rather generally agreed that the force of the *a priori* objections had been overestimated.

For the present, I will defend the theory at a fairly general level. In particular, I shall not attempt in this section to argue for a contingent as opposed to a necessary connection between universals. I will simply argue for the intelligibility of the conception of a law of nature (the law and not the true law-statement) as a connection of universals.

Let us suppose that a particular *a* has the property F and stands in the relation R to a particular *b* having property G. This state of affairs is immediately succeeded by *b*'s becoming H. What we have here is a certain sequence of states of affairs. *a*'s being F together with *a*'s having R to *b*, which latter is a G, is succeeded by *b*'s being H. The object *a* might be a guillotine in good working order, R its blade descending on the neck of an unfortunate person *b*, which is immediately followed by *b*'s being decapitated (H). Notice that so far we have only used the phrases 'succeeded by' and 'followed by'. Not a word about causing! We can go on to describe the *type* of sequence here instantiated. It is a type where something's being F, together with having R to a further thing *b* which is G, is succeeded by *that same further thing* becoming H. At this point we have reached a purely general description, and we may for the sake of the example treat F, R, G, and H as stand-ins for universals. Remembering our characterization of universals as state-of-affairs types, what we have described is a complex, or structural, universal, a structural universal involving sequence (3.722).

With our discussion of singular causation in the previous chapter behind us, we can now change the case a little. It may be the case that *a*'s being F and having R to *b* which is a G, not merely precedes but actually *brings about b*'s becoming H. That descent of that blade *causes* decapitation. By the argument of 14.6 we may even be able non-inferentially to *observe* causal sequences of this sort in favourable cases, observing that they are causal (doubtless not in this particular one).

We can now describe the sequence here instantiated in general terms, abstracting from particulars. It is one where something's being F and having R to a further thing G *brings about* that further thing becoming H. We again have the description of a complex, or structural, universal, a state-of-affairs type, one involving sequence, but now a state-of-affairs type involving (singular) *causal* sequence.

Now we wish to alter the case still further and make it a (deterministic) *law* that something's being F and having R to a further thing G causes that further thing to become H. (It is a deterministic law that guillotining in these circumstances *causes* decapitation.) What do we need to add? For a Regularity theorist, nothing but universal quantifiers, so that in all cases of something's being F and having R to a further thing of the sort G, this further thing is caused to become H. Indeed, according to this theory, we can eliminate the 'caused' and go back to mere regular succession.

Suppose though that, *contra* the Humeans, we have accepted the reality of irreducible singular causation, but still want to salvage what we can of the Regularity theory. We will not eliminate the 'caused'. We can say that the law takes the form just given: it is always the case that something's being F and having R to a further thing of the sort G causes the further thing to become H.

There is still a final step to be taken. Impressed, perhaps, by the regular succession, we put forward a hypothesis to *explain* the succession. The hypothesis is that there can be causal connections not merely between state-of-affairs tokens but also between state-of-affairs *types*. Something's being an F and having R to a further thing G, just that state-of-affairs type, brings about, causes, the further thing to become an H, a further state-of-affairs type. This direct connection of universals, an extra, higher-order state of affairs, is what is missing, for instance, from Peter Forrest's suggestion (15.1).

If this is an intelligible hypothesis, this hypothesis of causal connection at the level of state-of-affairs types, does it not *entail* the corresponding universal quantification? (Though there is still to come the qualification that this entailment holds only given the absence of further interfering factors. See 15.21.) The universal quantification, by contrast, does not by itself entail, though it may well suggest, the hypothesized causal connection between the state-of-affairs types.

Red is a colour. This entails that red things are coloured. This latter truth does not entail that red is a colour, as Frank Jackson has elegantly shown (1977). Heat is motion of molecules. This entails that if something is hot, its molecules are in motion. But this latter truth does not entail that heat is motion of molecules. It is compatible with heat and motion of molecules being no more than well-correlated.

Similarly, guillotining causes immediate decapitation. This entails that all who are guillotined, are immediately without a head. But that all who are guillotined are immediately without a head does not entail that guillotining causes immediate decapitation. Indeed, that all who are guillotined are *caused* to be immediately without a head does not entail that guillotining, a state-of-affairs type, causes immediate decapitation, a further state-of-affairs type.

To repeat. A *law*, it is our hypothesis, is something stronger than a universally quantified state of affairs, even a universally quantified state of affairs involving singular causations. It is a causal connection between state-of-affairs types. It is a 'direct' connection between these state-of-affairs types, that is, between universals. It does not hold between universals via their instances. This direct connection may suggest Platonism. Universals, whether instantiated or uninstantiated, stand above the flux and certain relations between the universals 'govern' their instances, lay down the law, to the instances. Perhaps this was Plato's picture of law-governed behaviour in the *Phaedo* (102–7). It is in any case a profoundly mysterious doctrine and is certainly not what is being advocated here.

The present idea is rather different. The law, the truthmaker of the corresponding true law-statement, is a connection between state-of-affairs types, of a sort that can at least be pictured in guillotining (that state-of-affairs type) causing immediate decapitation (a further state-of-affairs type). It is a second-order state of affairs, a relation holding between the universals involved. This second-order state of affairs must itself be a universal, a structural universal involving a certain linking of universals, a linking of state-of-affairs types. Now consider the guillotine, *a*, coming into suitable relation to a person, *b*, and so causing *b*'s immediate decapitation. This is an instantiation of the law, an instantiation of the structural universal that is the linking of certain universals.

The suggestion is then this. There is *nothing* to the law except what is instantiated in such sequences. Each sequence is an instantiation of that strictly identical 'thing' or entity: *guillotining causing the guillotined to be immediately decapitated*. The law, a certain special sort of universal, has no existence except in the particular sequences. (A consequence to be welcomed is that this analysis allows *as a possibility* something that seems independently quite a plausible possibility: a law having one instantiation only.)

Suppose that we now assume, what it seems there can be no proof of, but what seems a likely supposition especially to the scientifically minded, that every singular causal sequence is in fact governed by law. We can then advance the following reductive hypothesis (already put forward in 14.7). Each case of singular causation is a relationship between first-order states of affairs, but where this relationship instantiates a law (or laws), a law that is a causal connection of state-of-affairs types (universals) as spelt out above.

A reader who has been led through this argument, has first been presented with singular causation, and then has been asked to consider the suggestion that the same relation of causation which holds between suitable token states of affairs could also hold between state-of-affairs types. But as has but recently become clear to me, this is a ladder that can now be thrown away. *The fundamental causal relation is a nomic one, holding between state-of-affairs types, between universals.* Singular causation is no more than the instantiation of this type of relation in particular cases. When we experience singular causation, *what* we are experiencing is nomicity, law-instantiation. Or so my hypothesis goes. Of course, we do not *experience* it as nomicity, in the way that we do sometimes experience singular causation as causation.

This account would seem to answer the careful and penetrating assault that van Fraassen launches upon earlier presentations of this theory (1989, ch. 5, and 1993). In particular, he raises two problems which he thinks arise for this theory and other theories of 'strong' laws. There is first the Identification problem: which relation between universals is the relation of nomic necessitation? Second, there is the Inference problem: what information does the statement that one property necessitates another give us about 'what happens and what things are like' (the regularities)? He thinks that the two problems are connected in such a way that to make any fist of solving the one is to make it impossible to solve the other. It is a 'short sheet' or 'bulge in the carpet' problem.

The Identification problem is solved via our direct awareness, in certain favourable cases, of causation in the *token* case. One would hope that the problem could still be solved even if there is no such direct awareness of singular causation, solved by a postulation. But in fact we can solve the problem in the best Empiricist manner: causation is given in experience. Van Fraassen would deny this, of course. But, after all, he does not believe in the objective reality of *any* properties and relations. What was argued against him (14.6), putting it in terms that presumably he would prefer, is that the dyadic predicate 'causes' is as much an observational predicate as any other predicate in our language, especially in such cases as our awareness of pressure on our own body.

Whatever is the case for the Identification problem, the Inference problem can only be solved by a piece of theorizing. The theory being advanced is that when one particular state of affairs brings about another, then the *pattern* instantiated, one state-of-affairs type bringing about a further state-of-affairs type according to some pattern, is a 'direct' relation between the state-of-affairs types involved, *a relation that is the causality instantiated in the situation*. This would seem to solve the Inference problem. Wherever the antecedent state-of-affairs type is instantiated, then, assuming this law is a deterministic one, it must (subject to an already signalled qualification, to be discussed almost immediately) produce the consequent state of affairs.

It must be conceded that those of us who uphold the view that laws of nature are relations of universals have often used a *symbolism* that left the solution to the Inference problem obscure. The connection was represented as N(F,G) and the entailment of a universally quantified truth, a regularity, seemed a mystery. For N I am now substituting C for cause, and will discuss the question of non-causal laws in 15.3. But it was the '(F,G)' part of the formula that seriously underdescribed the situation.

The notation '(F,G)' invites the question: could there be a law of the form N (F,F)? No, one is then inclined to say, because how could a universal have a nomic relation to itself? But then we are in a bind. What symbolism is appropriate where like causes like? After all, like sometimes causes like in a law-like way. The problem is solved thus. It is the notion of a universal as a state-of-affairs type, the 'Fregean' notion of a universal, the eviscerated state of affairs with its particular particulars abstracted away, that delivers us the possibility of like causing like. There is no reason why something's being F should not cause something other (perhaps, in the simplest case, the next temporal part of the same thing) to be F also. The nomic connection analysed as a causal connection between state-of-affairs types handles this. The F→F causation just described is just such a connection between state-of-affairs types. In a certain sequence-type, the antecedent portion of the sequence brings about the consequent portion. And if this is so, then the inference from the law to *tokens* of the antecedent portion bringing about *tokens* of the consequent portion seems perspicuous, not to say analytic. Hume's edict against necessary connection between wholly distinct existences remains in force. The causal connection between state-of-affairs types remains a postulate, of course. But who ever thought that laws were not postulated, were not an inference from the regularities in the world? (Although Sorensen, 1992, has pointed to the likelihood of some minimal innate knowledge of nomic possibility thrown up as the result of natural selection.)

How then should we symbolize a law? Our discussion of complex or structural universals in 3.7 points the way. We analysed such universals as various sorts of conjunctions of state-of-affairs types. But we noted the necessity to link these types together by specifying that e.g. in certain conjunctions of these types, it was the very same particular involved in both. We could symbolize this by using subscripts to identify such sameness of particulars:

$$\_{}_1 \text{ being F } \& \ \_{}_1 \text{ being G.}$$

This tells us that the structure-type in question involves the *same* particular being both F and G. This, as it happens, gives us the structure of a conjunctive property.

In the same fashion, we can symbolize causal connection between state-of-affairs types. We might have:

$$(\_{}_1\text{being F } \& \ \_{}_1\text{having R to } \_{}_2 \ \& \ \_{}_2 \text{ being G) } \textit{causes } (\_{}_2 \text{ being H).}$$

This *is* a certain relationship in which the universals F, R, G, and H stand, where the conjunction of state-of-affairs types inside the first parenthesis causes the state-of-affairs type inside the second parenthesis. The analysis just given may be too simple to fit actual cases, but it shows what is envisaged.

The analysis can be adapted to fit cases where like causes like. The simplest schema would be:

$$(\_{1} \text{ being F}) \textit{ causes } (\_{2} \text{ being F}),$$

although this is somewhat too simple even where the two particulars are successive temporal parts of 'the same thing'. It must be conceded, though, that where like causes like the phrase 'relations between universals' begins to seem somewhat inappropriate, because only one universal is involved. But we can still speak of relations between state-of-affairs types, which preserves all that is essential. When like causes like, at the level of universals a state of affairs of type F brings about a further state of affairs of the very same type.

15.21 Iron laws and defeasible laws

Despite what has just been said, even a deterministic connection of state-of-affairs types does not entail the corresponding universally quantified truth about particulars, at least not without qualifications. The entailment actually holds only for the cases where it is given that *nothing further interferes*. To say this is not to trivialize the entailment to its always holding, except in the cases where it doesn't. Rather, the situation is one that we are quite familiar with in scientific laws. The gravitational laws give the gravitational forces holding between two bodies having certain masses and at a certain distance from each other. It is not necessary that these forces cause the two bodies to move towards each other. There may be many other bodies also exerting gravitational force in the situation, not to mention other types of force (three, according to contemporary theory) that may be operating. The two bodies are caused to move towards each other according to the law that governs just two massive bodies *provided nothing else interferes*.

But, it may be suggested, we ought to react to this situation by including in true laws all the forces that are operating in any situation. If there are just four fundamental forces, then the true force law for any situation, the causal law that connects state-of-affairs types, should involve all the four force-types.

Notice, though, that even if we were to adopt this suggestion, we would still not get an *entailment* between the connection of state-of-affairs types (in a deterministic law) and the corresponding regularity. We can never rule out the possibility, mere possibility though it may be, that further forces (for instance, irreducibly psychic ones) could be added to the situation which would alter the behaviour of the particulars involved. Hence we cannot get our entailment without adding the clause that excludes further factors. The clause itself seems to present no difficulty. It is, if our account of allness in chapter 13 has been correct, a higher-order state of affairs that certain state-of-affairs types are the *only* nomic factors operating in a certain situation. The entailment then goes through.

Rejecting negative universals as we do, the factors operative in a situation will all be positive. It is these positive factors, and these alone, that determine the situation. The state of affairs that these are *all* the factors causally operative in the situation is not a part of the cause, even the 'total cause'. It is simply the state of affairs that must hold if the *entailment* from the nomic connection of state-of-affairs types to a regularity of first-order states of affairs is to go through.

This, it seems, is a dialectical advantage for our theory. By indicating a further condition which must hold for the entailment to go through, the entailment between (deterministic) law and regularity, which is so often said to be a difficulty for 'strong' theories of law, is made that degree more plausible.

We can, though, distinguish between two types of law. If F→G (with some probability) is a law, and if it is *empirically* possible (nomically possible) that there is a universal F&H, and if in these circumstances the probability of an outcome of type G is altered, then F → G by itself is a *defeasible* law. Note that any law of the F&H→. . . sort may itself be defeasible, conceivably *ad infinitum*. (Armstrong 1983, 10.4, calls defeasible laws 'oaken'. The term 'defeasible' seems better.) It seems to be always possible that for any antecedent of a law there exists such an H. But it may not be empirically possible. If it is not empirically possible, then the law may be called an *iron* law.

15.3 ARE CAUSAL LAWS ENOUGH?

Not all scientific laws are causal laws. What is the nature of the connection between universals in a non-causal law? The hypothesis now to be put forward is of a sort that the reader has become familiar with, one hopes not sickened by! Given all the causal laws, then any further laws that there are *supervene*, are entailed. This needs to be argued for, of course, but before we do so we should consider the possibility (epistemic) that the supervenience is symmetrical. Could it be that non-causal laws supervene on the causal laws and the causal laws supervene on the non-causal laws? Given the position that we have taken about supervenience, this would be the claim that the two systems of law were ontologically identical. Two different systems of true propositions, perhaps, but the very same truthmaker for both. It is hard to get a clear picture of this suggestion, but if it had to be accepted it would not seem to prejudice our account. There would then be another way of describing the causal connections of state-of-affairs types (as functional correlations?), conceivably a more illuminating description. But those causal connections would still be there.

But leaving this suggestion aside, the *defence* of the supervenience hypothesis can proceed by the time-honoured, and not always corrupt, method of stretching the notion under discussion to avoid counter-examples. It will now be argued that the core, at least, of our conception of causality is so comprehensive that it can be extended to cover almost any candidate law that may be proposed as a plausible counter-example. The central notion of a cause is that of something which, being given, something further, a distinct existence, *has to be*. Its mental parallel is the inference, and causation is like an inference in nature. This being so, that further thing has to be or has a certain probability of having to be. That is why causation is associated with, indeed entails, counterfactuals, though in the case of singular causation the counterfactuals entailed are rather weak ones (14.5). If this thing had not been so, this further thing would not have been so, unless the further thing had to be because of the presence of other factors such as back-up causes.

But now consider laws. They are explicitly inferential, inference-tickets in nature, as it were. They have the same dyadic structure as causes have. Given these conditions, then this further thing must be so or has a certain probability of being so. If these conditions had not been so, this further thing would not have been so, unless other factors had also been present which, independently, nomically ensured the further thing.

For our larger purpose here, which is to argue that nomic connection can be understood as the sort of connection actually encountered in certain cases of singular causation, it seems that the core of what is *experienced* is the determining of a state of affairs by another state of affairs. This is the notion that we need for an account of nomic necessity, because having once got this notion we can go on to understand the notion of the determining of a state-of-affairs type by another state-of-affairs type. This determining seems to be the central notion, at least, involved in causality, even if some of the laws do not involve the sort of connection that ordinary language would call causal.

What we still do require, though, is a distinction between laws strictly so-called, and mere nomic truths. It is these latter that supervene, and perhaps include the 'non-causal laws'. This must be postponed to 15.5.

15.4 EXCLUSION LAWS?

We are, so far, attempting to work in terms of a single sort of nomic connective holding between state-of-affairs types. There may be different probabilities of a certain state-of-affairs type bringing about a further state-of-affairs type, and these different probabilities, if they exist, may be thought of as different determinates falling under a single determinable. But the different probabilities of causing are the only grounds so far introduced for postulating different nomic connectives.

Should we, however, introduce another sort of connective to deal with exclusion laws? Contemporary physics does find use for such principles; in particular we have Pauli's famous Exclusion Principle. One could deal with exclusions without multiplying nomic connectives by introducing negative universals. A certain positive state of affairs might ensure or probabilify that a certain particular lacked a certain positive property G, and *not being* G might be admitted as a property. Furthermore, one could admit negative properties in the selective or sparse way favoured by *a posteriori* realists about properties. But while this approach should not be decisively ruled out, it is not very attractive. Once negative properties are introduced as effects, presumably they would have to be allowed as causes also. If they do no causing, their presence would seem undetectable. But causation by negation will seem dubious to anybody who takes a reasonably robust, and in particular a non-Regularity, view of causality.

Disjunctive laws would seem a more attractive way of dealing with the situation, if the empirical facts allow. No disjunctive properties would be called for. On this account, a certain state-of-affairs type would have a certain probability, 1 or something less, of bringing about at least one of a certain *range* of effects (if the effect properties were necessarily incompatible, at most one of these effects). One would expect that the probabilities of a particular possible effect were weighted relative to the other possible effects, weighted by some number. This involves a disjunction of properties, but no disjunctive property. An *excluded* possibility would simply be one that failed to appear in the disjunction, and if it were a property that might otherwise have been expected to appear in the disjunction, then the description of the law as an exclusion law might seem natural. If the empirical facts permitted this type of law, this would seem the most intellectually economical treatment of so-called exclusion laws.

But suppose such a treatment is not possible. Could we introduce exclusion laws as a fundamentally new type of nomic connective, or, rather, nomic disconnective? This state-of-affairs type nomically excludes a certain further state-of-affairs type. The state-of-affairs types would all be positive universals, and so, according to us, would have to be instantiated *somewhere*. The relation itself would of course be symmetrical, unlike the non-symmetrical relation of ordinary 'causal' nomic connection (see 15.32). This would not create any combinatorial difficulties provided we identified the state of affairs of Fs excluding Gs with Gs excluding Fs, which would seem natural in any case (see ch. 9). No Fs would be Gs, but it would be *possible* that an F could be a G.

But perhaps a difficulty emerges when we consider what instantiation of an exclusion law comes to. That *a* is F but is not G cannot be a (first-class) state of affairs, unless we admit negative universals. The instantiation will have to be simply that *a* is F, or that *b* is G. Is this satisfactory? I leave the question unanswered.

15.5 THE FORMAL PROPERTIES OF NOMIC CONNECTION

But in any case, not all connections that we would normally call nomic connections are ones that should be thought of as involving a direct connection between universals, a direct connection between state-of-affairs types. Suppose that we symbolize the nomic connection between universals F and G in the now conventional if, as we have conceded, rather misleading way and say that N(F,G). As we have noted in 15.2 the symbolism has been a source of problems because it conceals the exact nature of the relationship that we have tried to spell out. But it is convenient here where we want to illustrate the limits of application of the nomic relation. Suppose, then, that N(F,G) and N(G,H), where both are deterministic laws. It by no means follows, and will very likely not be true, that N(F,H). Given an instantiation of F, and given that the laws are iron ones (15.2), one can *infer* the instantiation of H in a suitable relation to the F. One can say that in these circumstances it is nomically necessary that H be so instantiated, and even that it is a law that Fs and Hs are so linked. But for N(F,H) to hold in these circumstances would be for the instantiation of H to be *overdetermined*. One could certainly distinguish between N and N*, with N the ancestral of N*. One would then go on to allow N(F,H), because N*(F,G) & N*(G,H), while denying N*(F,H). But then it is N* that is the genuine nomic connection that we are talking about, and N is a relation that supervenes. This, of course, will remind us of the distinction between causes and causes* that we drew in 14.2. Causes* is the more fundamental, ordinary causing being a chain of causings*.

In general, one would hope that the basic nomic connection respects the principle of Independence, which will mean in particular that the relation is non-transitive and non-symmetrical. Non-symmetry will mean that if N(F,G) obtains then both N(G,F) and its denial are possibilities. N(G,F) will be, perhaps, the more controversial possibility. It would involve either nomic coexistence of a thing or things with the two properties, or, more bizarrely, a very small causal temporal loop.

If this is correct, then the identification of causation with nomic necessitation, and singular causation with instantiation of nomic necessitation, or, as we can also put it, the identification of cause* and N*, seems more plausible. Of course, it may turn out that it is useful to restrict the term *causal* law to a particular sub-species of law, for instance ones that involve succession or even more narrowly. But that will be relatively superficial, something like the manoeuvre in the Mill-Ramsey-Lewis theory which tries to tame the Regularity theory of law by introducing a relatively superficial distinction between 'good' and 'bad' cosmic regularities.

15.6 LAWS AS PROVIDING EXPLANATIONS

Laws as relations holding between universals, relations of a causing sort between state-of-affairs types, provide *explanations* of regularities in the behaviour of things in the way that a Regularity theory is, by hypothesis, unable to do. The premiss required here is that, as argued by Michael Friedman (1974), in the natural sciences what, before anything else, counts as a good explanation is something that unifies the phenomena. (Friedman provides excellent brief criticism of other accounts of scientific explanation.) This has been followed up by Philip Kitcher (1981). The same idea was put forward briefly in Armstrong 1991b, in ignorance of the work of Friedman and Kitcher. (Thanks are due to John Wright and Ken Gemes for calling attention to these references.)

As a matter of fact, simply to discover universals, or even properties and relations that constitute good approximations to universals, is already to unify phenomena by discovering identities. But when a law is discovered, or even approximated to, then provided it is conceived of as a linking of universals or near-universals, further unification takes place. On a Regularity view, the truthmakers for the true law-statement may be spread throughout the spacetime world, and even then a higher-order state of affairs will be required: viz. that these states of affairs are *all* the states of affairs of a certain sort. But on the view that the law is a relation between state-of-affairs types an extraordinary unification is made. The law may be higher-order, but, as Michael Tooley has insisted, it is *atomic*. As in the case of ordinary universals, it is just one and the same thing that occurs at each instantiation of the law.

Furthermore, some aid and comfort is given in dealing with the Problem of Induction. It may be that some shifts can be made with this problem even within the Regularity theory of laws, although it is certainly no accident that near-despair of seeing *why* induction is rational comes in with Hume. But if the theory of law being advocated here is correct, then the argument from regularities to possible laws, and from this to predictions about unobserved instances falling under the putative laws, is assimilated to a fairly simple *abduction*. (This assimilation is itself a unification within the theory of inductive reasoning, because induction and abduction are brought together, and so perhaps is an *explanatory* because unifying assimilation.) A regularity in nature is observed. It is postulated that behind this regularity, explaining it, and predicting further observations, is some connection of properties, some connection of state-of-affairs types. The instantiations of the actually observed properties which constitute the regularity need not be universals. They may be (ontologically) second-class properties. Even the deeper properties postulated to explain the regularity need not be universals. But these deeper properties must be on the road to being universals, and the unifying power of the explanation depends on the true and ultimate laws being connections of universals.

Following Gilbert Harman (1965) I have in the past described this sort of explanation as inference to the best explanation, and am still prepared to do so. (See 1983, 4.5 & 6.7, and 1991b. See also Foster, 1983.) But I note that Evan Fales (1990, ch. 4) has argued in detail that there is a more intellectually economical way of seeing the inference. All that is demanded is that we give the hypothesis of a certain nomic connection of universals some positive initial probability. Given this, if and when further favourable evidence is encountered, we can then use Bayesian reasoning to increase that probability without limit, and rather quickly. I mention this suggestion without either endorsing it or rejecting it.

In all this, tropes appear to have a major disadvantage when compared to universals. If all properties and relations are particulars, so that the 'universal' is nothing but an equivalence class of exactly resembling tropes, then what theory of laws is available? What, in particular, can the truthmaker for true law-statements be? The principle required is that exactly resembling tropes should bestow the very same nomic powers. But what is the truthmaker for this principle? Can it be anything more than the state of affairs that all the token states of affairs do in fact behave according to this principle? And what is this but a Regularity theory of law? Our theory, however, is able to *explain* the regularity of the world in some degree. It is not a decisive advantage, and in the philosophical balance-sheet it might be outweighed or at least balanced by other advantages for tropes over universals. But what are these other advantages?

15.7 PROBABILISTIC LAWS

It may well be that some or all laws of nature are irreducibly probabilistic. So it is an important question for us whether the account of laws given in the previous section can be extended to cover such laws. It does not seem too difficult to do this, but a number of quite delicate and disputable issues do arise. We have already said something about probabilistic causation at 5.4, but the issue is important enough to bear some repetition.

The idea is that, instead of a state-of-affairs type that ensures, determines or necessitates a further state-of-affairs type, the first state-of-affairs type will give a certain *objective probability* (which presumably can be given some definite value) that an instance of the second state-of-affairs type will be caused to exist in suitable relation to the first state of affairs. This probabilistic connection between state-of-affairs types will automatically yield a single-case chance whenever the antecedent universal is instantiated. We can say that the antecedent state of affairs, as it is convenient to call it, has a certain *propensity* to bring about the consequent state of affairs. A 'deterministic' law can then be thought of as one where the propensity takes the value 1 (not, be it noted, 1 minus an infinitesimal, which would not be a deterministic law). Whether such propensities are to be thought of as *pure* propensities, or whether instead they must or do have a 'categorical basis', is a great issue that was already raised in chapter 5. My vote is for categorical basis.

Suppose, then, that something's being an F has a certain propensity, less than 1, to bring about a change, G, in a later state of the thing that is an F. Perhaps the emission of a particle from a uranium 235 atom after a certain period of time is a law of this sort, immanent causation with no factors external to the atom having any influence on the probability of emission. The instantiations of F divide into two sorts of case: Fs that produce Gs and Fs that do not produce Gs. Call these the positive and the negative cases. There is an obvious sense in which the positive cases have primacy. In these cases the law as it were 'fires'. It really is instantiated.

(As a matter of fact, there seems to be a further possible or at least conceivable case, as Michael Tooley has pointed out. There might also be Fs that are succeeded by Gs by sheer random chance. They would not be instantiations of the F→G law. Such a distinction between the two sorts of FG sequences could not be drawn within a Regularity theory. However, although it is intellectually illuminating to recognize that a 'strong' theory of law apparently allows for such a possibility, there seems to be no particular reason to think that such totally random states of affairs ever occur in our world. It seems a plausible assumption that every event has a cause. Perhaps a law is involved. See ch. 17 for a brief further discussion.)

We are supposing that the law is one that is uncontroversially a causal law. The positive cases will be ones where there is actual causation. In the negative cases there will be no causation. For this reason, the phrase 'probabilistic causality', which is often heard, is really inappropriate. What a probabilistic causal law gives us is not probabilistic causality but a certain probability that causation will occur, an ordinary causation which occurs whether the law governing the causation is deterministic or merely probabilistic. In a law that is not causal, if there are such things, there will likewise be a certain probability that a positive case will occur, a certain probability of instantiation of the consequent. The law, in our theory, lives in its positive instantiations. This shows, incidentally, that the proposition that every event has a cause is compatible with *no* causal law being deterministic. Determinism entails that every event has a cause, but the converse entailment does not hold.

This line of thought may be thought to lead to a difficulty. Given independence of chances, which is at least the simplest supposition, then there will be no *contradiction* in the idea that the experimental results should always and everywhere fail to agree with the propensity, and even although those results are the best evidence we can have for what the strength of the propensity is. There is, for instance, no contradiction in a fair coin being tossed an infinite number of times, and coming down heads every time.

This in turn leads us to consider the two extreme cases. Can there be a merely probabilistic law connecting the Fs and the Gs, yet every F be a G? And in the same circumstances, can no F be a G? Given our account of laws, there would seem to be little difficulty in the former case. It is some, though no more than some, embarrassment for a Regularity theory, but there seems no objection to a mere propensity 'firing' every time. But should we not also allow that, by chance, a propensity never fires and yet exists? This seems to show that a law can exist in the absence of a positive instantiation of that law. To admit this, however, is to give up the idea, to which I attach great importance, that laws exist nowhere and nowhen except in their positive instantiations, and the connected idea that laws are themselves a special sort of complex universal. So, not without some misgiving, I deny the possibility of a propensity that exists yet never fires.

There appear to be two ways to go if we do accept the ontological reality of such uninstantiated laws. The one way, favoured by Michael Tooley in particular, is to accept uninstantiated universals, not necessarily any old uninstantiated universals, but whatever uninstantiated universals and relations between them that are required as truthmakers for uninstantiated laws. (He calls this Factual Platonism.) The great cost of this way of going is that it involves abandoning Naturalism, the view that the world is exhausted by the spacetime system. Naturalism in this sense is certainly not to be regarded as sacrosanct. We can readily conceive of evidence that ought to persuade us to abandon it. But among the larger principles that we have steered ourselves by in this work – Factualism (obviously controversial), Naturalism and Physicalism (somewhat controversial) – Naturalism does seem to be something rather plausible which should not lightly be abandoned.

A more plausible alternative, it may be suggested, is to give an account of uninstantiated laws in terms of *unmanifested powers*. To take this line, however, is to revive the dispute discussed in chapter 5 about the nature of properties, the dispute between Categoricalism and Dispositionalism. The Dispositionalist view is that a property is essentially a power, a power to act or be acted upon, and is nothing more than a power. We can certainly try to give an account of unmanifested powers in terms of properties as the Dispositionalists conceive them. (Though there may still be difficulties where the particulars involved do not exist. Suppose the world has a finite mass. It might still be reasonable to hold that if a particular with greater mass had existed, it would have had certain gravitational powers.)

Certain difficulties about Dispositionalism, however, inclined us to the Categoricalist view that properties are self-contained entities, and do not involve powers essentially. This, as we have already noted, involves giving an account of powers in terms of the laws that govern these categorical properties as a matter of contingent fact. And if the laws are relations of universals, then we are brought back to the problem of uninstantiated laws. Do we require uninstantiated universals for these laws? We will postpone a final showdown on these matters until the next chapter.

15.71 *Van Fraassen's problem about propensities*

Van Fraassen (1987) has proposed an ingenious difficulty for the theory of objective propensities defended in this essay. It appears to apply to all propensity theories. The propensity may be any number, rational or real, between 0 and 1. It gives the objective chance that an F-type state of affairs, say, gives rise to a G-type state of affairs, with F and G universals. Suppose, then, that the omnitemporal number of instantiations of the F→G law is finite. The proportion of the Fs that are Gs may then fail to be equal to the value of the propensity P. (Suppose that P=.25 and F is instantiated just five times.) Given independence of chances, there is, of course, no inevitability that the proportion of positive instantiations of the law will equal P for *any* such law. But can we attach any sense to a value of P for which, given the actual number of instantiations of F, the proportion of positive instantiations *could* not be equal to P?

The suggestion for meeting this difficulty in Armstrong 1988b is that one should appeal to a counterfactual about the limit that the proportion of positive instantiations of F would in all probability tend towards, in a world where the number of instantiations was infinite. The truthmaker for this counterfactual would be provided by the nomic relation between the universals F and G: the higher-order state of affairs that the F-type state of affairs had propensity P to give rise to G-type states of affairs. If that is thought of as a categorical relation between state-of-affairs types, perhaps it will serve as a satisfactory truthmaker. After all, universals and relations between universals, being 'predicable of many', may be thought to be indifferent to the number of their instances.

It may be objected that the extension from the finite to the infinite case makes the truth of the counterfactual much more dubious. The merely possible particulars involved would presumably be *alien* particulars, ones belonging to the somewhat dubious 'outer sphere' of possibility. But to this, it seems, it may be replied that we are only required to *make sense* of the possibility that the value of P and the number of instantiations of a certain law should be at odds with each other in the way described by van Fraassen. It is not as if the objection is based on empirical data from physics or elsewhere. For the possible case, we have provided a possible truth-maker. That seems to be all that is required.

The next chapter will first consider the enormously important question of *functional* laws. Without an account of these laws, the Prince of Denmark is lacking from the play. We will then be in a position to be a little more decisive on the topic of uninstantiated laws and unmanifested powers. This will involve confronting the Categoricalist accounts of properties and laws with the important position of C. B. Martin. His view is in part Categoricalist, but looks to irreducible powers rather than laws. It will be the 'last showdown' in this essay.

16

Laws II

16.1 FUNCTIONAL LAWS

16.11 The problem of functional laws

The discussion up to this point has had, inevitably, a somewhat unrealistic air. This is because the form of the laws that we have been discussing remains within what one might call the *ravens are black* paradigm. This is no better than a respectable generalization at the edge where ordinary experience begins to merge into science, having the form *being a raven* ensures (more or less) *being black*. The terms do not pick out universals, although no doubt there are universals whose connections ensure the truth or near truth of the generalization. But it is the suggestion that a typical law connects just two universals that chiefly misleads. The laws that have the best present claim to be fundamental are laws that link together certain classes of universals, in particular certain determinate quantities falling under a common determinable, in some mathematical relation. They are functional laws. If we can give some plausible account of functional laws, then and only then do we have a theory of lawhood that can be taken really seriously.

There are two particularly notable characteristics of functional laws. (1) They are determinable laws, and under each such law falls a large, perhaps infinite, class of determinate laws. (2) A great many of the determinates are likely to be uninstantiated. The latter point poses a special difficulty for our metaphysical system. Take these characteristics in turn.

Consider the Newtonian gravitation law. The gravitational force holding between two bodies depends upon the product of the two masses divided by the square of the distance. This gives us three different quantities (two of them masses) that can vary independently. For each different triple of numbers that measure these quantities one can calculate a force. One can think of this calculation as yielding a gravitation law that holds for just these two mass-values and just this distance-value. There are innumerable, perhaps infinite, numbers of these determinate laws. They involve determinate masses and distances, which we may assume are genuine universals, strictly identical in their different instances. (For simplicity of discussion, we accept the fundamental concepts of Newtonian physics as picking out true universals.) What we appear to have in these determinate laws are first-order laws linking first-order determinate universals.

Now we can conceive, and indeed it appears actually possible, though no doubt merely possible, that each of these determinate laws should be laws in their own right, meaning by this that each law should be an independent existence, holding independently of the holding any other determinate law that falls under the determinable law. As a matter of fact, an upholder of the Regularity theory must uphold such independence. This ought to be a reproach to that theory, because, although it is a bare possibility that all these laws are wholly distinct existences, their co-ordination cries out for further explanation. The co-ordination is far more extraordinary than regularities such as the monotonous way that the feathers of ravens keep on being black. If, however, the functional law is a *unitary entity* of some sort, then all the determinate laws can be deduced from the existence of that law plus the assumption of appropriate antecedent conditions – viz. two objects with certain masses at a certain distance. And not only is there deduction, but there is *explanation* because of the unification that the determinable law brings to the huge class of determinate laws. It turns out to be the same damned thing going on in each case.

The functional law is therefore in some sense a higher-order law, the law that determines and unifies the determinate laws. It will be seen, therefore, that much hangs on giving an appropriate account of what a functional law is. For us this account will have to be consilient with the general plan of exhibiting all laws as relations between universals, between state-of-affairs types. But we leave this central problem aside for the moment to look at the question of uninstantiated values of functional laws.

16.12 Uninstantiated values of functional laws

It appears to have been C. D. Broad (1935) who pointed out that functional laws were likely to have uninstantiated values, cases where the antecedent conditions were omnitemporally not instantiated, but where the law mandates a certain consequent state of affairs. Important cases are (1) limiting cases where antecedent values go towards zero – Newton's First Law is a particular case; and (2) cases where antecedent values are too large. The second sort of case would occur for the gravitation law if the total mass of the universe is finite. For presumably the law holds for masses that exceed this total.

Among those philosophers who take laws seriously, and in particular among those who accept 'strong' laws, there appear to be three reactions to the problem posed by uninstantiated laws. The first is the Platonist solution. Uninstantiated laws are accepted as denizens of the world, alongside instantiated laws, but as transcendent things, things not in spacetime. The second view we will call the Power view. An uninstantiated law is an unmanifested power (disposition, etc.) of particulars, where powers are taken with full ontological seriousness. This is a natural solution for a Dispositionalist, for whom the essence of properties lies in their power-bestowing nature (see ch. 5). The third solution, which is my own preference, will be called the Counterfactualist account. It is the solution that will naturally attract a Categoricalist about properties who is also a Naturalist, postulating nothing that exists over and above spacetime. Statements of uninstantiated laws become counterfactuals about what laws would hold if certain unrealized conditions were realized. Their truthmakers must be sought in the real or instantiated laws. It is a *deflationary* but not (I hope) an *eliminativist* solution. It runs parallel to the account already offered of unmanifested powers and dispositions of particulars in chapter 5. Now to say something more about the three positions in turn.

(1) Platonism is defended by Michael Tooley (1987, p. 119). He calls his view *Factual* Platonism, 'Factual' to mark his view, shared in this work, that universals are no more necessary beings than particulars are. The advantage of this position is that many statements of uninstantiated law appear to be true, and for them a truthmaker is supplied parallel to the truthmaker for true statements of instantiated law: a relationship of universals. A particular dialectical advantage over the Powers view will appear if it turns out that e.g. the mass of the universe is finite. Since there will exist no particular having a mass greater than this, there will be no actual thing to have the powers of gravitational attraction associated with such very large masses. The disadvantage of Factual Platonism is obvious. It breaks with Naturalism, postulating entities that lie outside spacetime.

(2) The second solution, the Powers account, which postulates ontologically irreducible powers, has obvious advantages when it comes to uninstantiated laws that apply to really existing particulars. It may well be that

omnitemporally nothing instantiates the First Law. But innumerable particulars may be thought of as possessing at all times the never actually manifested power to remain in their present state of motion or rest *if* no forces (or exactly equal forces) act upon them. As already indicated, the solution in terms of powers has to start talking faster when it comes to uninstantiated laws involving uninstantiated properties (masses greater than the total mass of the universe). What seems to be needed here is some property of massiness that a thing with mass has whatever particular mass it has, a property which bestows on its particulars the powers associated with any determinate of massiness. As we shall see in 16.13, perhaps such a property can be provided.

(3) So we come now to the Counterfactual position. On this view there are none but categorical properties and relations, and none but categorical relations between these universals, relations that constitute the laws of nature. The laws do not exist except in their instantiations, pleonastically in their positive instantiations. What are uninstantiated laws on this view? They are truths of an ontologically second-rate sort: true counterfactuals. Thus, suppose that we have a functional law. We know that an ordinary first-order law, an F→G law, 'sustains counterfactuals'. The statement of the law, plus the false (but nomically possible) supposition that a certain particular is an F, allows us to conclude (subject to some escape clauses) that this particular, or some other related and relevant particular (depending upon the detail of the law), is a G. What we have in the case of a functional law is the same thing one order up. It is a determinable law that governs a class of determinate laws. Sometimes there is, strictly, no determinate law for certain particular values falling under the determinable law, because the antecedent value is omnitemporally never instantiated. But we can conjoin the statement of determinable law with the false statement that the antecedent is somewhere instantiated, and then deduce the determinate law that would have obtained given this false condition. We can even call it a law, if we like. (Newton did, for the case of the First Law.) But according to the present metaphysics, it is not strictly a law because it is not instantiated. It is probably best to call it a law in a secondary sense.

These counterfactual truths are supposed to supervene upon the actual, instantiated, laws. Given just the instantiated laws, the uninstantiated laws are entailed. This makes this view deflationary, and so, to a degree, sceptical. But it is not eliminativist. The reader is referred back to the account given of unmanifested dispositions in 5.6. The argument between the Platonist and the Power views of uninstantiated laws, on the one hand, and the Counterfactual view, on the other, will be continued at a later point in this chapter.

What is needed at this point, of course, is a plausible account of the determinable law, the functional law, which will sustain the counterfactuals to which this view reduces uninstantiated laws. Platonist and Power theorists also require an account of functional laws, but the matter is peculiarly urgent for the Counterfactualist. So let us turn to this task.

16.13 The nature of functional laws

Like the determinate laws, we want the functional or determinable law to be an atomic fact or state of affairs. How is this to be achieved? It seems that what is wanted is a single property, an antecedent property, linked in the simplest case with a second or consequent property. Consider the class of all the mass-universals, actual and possible: the kilo, the pound, and so on, perhaps a class with an infinite number of members. If we are to have functional mass-laws, we want a common property of all these properties.

It will at this point be useful to distinguish between *logical* and *real* determinables. All real determinables are logical determinables, but not all logical determinables are real ones. Logical determinables are W. E. Johnson's determinables. They are whatever obey the logical laws that Johnson laid down for determinables. Colour is a logical determinable, with the individual colours as determinates, standing in the familiar logical relations. But it is likely enough, or at least a Physicalist will think it likely enough, that it is not a *real* determinable. The individual shades of colour do not really have, even if in the manifest image of the world they may appear to have, a genuinely common property, a property that is a universal. So perhaps for all or most of the secondary qualities. But the collection of determinate mass-properties, of the length and duration properties, and other such classes, appear to be much better candidates for classes of universals that are united not in some loose way only, but by their possession of a common property, a property that is itself a universal. Such universals will be the *real* or *ontological* determinables. Unlike logical determinables, which are properties of particulars, the real determinables are genuine, and non-relational, properties of determinate properties, providing a universal to unify suitable classes of determinates.

It was argued in 4.13 that classes of determinates falling under a common determinable are classes united by various more or less complex patterns of *partial identities* holding between the determinates concerned.

Each such class forms an equivalence class, so its members may be said to be identical in a certain respect, provided that the identity involved is no more than *loose* identity (2.31). But, I am now suggesting, *some* of these classes, though united in this way, are also united by a *strictly* identical property that is a property of all and only the determinates that are the members of that class. It is these strictly identical second-order properties, where they exist, that we are calling the real, as opposed to the logical, determinables.

The idea is then that functional laws of nature are relations between these determinable universals.

It is to be emphasized as usual that the discovery or postulation of these higher-order properties is an *a posteriori* matter, to be decided, to the extent that it can be decided, in the light of total science. The 'Newtonian determinables' that we have been using, have been used for convenience and simplicity of exposition, not to mention my scientific incompetence. For real ontological determinables one might have to go to such properties as space-time interval. It is a plausible conjecture that all ontological determinables are *quantities*.

But although these universals are to be postulated *a posteriori*, it seems that it cannot be a contingent truth that certain classes of determinate universals fall under *real* determinable universals. It is not possible that these determinate universals should exist and yet 'in some other possible world' should lack this common property. The existence of the determinable universal is entailed by, and so supervenes upon, the existence of each and every determinate universal falling under it. And, if the doctrine of the ontological free lunch is correct, the determinable is already 'in' the determinate, and so is no increase of being.

This point was for long a stumbling block for me in working out an account of functional laws, which I thought of as contingent like all other laws. But it seems that it should not have been an obstacle. Just because a ton or a kilo is necessarily a mass, and a mile necessarily a distance, is no reason why the determinables of mass and distance, taking them to be real universals, should not be *contingently* connected with the force they generate, according to some functional relationship. Two particulars each have a particular mass, and so must have mass. They are at a certain distance. This complex state of affairs is of a type that nomically ensures that the particulars each generate a certain quantity of force (ultimately, perhaps, mediated by a stream of intermediate 'particles') according to the gravitational formula. It is a non-supervenient law involving (and here is the trick) the supervenient determinable property of mass and the supervenient determinable relation of distance. Like other laws, it is an atomic state of affairs. And it exists nowhere except in its instantiations. It can be called a higher-order *law*, because it is a law that governs the determinate laws. But it is not a higher-order state of affairs than the states of affairs that are the determinate laws. (Remember that higher-order states of affairs are, in this system, supposed to be *non*-supervenient.)

Before leaving this topic, I take note of a suggestion of Jim Franklin which, if it could be applied, would in many ways yield a simpler treatment of functional laws. The idea is to have a functional law supervene on a non-functional law. Consider gravity, and take it, for simplicity, that space, time and matter are all made up of a finite number of atoms. A spacetime point is either occupied by a matter atom, or not. Suppose it is so occupied. It will be a non-functional law of nature that atoms give a small 'pull' to immediately adjacent points, at the next time point. Even if empty of matter, such a pull will be passed on to the next adjacent points. (This is a further non-functional law.) The pull gets passed across spacetime in this fashion to distant bodies. The resulting equation of pull is the functional law of gravity. Basically, though, it is all a 'propagation of local actions'. The functional law supervenes on the local propagation. The tactic here, as Franklin points out, is similar to treating such a relation as *before* as the ancestral of a relation *before** which holds only between adjacent instants. See chapter 9.

Franklin's illustrative example, just given, depends upon the rejection of action at a distance, and this is at present controversial in fundamental physics. And there is a mathematical question whether actual functional laws can be all recast in this way. But he has proposed an interesting alternative to my treatment.

16.2 DISPOSITIONALISM AGAIN

Our present concern is with the laws of nature. But, of course, views on the ontology of properties greatly affect views on the ontology of laws. An important part of this chapter, the business of the next section, is to examine the view of laws that comes out of the 'Two-sided' theory of properties, the view of C. B. Martin (5.7). It will be useful first to run over again what I judge to be the less plausible Dispositionalist theory of properties (5.5) and the stand that a Dispositionalist takes on laws.

On this view, all properties, the genuine, non-relational properties, are *purely* Dispositional, mere powers. They have nothing categorical (non-dispositional) about them. As we pointed out in our earlier discussion of Dispositionalism (5.21), this has the consequence that when a thing has a certain disposition, and conditions for its manifestation are satisfied (conditions, presumably, that are a matter of certain particulars having certain dispositions), then the manifestation occurs of necessity. This is an intellectually very transparent necessity. Once this account is given of properties, it seems trivially true that they exercise the powers that they bestow with necessity. Incidentally, there seems to be no *other* account of the laws of nature that makes it plausible that these laws hold 'in every possible world'.

Dispositionalists generally go on to point out that they do not deny that it is contingent that particulars have the particular disposition-properties that they have. This seems a correct development of their theory. But it does have a consequence that may be less welcome to them. Faced with the question why particulars should continue (other things being equal) to have the same properties, and so produce the same effects, they can only say that their warrant is induction. They can offer their laws as explanations of observed regularities (15.6) but they will need further reasons for thinking that the regularities will be sustained.

The strongest argument for Dispositionalism is the fact that many of the properties with which the advanced sciences deal seem only to be characterized in terms of what powers these properties bestow on the particulars that have them. As we saw in chapter 5, the most striking examples are those vector properties which figure in physical explanations. It is difficult not to treat e.g. the velocity that a thing is said to have at an instant, as anything but a property of the object that genuinely qualifies the object at that instant, with the property at least a good candidate for a universal. Yet, if this is accepted, how is this property to be characterized except in terms of what the object is disposed to do in the immediate future, if not acted upon by some further force? It is a somewhat unappetizing feature of the Categoricalist programme that it must simply declare that there are categorical bases for such vectors. I do so declare, but we should not forget that the scientific facts may in the end declare against the Categoricalist view.

But, as already argued at greater length in 5.5, there are two arguments against the Dispositionalist view that make it, in my view, profoundly unsatisfactory. The first is that, on this account, a never manifested disposition of a particular must contain within itself, essentially, a reference or intentionality directed towards the manifestation that never occurs. Or, if it is thought that this is putting the point in too psychologistic a way, a particular must be credited with a *relation* to a non-existent outcome. A Meinongian view of this sort is very strange. The second, still more unsatisfactory, feature of the view is that, since on this view manifestations of dispositions can be no more than the acquiring of further purely dispositional properties by the particulars involved, potentiality can never pass over into genuine act, genuine non-potentiality. For these reasons, we here turn our face against a pure Dispositionalism.

It is true that there can be a Dispositionalism that is less than pure, one for instance that excepts the spatial and temporal properties and relations, allowing them to be categorical. The difficulty with this view seems to be its arbitrariness. What reason is there to except these universals? If these can be excepted, why not others? After all, will it not have been tacitly conceded that there is nothing incoherent in the notion of a categorical property?

16.3 THE TWO-SIDED THEORY AGAIN

More plausible, then, seems the more moderate position of C. B. Martin. For him every property has two sides: a categorical and a dispositional (power) side. One might speak of a Double-aspect theory, if this name was not so closely associated with a position in the mind-body debate. The two-sided view is marked off from Categoricalism by the *irreducibility* of the dispositions or powers. The Categoricalist, at any rate as I have tried to develop the position in this work, tries to play down the power side, making it supervenient upon the categorical nomic relations holding between the categorical universals.

This Weak Dispositionalism of Martin (which could also be called Weak Categoricalism!) can actually dispense with ontologically primary laws of nature, and use instead the powers associated with each different property and relation. There is a set of powers associated with each universal (or with each class of tropes under the equivalence relation of exact resemblance in the case of a trope theorist). As in the Dispositionalist theory, these powers are necessarily connected with their nomically possible manifestations. The powers associated with each universal, or equivalence class of tropes, can constitute the laws governing that property. Functional laws could doubtless be accommodated within the scheme, although the problem constituted by uninstantiated values of functional laws where there is no particular that has, say, the required mass, and so there is nothing to carry a power, has not been addressed by Martin as far as I know. The solution suggested in 16.31 could perhaps be adapted to his position.

We have seen, of course, (in 5.23, noted again in 16.2) that there is a cost for Two-sided theories, shared with Dispositionalism, though one that may be differently estimated by different philosophers. This is the strange nature of these properties, their ability to point beyond themselves, or at all events to be related to, manifestations that may never exist. The non-existent has a place in the two-sided ontology, as a term in a relation!

We should also think about something which is not present in thoroughgoing Dispositionalism: the apparent reappearance of contingency in this theory. Where circumstances are such that the powers of the particulars in some situation combine to produce a manifestation, there is a necessary connection between the possession of these powers and the manifestation. But the property has a categorical as well as a power side, on this theory. Is the power side necessitated by the categorical side, or is the link contingent only? (Or, as Peter Anstey has put it to me, is the relation between categorical and power side internal or external?) Given the categorical side, do you have to have just that power? The necessity, if there is one, seems totally opaque, a totally brute necessity. It is unlike the transparent and obvious necessity that holds in the Dispositionalist theory between property and manifestation in suitable conditions. Why believe that there is a necessity here?

Martin has made some gestures here, appealing, like Locke, to the relation between a key and its lock. See Martin, 1993, sec. VI. Keys turn locks in virtue of similarities of shape of the business end of the key, and the shape of the lock. This is because of the unyielding natures of key and lock, unyielding except for their ability to turn with each other when the key is inserted. This unyieldingness of key and lock is a power. The necessary connection between the active power of the key and the passive power of the lock may therefore be accepted. But what is there in the categorical sides of the properties involved that necessitates these powers? It is hard to see necessity here. Contingency has been expelled at one place, only to reappear at another. That being so, why not cut out the middleman and have a straight contingent connection between the categorical element or side in the cause and the categorical element or side in the effect? We arrive back at the Categorical view.

Such are the weaknesses of the Two-sided view, as I see them. But it rains on the enemy as well, as Marshal Foch observed. The powers are not *just* an idle wheel in the two-sided scheme. They make it possible to give a Realistic (but not Platonic, not transcendent) account of uninstantiated laws, something not available to the Categoricalist.

Consider, first, the case where a certain antecedent value of a functional law is omnitemporally missing. Is there a *law* which governs that determinate value? Martin can, in general at least, say yes, there is. Certain particulars really do have the power such that, if they were to instantiate that antecedent value (by happenstance they never do), then the appropriate consequent value of the function would be instantiated. Powers and laws are not different on this theory, so the uninstantiated law is a law in as good standing as an instantiated law.

What can the Categoricalist, or at any rate the Categoricalist who, like us, denies the existence of uninstantiated universals, say? One can certainly assent to a counterfactual: 'If the antecedent value were at some time instantiated, then a certain determinate law would be instantiated, yielding a certain consequent value'. But what is the truthmaker for this law? Nothing but the *determinable* functional law, linking determinable universals, state-of-affairs types. This law lives (exists) only in its instantiations. The 'uninstantiated law' is nothing but the truth of the counterfactual, and so is not fullbloodedly a law. Certainly, by comparison with the Two-sided view, a deflationary account of uninstantiated laws.

Martin and Tooley have tried to twist the knife further here with an ingenious case, Tooley, of course, in the interest of uninstantiated nomic connections of universals rather than powers. (See Martin, 1993, p. 180, and Tooley, 1977, p. 669.) Tooley states the case thus:

> Imagine a world containing ten different types of fundamental particles. Suppose further that the behavior of particles in interactions depends upon the types of the interacting particles. Considering only interactions involving two particles, there are 55 possibilities with respect to the types of the two particles. Suppose that 54 of these possible interactions have been carefully studied, with the result that 54 laws have been discovered, one for each case, which are not interrelated in any way. Suppose finally that the world is sufficiently deterministic that, given the way particles of the types X and Y are currently distributed, it is impossible for them ever to interact at any time, past, present, or future. In such a situation it would seem very reasonable to believe that there is some *underived* law dealing with the interaction of particles of types X and Y.

The sting here is that there would be a law, but the Categoricalist can find no truthmaker for the law. All parties to the dispute agree that the law must be for ever unknown. But Martin and Tooley do have truthmakers for the unknown truth about it.

What should the Categoricalist do in the face of this case? The only counterfactual available for which the Categoricalist can provide a truth-maker is that, if these particles had met, then their interaction would have been governed by some idiosyncratic law. But if so, must it not have been some definite law? Yet the Categoricalist has no truthmaker available for this definite law.

Now to reply on behalf of the Categoricalist. The first point to be made is that the case given is no more than a possible one. We are committed in this work to the proposition that fundamental ontology is not sharply cut off from natural science, and so that scientific results may properly sway metaphysical theories. If the case envisaged by Tooley were an actual case, we should have to take it very seriously. It would constitute some *evidence* for postulating unknowable because never manifested powers or else uninstantiated universals. But we can afford to take it less seriously if it is a mere possibility. One might call this the 'Cross-the-bridge-only-when-one-comes-to-it Defence'.

The second point is that it is perfectly possible for counterfactuals to be to a degree indeterminate without there being an unknown determinate truth lying inaccessibly behind the indeterminate truth. Suppose that there is an irreducibly probabilistic law that P-type states of affairs have an 0.5 chance of developing in a Q-type way, and an 0.5 chance of developing in an incompatible R-type way. Now consider a true counterfactual that if a certain token state of affairs had been, as it was not, of the P-type, then it would either have developed in a Q-type or an R-type way. Such true counterfactuals will surely be available in favourable cases. But which of those two ways would it have developed in? No one would want to say, I take it, that there is a truth of the matter here, though a truth that we cannot ever know, about which of the two types, Q and R, would have been the outcome. This shows, I take it, that counterfactual discourse is, ontologically, second-rate discourse. It permits of truth, but Excluded Middle may fail.

So it seems at least permissible to argue that in the Martin/Tooley case, if it were actual, although there would be a true counterfactual to the effect that if Xs and Ys had ever met then the resulting interaction would have been idiosyncratic, *nevertheless* there is no specific idiosyncratic interaction that is the interaction that would have occurred. No attempt is being made to prove this point, and so to *establish* Categoricalism. It is simply being argued that this way is open. I concede that it is a much less attractive resolution of the case than the robuster realism of powers or uninstantiated universals. But if we draw up a balance sheet for the opposed theories *taken as a whole,* my claim is that what is lost on the roundabouts at this particular point is more than made up on the swings. Taken as a whole, I claim, the Categoricalist theory is ahead. It is true, of course, that the choice to be made here is a relatively delicate matter, one involving difficult judgment.

It seems, in any case, that a Powers view, whether Dispositionalist or Two-sided, has a psychological advantage, but one that ought to be discounted. The point has already been made in 5.6, but is worth developing again. There may be quasi-biological advantages in thinking about the world in terms of real powers. For all animals, even human beings, even philosophers, practice is primary. Practice, for us humans at least, involves planning, and planning involves moving concepts around in our heads in an imaginative, often image-bound, way. Now it energizes our thinking, and so assists our practice, to think of things as possessed of powers. (And, of course, they *are* possessed of powers, in the sense that it is true that if they are treated in a certain way, then they are liable to react in a certain way.) It is *good*, practically good, picture-thinking to see the things as making threats and offering rewards, having a semi-anthropomorphic intentionality within themselves. This practice, metaphysically mistaken as I take it to be, helps one to reason better, especially in a practical context. This may help to explain the seductiveness of a power theory of properties. (And the seductiveness of anthropomorphism generally.)

From the standpoint of Categoricalism, it is the old business of 'projection'. Here, the Categoricalist can say, we are projecting the strong laws back into the things and properties that are governed by the laws. As a result, we, or some of us, engage in metaphysical overestimation of what it is for objects to have unmanifested powers. It is true to *say* that objects have unmanifested powers – the Categoricalist can provide truthmakers for such statements – but unmanifested powers are not as big a deal as a Powers theory imagines.

16.4 THE CAUSAL NET AND THE POWER NET

Thick particulars, the full-blooded particulars, are states of affairs. These states of affairs are a matter of the corresponding thin particulars having the totality of their non-relational properties. These particulars persist (perdure) through time (their proper parts may be interacting with each other) and they interact continuously with further particulars. The interaction is causal by definition, but the persistence of the particulars, we have argued (7.22) is also a matter of causation, with an earlier temporal part producing a later temporal part of the one particular.

The unimaginably huge number of singular causal relationships involved are all to be taken with complete ontological seriousness. They are not to be analysed away in terms of embeddings of these sequences in regularities, in terms of raisings of probabilities of the effect (though they almost always do raise that probability), or in terms of counterfactual truths. Some of these sequences are even perceivable *as causal*, perceivable in as strict a sense as anything else is perceived *as*. All these sequences are a matter of one complex state of affairs *bringing about* a further state of affairs. We can think of their totality as a huge causal net. It is thus that the world's work is done. I am here, as I conceive, in large agreement with Nancy Cartwright (1989).

Although it seems not possible to prove the matter *a priori*, it is a reasonable explanatory inference from the regularities exhibited by these singular sequences to conclude that each such sequence is, essentially, an instantiation of some fundamental law. In such a law, instantiation of a complex universal, a state-of-affairs type, the antecedent, the cause, brings about the instantiation of a certain complex universal, a state-of-affairs type, the consequent, the effect. The properties of the singular cause, the state-of-affairs type that it is a token of, are causally/nomically efficacious in producing the properties of the singular effect, the state-of-affairs type that *it* is a token of.

It is worth contrasting this position with that of Martin. He, too, postulates something that he perhaps would not describe as a net of singular causes, but which is nevertheless very close to it. But instead of laws he has the unreduced, ontologically real, powers of things, though powers having a categorical side to them. Manifestations of his powers correspond to my singular causes. (But his powers are particulars, not universals. For myself, I think he would do better to make his powers into universals and think of each universal as a unique set of powers associated with that universal. But, here in this context, that is a relatively minor dispute.)

But powers do not have to be manifested, and any particular will have innumerable powers, both passive and active, that are not manifested, at every stage of its existence. This gives Martin the conception of the world as a *power net* (personal communication) and I have taken over his phrase, but modified it to *causal* net, because my net is but a sub-net of his. Martin gives unmanifested powers a reality that I deny them. But, of course, I do not deny that there are innumerable *truths* about the might-have-been, corresponding to Martin's unmanifested powers. I believe that I have provided reasonably satisfactory truthmakers for these truths, using my strong laws.

16.5 FURTHER TOPICS

16.51 Smith's garden

Michael Tooley (1977) considers a conceivable case where a *particular*, simply as a particular, has nomic powers (pp. 686–7). The case goes as follows:

> All the fruit in Smith's garden at any time are apples. When one attempts to take an orange into the garden, it turns into an elephant. Bananas so treated become apples as they cross the boundary, while pears are resisted by a force that cannot be overcome. Cherry trees planted in the garden bear apples, or they bear nothing at all. If all these things were true, there would be a very strong case for its being a law that all the fruit in Smith's garden are apples. And this would be no way undermined if it were found that no other gardens, however similar to Smith's in all other respects, exhibited behavior of the sort just described.

Tooley argues that the case shows that we might be forced to accept laws that bestowed nomic power on particulars rather than universals. I agree. The conception of universals as emasculated or unsaturated, Fregean, states of affairs, what I have called in this work state-of-affairs types, is helpful here. We can think of the case Tooley envisages as one where the antecedent condition of the law plugs in a particular, though one having certain universal properties – fruit in *Smith's* garden – creating a state-of-affairs type that is not purely universal. It does seem that such a bastard state-of-affairs type might have unique causal power. (We may call such a type a quasi-universal.)

Tooley's point, that laws might involve an irreducible element of particularity, seems to apply to all theories of laws. A Regularity theorist can hardly deny the possibility of such laws. Neither can a Necessitarian. Contemporary Necessitarianism about laws leans to a Dispositionalist theory of properties. Given such a theory, the essence, or part of the essence in Two-sided theories, lies in the effect an instantiated property has in suitable circumstances. A property is a power. But if Tooley's case is good at all, a certain particular's having that power might constitute a quasi-universal, with *the fact that it is that particular particular* an essential component for the exercise of the power.

Why is this case important? It is important because the case raises once again the inductive problem. The regularities in the world, as we experience them, seem to link universals with universals. But may we not be living in a giant Smith's garden, so that our laws are no better than local laws, laws whose scope embraces no more than a limited spatiotemporal area? Laws may take some such form as:

$$\text{(1) F \& Spacetime}_1 \rightarrow \text{G}$$
$$\text{(2) F \& Spacetime}_2 \rightarrow \text{H.}$$

The view that laws of nature are relations between universals shows promise of easing the problem of induction. It does this by the suggestion that the existence of such relations are abductive or 'best explanation' inferences from observed regularities. Tooley's case, though, tends to reinstate sceptical doubts about the inference by pointing to a less welcome alternative explanation.

16.52 Can relations between universals change?

A closely connected point, one often raised in discussion, is this. Why cannot a law of nature, if conceived of as the holding of a contingent relation between categorical universals, change? Why may it not be that F has the nomic relation G at one time, but later, since the connection is contingent, this relation lapses, perhaps being succeeded by F's being related to H?

I used to argue that no such change is possible, that although the relation is contingent, nevertheless 'within the one world' the nomic relations between two universals cannot change. Suppose that at a certain time and place, an F brings forth a G, in virtue of these properties. (For simplicity, let the probability be strictly 1.) 'In another world, it might have been different.' But, I thought, given that all other causally relevant factors are the same, *in this world* another F must also produce a G. The *intra*-world nomic relations between universals cannot change.

David Lewis has an argument, considered in 7.21, which, if sound, seems to strengthen this position. Lewis argued that two particulars that have strict identity over time (classical atoms, perhaps) cannot change their relations to each other over time, because then the two particulars would both have and would lack some relation, which would be self-contradictory. If Lewis' argument is correct, then it seems that it will have to apply also to genuinely, ontologically, dyadic relations holding between two universals. The thesis of intra-world stability is upheld.

Ironically, though, this led me away from my original upholding of intra-world stability. For it was argued against Lewis in 7.21 that two strictly identical atoms, atoms that lack temporal parts, although they could not change their own nature over time, *could* change their spatial relations over time. The two atoms, for instance, might be related by distance d_1 at t_1 but related by d_2 at t_2. (The argument, it may be remembered, depended on introducing states of affairs, entities that Lewis thinks he has reason to bar.) So why should not a universal, also, lose or gain nomic relations to another universal over time?

I am not perfectly certain that the case of the atoms and the case of the universals are really parallel. One interesting consideration is that the places and times occupied by unchangeable entities would appear to be *accidental* properties of the entities. It is these places and times that mediate the different spatial relations of the unchangeable atoms at different times. Strictly, perhaps, it is the places and times that are different and so differently related to each other. No such mediation is present in the case of the nomically connected universals. Although the relations are external, they depend on the universals involved alone. Perhaps external relations of this second sort, and only this sort, are subject to the Lewis argument. Nice as it would be for me, though, I do not have enough confidence in this suggestion to base my argument upon it.

The following appears clear enough, though. (1) If Lewis' argument succeeds wholly, then a contingent connection of universals is as little subject to change as a necessary connection of universals. On the other hand, my contention in chapter 7 that particulars that are strictly identical through time are at least possible, also becomes very dubious. That latter contention, though, is not one in which I have a great investment.

(2) Suppose, however, that the Lewis argument fails wholly. (As I tend to think.) It seems that I have to allow that contingent relations between universals can change. (As a small consolation prize, my contention that such things as atoms that are strictly identical through time are at least possible, can be upheld.)

But now it seems that both Regularity theorists and Necessitarians may triumph. Regularity theorists can argue that if relations between universals are subject to change, then inductive scepticism is as much a problem for Contingency theorists as it is for them. Necessitarians can be even more triumphant. Necessary relations between universals cannot change. So Necessitarians seem to have epistemic advantage over both of the other parties to the dispute.

It is convenient at this point to turn to the subject of laws and counterfactuals. We will be led to substantially the same issue as the question whether the laws can change.

16.53 Contingent laws and counterfactuals

True law-statements are thought to 'sustain counterfactuals' in a way that merely accidental generalizations do not. This property of law-statements is regularly made a reproach to Regularity theories. Let us begin by seeing why. Using the doctrine of the truthmaker, the difficulty can be brought out with special clarity. Suppose that we have a true statement of law, which for simplicity can be a deterministic law: it is a law that an F must be a G. What is the truthmaker for this truth, given a Regularity theory? It will be a *molecular* state of affairs, having the form (F*a* & G*a*) & (F*b* & G*b*) . . . together with the higher-order state of affairs that this conjunction covers *all* the Fs. Now suppose that we consider *c* which is not F and (truly) assert of it that if it had been F, then it would have been G. This will not change the *meaning* of the statement that all Fs are Gs. But it will change its *truthmaker*. When it is assumed for the sake of argument that *c* is F, then the truthmaker is enlarged in the imagination to include the states of affairs F*c* and G*c*. Now the problem emerges. Granted that F*c* has been added in imagination, what justification is there for adding G*c* also? The actual law, for a Regularity theorist, is just the original molecular state of affairs. If the extension of F is changed, we need some argument for thinking that the extension of G will change to keep step.

The force of the argument may best be appreciated by contrasting the situation where the law is taken to be a relationship between universals, between state-of-affairs types. The law, a single entity, a higher-order state of affairs, remains exactly the same, strictly identical, regardless of the number of its instantiations. So when it is supposed that *c* is F, the truthmaker for the law-statement has not changed. The extension of the law to the new case requires no justification. (This, incidentally, is an advantage that universals here have over the tropes. A trope theorist would have to enlarge the truthmaker.)

Returning to the Regularity theory, the difficulty about counterfactuals has been appreciated by one Regularity theorist, J. L. Mackie. In his 1966, he suggested a solution. His idea was that when we contemplate the imaginary case of *c* being F, what we do is to apply inductive reasoning to the pretended F. Other Fs have all turned out to be Gs. So we have inductive warrant for thinking that this imagined F will also be a G. That is why we hold the counterfactual true. Criticism of this ingenious attempt to meet the difficulty will be found in Armstrong, 1983, 4.4. Mackie notes that in any case his idea depends upon there being a solution to the Problem of Induction compatible with a Regularity theory of law. It is dubious whether there is such a solution. See Armstrong, 1983, 4.5.

But is a *contingent* connection between universals enough to solve the problem of sustaining counterfactuals? Some philosophers have doubted it. Martin Tweedale (1984) argues that if laws are contingent relations between universals, then:

> How could such a relationship possibly sustain the counterfactual implications of laws of nature? Since it is contingent and totally unaccounted for, there is nothing to say whether it would hold, or not, if the related universals existed in circumstances in any way different from the actual ones. We no longer have a genuine solution to the difficulties besetting the Humean view.
>
> (pp. 185–6)

It will be seen that the difficulty Tweedale is raising is dependent on the premiss that contingent relations between universals can change over time. If such change is allowed, and we *have* allowed it, what reply can be made to Tweedale?

I do concede that the Necessitarian theory has an advantage over the Contingency theory here. All I can plead is that, when *all* advantages and disadvantages of the two theories are weighed, the balance tips towards the Contingency view. See in particular the difficulties raised for Dispositionalist and Two-sided theories of properties in chapter 5 and in this chapter. Yet without such accounts of properties, Necessitarianism is not very plausible. In the rest of this section two arguments will be advanced. (1) The Contingency view (along with the Necessitarian view) has real epistemic advantages over the Regularity theory. (2) Tweedale has exaggerated the epistemic advantages of the Necessitarian over the Contingency view.

First, then, the advantages of strong theories of law over Regularity theories. Go back to an ontological point already made. Given strong laws, enlarging the extension of the law does not in any way change the truthmaker for a true law-statement. Whether it has one instantiation or many, the law itself is the same. It is an atomic state of affairs. The law will therefore be the truthmaker both for the law-statement and certain counterfactuals. In a Regularity theory, however, those counterfactuals demand an imagined extension of the molecular truthmaker.

This has epistemological consequences. For the Regularity theory the inference involved in such a counterfactual involves an extra step: that the law can be legitimately extended to this new case. Given the 'loose and separate' world of the Regularity theorist, it is not clear that this extension is legitimate. More generally, why, given an observed regular succession, should there be any good reason to believe that this regularity will continue?

Upholders of strong laws have epistemic advantage here. They can appeal to simplicity here *in a way that a Regularity theorist cannot.* Consider this situation. The observed Fs are all Gs. Our explanatory hypothesis is that F-ness actually produced the G-ness of the things that are F in those particular cases. (Perhaps it is backed up by experiment, the application of such canons as Mill's methods of Agreement and Difference.) If F-ness produced G-ness, then F-ness has the power to produce G-ness. It may only have this power within a certain spatiotemporal area. It may at some point lose this power. It may turn out to have the power to produce other effects also. But it did have this power at a certain point. Is it not an attractive and simple hypothesis that it will continue to have this power at all times and places? (Power here, of course, does not have to be understood according to the Dispositionalist model.) This justification may not be quite all one might hope for, but it seems to have real value. Nothing comparable is available to Regularity theorists, because they have such a deflationary view of singular causation.

It is this same point that mitigates the force of the epistemological point made by Tweedale against the Contingency theory. We appear to observe, or have other good reason to think, that on certain occasions, Fs actually produced Gs, and that there is a real connection, in those cases, between F-ness and G-ness. The universal F has that power. It is true, though, because this is the Contingency theory, that F may come to lack that power in other situations. That debt must be paid to inductive scepticism.

But the Necessitarian theory also has at least one debt to pay, and I think it is a debt of equal size. Grant that in the observed cases property F produced G, and that by necessity. In future cases, might it not produce something else instead of G, and that by necessity too? Who is to say that the property F is not the power to produce one out of a whole range of effects, of which G is only one of the possibilities, or even sometimes no effects at all? What the Necessitarian needs to bar this, is that F must produce G and can produce nothing else. That will support the counterfactual. But, again, if the Contingency theorist is allowed a law that F produces G and produces nothing else, the counterfactual seems equally supported. So I suggest that Tweedale's argument has much less power than he claims for it.

Another way that the Contingency theorist may argue (perhaps it is the same way at bottom) is this. In considering the truth values of counterfactuals that are sustained by causal/nomic knowledge and belief, we keep important circumstances fixed. In Lewis' terminology, we go to near worlds. Laws of nature, if considered as contingent relations between universals, are important and it is easy and natural to keep them fixed. So we do so in our counterfactual reasoning.

17

The unity of the world

This essay has upheld many of the central theses of the Logical Atomist programme, although the existence of *atoms*, simples, whether particulars or universals, is held to be a question for science rather than metaphysics, and one that we should at present remain agnostic about. The world divides, as Wittgenstein wrote, but it may divide *ad infinitum*, and there be no terminus even at infinity.

Logical Atomism owed a great deal to Hume, to his deflationary doctrine (or alleged doctrine as some have it) of causation as regular succession, and, more centrally, to the core Humean view that in metaphysics there are no necessary connections between distinct existences. We have rejected the Regularity theory, re-instating singular causation, real bringing about in the singular case. But we have accepted the Distinct Existences principle with no more than a clarificatory, though very important, amendment: there are no necessary connections between *wholly* distinct existences.

The world divides, we have maintained, into contingent states of affairs, whose constituents are (thin) particulars and universals, the latter comprising properties and relations. But a philosophy that divides the world must make provision for its unity. What provision have we made?

(1) The world is a mereological unity, a mereological whole embracing every part and constituent of the world. This is a 'unity' that does not unify. It is true that the parts supervene, are entailed by, the whole. But equally the whole supervenes on the sum of the parts, and is nothing more than these parts. Those who hold that mereological unity is the only unity to be found in the world are really maintaining that the world has no unity. This is an extreme, and implausible, metaphysical Pluralism. Hume has been traditionally accused of such a pluralism. David Lewis is perhaps a modern instance.

(2) Every particular is linked to every other particular, either directly or recursively, by some external relation. The world is a relational net. This

is not a necessary truth. *Contra* Lewis, in particular, there could be 'island universes' (to adapt the Kant-Hubble term for the galaxies) in a world where these islands stood in no external relation to each other. (For Lewis, the two islands would be merely possible relative to each other.)

Thus, consider a small world which contains just two wholly distinct atomic particulars, each having just one atomic non-relational property (F*a* & G*b*), and where they are related by just one external relation R. If *a*R*b* is a contingent state of affairs, then presumably it might not have existed in that world, nor is there any necessity that some other external relation has to replace this relation. The two states of affairs F*a* and G*b* would then have been island universes in the one world.

Not only are island universes possible, but it is also difficult to see how one can be certain that our world does not contain such islands. At the same time, though, it is also difficult to see what positive evidence there could be *for* the existence of islands. We appear to have good pragmatic grounds, if nothing else, for assuming that everything that exists (past, present, future) is 'reachable' from *here* via a chain of external relations.

(2.1) We can be more specific. It is plausible that the world has (a) a spatiotemporal unity; (b) a causal unity. First, considering just the spatiotemporal relations, it is plausible that from any first-order spatiotemporal particular, there is a 'path' of fundamental spatiotemporal relations that links the original particular to every other, recursively at least. This is part of the hypothesis of Naturalism, the further hypothesis needed to yield a full Naturalism being that this linking embraces *every* first-order particular, because all particulars are spatiotemporal. It is to be noted that this spatiotemporal linking would be satisfied by a spacetime of very eccentric 'shape', quite different from the traditional four-dimensional continuum. For instance it would be satisfied by a world that was continually splitting into different 'worlds' which from that point onwards had no further spatiotemporal or other external relation. From our point of view, this is not a 'many *worlds*' hypothesis. (For Lewis also, these split paths would be 'world-mates'.)

(2.2) We have argued for the ontological reality of singular causation, where the relation holds between first-order states of affairs. This yields a further dimension of unification. It is plausible that from any state of affairs there is a chain of causal relations, either from cause to effect, or from effect to cause, that leads recursively to any other first-order state of affairs. C. B. Martin has spoken of the world as a 'power net'. Without underwriting a doctrine of irreducible powers, we may still hypothesize that the world is a *causal* net.

A strong, and attractive, form of this hypothesis would be that (i) Every state of affairs has a cause. (This would be compatible with the laws, if any, governing these singular causal relations being probabilistic only.) (ii) Every state of affairs has an effect. No state of affairs is epiphenomenal. It may well be a true nomic conditional that a simple or relatively simple state of affairs not in causal relation to any other state of affairs, would even so give rise to an exactly resembling state of affairs involving further temporal parts of the particulars involved. (See Russell, who calls this a generalized form of Newton's First Law, 1948, p. 475.) It may be noted that the strong hypothesis formed by the conjunction of (i) and (ii) just above would be compatible with a finite world provided that the causal relation comes in a circle. That such a causal loop is possible has been suggested in chapter 9. But I know of no reason to think that this possibility is more than a *mere* possibility.

(3) The Aristotelian Realism about universals defended in this work brings universals, properties and relations, within states of affairs. The states of affairs, organized as they are organized, in turn constitute the whole of reality (spacetime if the thesis of Naturalism is accepted). Given these universals, the world is unified in a way that it is not unified in a Nominalist ontology. Identities run across the states of affairs. These identities are somewhat mysterious because, as we have noted, they seem to be compatible with two states of affairs that involve these identities being wholly distinct in the sense that it is possible for either state of affairs to exist in the absence of the other. If *a* and *b* are wholly distinct particulars, the monadic states of affairs of *a's being F* and *b's being F* are wholly distinct in the sense of being independent, yet they have a common constituent. The same holds for *a's being F* and *a's being* G for suitable (wholly distinct) F and G.

I do not really understand this situation. It is perhaps connected with 'the victory of particularity' (8.4), the fact that a state of affairs whose sole constituents are first-order particulars and first-order universals is, because it is unrepeatable, a first-order particular. But while a state of affairs is a particular, a nugget of being, something capable of independent existence, in that sense a substance, it is not so clear why it lacks partial identity with another state of affairs having common constituents. (Is this a reason that lies behind Scotus' doctrine of the 'contraction' of his 'common natures' when such a nature is instantiated by a particular? See, for instance, Boler, 1963.)

What does seem plausible to say is that two genuinely atomic states of affairs are, because they are impenetrable by mereology, mereologically wholly distinct. If that is so, then the Distinctness principle can be upheld for *mereologically* wholly distinct existences. This may be all that is needed.

(4) Do totality states of affairs, and in particular the grand totality state of affairs, provide unity? We have seen that, in the absence of totality states of affairs, mere conjunctions of states of affairs do not provide for any setting of limits. Suppose, for instance, we are given all the properties of a particular thing. That conjunction of states of affairs, we have argued, is not a sufficient truthmaker for the truth that the conjunction contains *all* the properties of the thing. Since it is always possible that the thing has further properties, we need a further state of affairs as truthmaker for this truth. We need the state of affairs that there are *no more* of these properties, that what we have is the *totality* of these properties.

We can actually perceive totalities, though the perception will always involve some theory. It can be perceived that X, Y, and Z are the only persons in the room at the present time. Allness is thus a quasi-empirical concept. A counterfactual will often be true: if there had been others in the room, then we would have perceived them. Like all higher-order states of affairs, totality states of affairs do not supervene. The lower-order states of affairs do not entail the totality states of affairs. But the totality states of affairs do entail the existence of the states of affairs, or whatever, that they total, and so limit them. There are no more of that sort of thing, say persons now in the room, or whatever. *Given the totality state of affairs*, Independence fails for the entities limited.

Totality states of affairs may therefore be said, in some weak sense, to unify the lower-order states of affairs that they set a limit to. But it is a weak sense only because what is thus 'unified' may not be unified in any other way. A number of 'island universes' are not conspicuously unified by being the totality of such islands!

(5) With the introduction of laws of nature as connections between universals, connections between state-of-affairs types as we have presented the matter, a major source of unification is introduced. While universals give identities of a sort across wholly distinct particulars, *connections* between universals introduce linkings between states of affairs so that state-of-affairs types are welded together. Given the instantiation of a certain state-of-affairs type, instantiation of a further state-of-affairs type is mandated or probabilified. Furthermore, laws at the level of determinate universals are regularly subsumable under connections of determinable universals,

connections which take a functional form. In this way, first-level laws are subsumable under a relatively small number of functional laws. In the physicalist 'dream of a final theory' (Weinberg, 1993) a single unified equation is the sole fundamental law. It is laws above anything else that give the world its unity. The causal net is most deeply understood as a *nomic* net. From the same causes, the same effects flow.

(6) I have left to the last the unification of (thin) particulars and universals that is found in atomic or relatively atomic states of affairs. This cross-categorial unity is the most puzzling unity of all (no doubt because it is cross-categorial). The puzzle is about the status of the truth, as I take it to be, that particulars and universals are found only as constituents of states of affairs. (We consider here only first-order states of affairs. That thin particulars instantiate the particular universals that they do instantiate is, of course, contingent.) There are three hypotheses about this connection, none of which I find to be quite satisfactory. (1) It is a contingent connection; (2) It is a necessary connection; (3) It is neither contingent nor necessary. Consider these hypotheses in turn.

If the connection is a contingent one, then it is possible for there to be (i) bare particulars, particulars that have neither properties nor relations and (ii) uninstantiated universals, properties and relations that are not properties or relations of anything. It is not at all obvious that these are real possibilities. Could a particular be of no sort or kind? Again, if it is accepted that universals are unsaturated entities, hungry, as it were, for a certain number of particulars; and if it is also accepted that universals are ways particulars are or ways particulars stand to each other, it is at least rather plausible that uninstantiated universals are impossible. The case against contingency is not overwhelming, but it is pretty strong.

So is the relation between particulars and universals a necessary one? The contingency of states of affairs cannot be abandoned, I think. But it is not implausible to argue that it is necessary that a particular have some non-relational property (or just possibly some property, non-relational or relational), although just what that property is, is not necessary. Similarly, it would be necessary that every universal be instantiated, although not necessary that it be instantiated by the particular particulars it is actually instantiated by.

My problem with this position is that, if there are necessities here, there may be no truthmaker for the necessary truths involved except in the structure of the world. The necessity seems like a necessity *in re*. The only truthmaker that is available is the nature or constituting principle of particulars (*qua* particulars) *plus* the nature or constituting principle of universals (*qua* universals). But suppose that we follow the line taken in this essay, which has linked necessity with identity. Then we shall have to say that particulars and universals are not 'distinct existences' but that their identities are in some way entangled with each other. This does not violate Independence, which has been put forward as a thesis about states of affairs, as opposed to their constituents. Furthermore, the truly bare particular and the uninstantiated universal, be it property or relation, are strange creatures, as has been argued in the course of the essay. Nevertheless, I remain distinctly uneasy about this second horn of the trilemma.

As between the two views so far considered, I certainly lean to the necessitarian hypothesis. But there is a third position that demands consideration. It may be that, although most truths are either necessary or contingent, the ultimate metaphysical truths are neither necessary nor contingent. The thought behind this view is that the necessary/contingent distinction is drawn *within the theory of modality*. What, then, is the status of the truths that constitute this theory?

A Combinatorialist theory of possibility, which we have argued for, can be developed in two ways, a less and a more ambitious one. The less ambitious view sees Combinatorial principles as doing no more than set out the modal structure that reality has, without any reductive account of what possibility and necessity are. Such an account, valuable as it might be, would be compatible with recognizing that we need necessary states of affairs alongside contingent states of affairs in giving an account of the world.

The more ambitious view, which has been espoused in this work, even if with an appreciation of the difficulties that it faces, sees combinatorial principles as actually rendering the essence of possibility. Suppose this more ambitious view to be correct. What then of the combinatorial principles themselves? What modal status do they have? Can they themselves be necessary?

If they are necessary, what is their truthmaker? If we are trying to avoid falling back upon a modal structure of reality, what answer can we find to this question? The only answer available would seem to be that their truthmaker is nothing more than our concepts of necessity and possibility, properly understood. It is hard to feel much confidence in this answer.

So perhaps we should reject the view that *every* truth is either necessary or contingent. Perhaps the truths that lie at the basis of the theory of modality are simply true. We still have to face the problem of their truthmaker. I can only suggest that the truthmaker is the fundamental (but nonmodal!) structure of the world. Perhaps it can be argued that this structure is some sort of law of the world. If *being a state of affairs* can be taken to be an overarching (determinable) universal, then the law will govern this universal. But the corresponding law-statement can be neither a necessary nor a contingent truth. We might interpret the traditional doctrine of the categories as the laws of states of affairs *qua* states of affairs. We might be able to link this up with questions of law and causality. Perhaps it is a fundamental law governing the universal *being a state of affairs* that, for instance, all states of affairs have causes and effects. Whether such lines of thought can be plausibly developed, I do not know.

References

[ ] indicates date of first publication, prefix *c.* (*circa*) indicates estimated date

Anderson, John, 1962, *Studies in Empirical Philosophy*, Sydney: Angus and Robertson.

Anscombe, G. E. M., 1971, *Causality and Determination*, Cambridge: Cambridge University Press. Reprinted in *Causation and Conditionals*, ed. Ernest Sosa, Oxford: Oxford University Press, 1975.

Aristotle, 1941, *The Basic Works of Aristotle*, ed. Richard McKeon, New York: Random House.

Armstrong, D. M., 1968a, *A Materialist Theory of the Mind*, London: Routledge and Kegan Paul.

1968b, 'The Headless Woman Illusion and the Defence of Materialism', *Analysis*, 29, 48–9.

1973, *Belief, Truth and Knowledge*, Cambridge: Cambridge University Press.

1978a, *Nominalism and Realism* (Vol. 1 of *Universals and Scientific Realism*), Cambridge: Cambridge University Press.

1978b, *A Theory of Universals* (Vol. 2 of *Universals and Scientific Realism*), Cambridge: Cambridge University Press.

1980, 'Identity through Time', in *Time and Cause: Essays Presented to Richard Taylor*, ed. Peter van Inwagen, Dordrecht: Reidel, 67–78.

1983, *What is a Law of Nature?*, Cambridge: Cambridge University Press.

1986, 'In Defence of Structural Universals', *Australasian Journal of Philosophy*, 64, 85–8.

1988a, 'Are Quantities Relations?: A Reply to Bigelow and Pargetter', *Philosophical Studies*, 54, 305–16.

1988b, 'Reply to Van Fraassen', *Australasian Journal of Philosophy*, 66, 224–9.

1989a, *Universals: An Opinionated Introduction*, Boulder, Colorado: Westview Press.

1989b, *A Combinatorial Theory of Possibility*, Cambridge: Cambridge University Press.

1989c, 'C. B. Martin, Counterfactuals, Causality, and Conditionals', in *Cause, Mind, and Reality*, ed. John Heil, Dordrecht: Kluwer Academic Publishers.

1991a, 'Classes are States of Affairs', *Mind*, 100, 189–200.

1991b, 'What makes Induction Rational?', *Dialogue* (Canada), 30, 503–11.

1995, 'Reply to Rosen', *Australasian Journal of Philosophy*, 73, 626–8.

Austin, J. L., 1950, 'Truth', *Proceedings of the Aristotelian Society*, Supp. vol. 24, 111–28.

Bacon, John, 1995, *Universals and Property Instances: The Alphabet of Being*, Aristotelian Society Monograph, Vol.15, Oxford: Blackwell.

Bacon, John; Campbell, Keith; and Reinhardt, Lloyd (eds.), 1993, *Ontology, Causality and Mind*, Cambridge: Cambridge University Press.

Bergmann, Gustav, 1967, *Realism: A Critique of Brentano and Meinong*, Madison: The University of Wisconsin Press.

Berkeley, George, 1965 [1713], 'Three Dialogues Between Hylas and Philonous', in *Berkeley's Philosophical Writings*, ed. D. M. Armstrong, New York: Collier Books.

Bigelow, John; Ellis, Brian; and Lierse, Caroline, 1992, 'The World as One of a Kind: Natural Necessity and Laws of Nature', *British Journal for the Philosophy of Science*, 43, 371–88.

Bigelow, John and Pargetter, Robert, 1988, 'Quantities', *Philosophical Studies*, 54, 287–304.

1990, *Science and Necessity*, Cambridge: Cambridge University Press.

Black, Max, 1952, 'The Identity of Indiscernibles', *Mind*, 61, 153–4, reprinted with additional notes in *Problems of Analysis*, by Max Black, London: Routledge and Kegan Paul, 1954.

Boler, J. F., 1963, *Charles Peirce and Scholastic Realism*, Seattle: University of Washington Press.

Bradley, F. H., 1893, 'On Professor James' Doctrine of Simple Resemblance', *Mind*, 2, 83–8, 366–9, and 509–10.

Bradley, Raymond, 1992, *The Nature of all Being: A Study of Wittgenstein's Modal Atomism*, New York: Oxford University Press.

Broad, C. D., 1935, 'Mechanical and Teleological Causation', *Proceedings of the Aristotelian Society*, Supp. Vol. 14, reprinted in *Induction, Probability and Causation*, by C. D. Broad, Dordrecht: Reidel, 1968.

Burnheim, John, *c.* 1968, 'Intentionality and Materialism', unpublished paper given to the Department of Philosophy, Sydney University.

Butler, Joseph, 1906 [1736], *The Analogy of Religion*, London: J. M. Dent (Everyman).

Campbell, Keith, 1991, *Abstract Particulars*, Oxford: Blackwell.

1994, 'Selective Realism in the Philosophy of Physics', *The Monist*, 77, 27–44.

Carnap, Rudolf, 1962, *Logical Foundations of Probability*, Chicago: University of Chicago Press.

Cartwright, Nancy, 1989, *Nature's Capacities and their Measurement*, Oxford: Clarendon Press.

Castañeda, Hector-Neri, 1975, 'Identity and Sameness', *Philosophia*, 5, 121–50.

Davidson, Donald, 1975 [1967], 'Causal Relations', *Journal of Philosophy*, 64, 691–703. Reprinted in *Causation and Conditionals*, ed. Ernest Sosa, Oxford: Oxford University Press, 1975.

Ellis, Brian and Lierse, Caroline, 1994, 'Dispositional Essentialism', *Australasian Journal of Philosophy*, 72, 27–45.

Fahrnkopf, Robert, 1988, *Wittgenstein on Universals*, New York: Peter Lang.

Fair, David, 1979, 'Causation and the Flow of Energy', *Erkenntnis*, 14, 219–50.
Fales, Evan, 1990, *Causation and Universals*, London and New York: Routledge.
Feinberg, Gerald, 1966, 'Physics and the Thales Problem', *Journal of Philosophy*, 66, 5–13.
Fine, Kit, 1982, 'First-Order Modal Theories III – Facts', *Synthese*, 53, 43–122.
1994, 'Essence and Modality', *Philosophical Perspectives*, 8, (*Logic and Language*), 1–16.
Forrest, Peter, 1993, 'Just like Quarks? The Status of Repeatables', in *Ontology, Causality and Mind*, ed. John Bacon, Keith Campbell and Lloyd Reinhardt, Cambridge: Cambridge University Press.
Forrest, Peter and Armstrong, D. M., 1987, 'The Nature of Number', *Philosophical Papers*, 16, 165–86.
Foster, John, 1979, 'In *Self*-defence' in *Perception and Identity*, ed. G. F. Macdonald, London: Macmillan.
1983, 'Induction, Explanation and Natural Necessity', *Proceedings of the Aristotelian Society*, 83, 87–101.
Frege, G., 1950 [1884], *The Foundations of Arithmetic*, trans. J. L. Austin, Oxford: Blackwell.
Friedman, Michael, 1974, 'Explanation and Scientific Understanding', *Journal of Philosophy*, 71, 5–19.
Gasking, D. A. T., 1949, 'Anderson and the Tractatus Logico-Philosophicus', *Australasian Journal of Philosophy*, 27, 1–26.
Geach, Peter T., 1980 [1962], *Reference and Generality*, Ithaca and London: Cornell University Press.
Gödel, Kurt, 1990 [1949], 'An Example of a new Type of Cosmological Solutions of Einstein's Field Equations of Gravitation', in Kurt Gödel's *Collected Works*, Vol.II, ed. Solomon Feferman, New York: Oxford University Press, 190–8.
Goldman, Alvin, 1993, 'The Psychology of Folk Psychology', *Behavioral and Brain Sciences*, 16, 15–28.
Goldstein, Laurence, 1983, 'Scientific Scotism – The Emperor's New Trousers or has Armstrong made some Real Strides?', *Australasian Journal of Philosophy*, 61, 40–57.
Goodman, Nelson, 1958, 'On Relations that Generate', *Philosophical Studies*, 9, 55–6.
1966, *The Structure of Appearance*, (2nd edn.), Indianapolis: Bobbs-Merrill.
1964 [1956], 'A World of Individuals' in *Philosophy of Mathematics*, ed. Paul Benaceraff and Hilary Putnam, Oxford: Basil Blackwell.
Grandy, Richard E., 1976, 'Anadic Logic and English', *Synthese*, 32, 395–402.
Grossmann, Reinhardt, 1983, *The Categorial Structure of the World*, Bloomington, Indiana: Indiana University Press.
1992, *The Existence of the World*, London and New York: Routledge.
Guth, Alan and Steinhardt, Paul, 1989, 'The Inflationary Universe', in *The New Physics* , ed. Paul Davies, Cambridge: Cambridge University Press.
Harman, Gilbert, 1965, 'The Inference to the Best Explanation', *Philosophical Review*, 74, 88–95.

Heathcote, Adrian and Armstrong, D. M., 1991, 'Causes and Laws', *Noûs*, 25, 63–73.

Hochberg, Herbert, *c.* 1964, 'Things and Qualities', in *Metaphysics and Explanation*, ed. W. H. Capitan and D. D. Merrill, University of Pittsburgh Press.

Hume, David, 1888 [1739], *A Treatise of Human Nature*, ed. L. A. Selby-Bigge, Oxford: Clarendon Press.

1902 [1751], *An Enquiry concerning the Principles of Morals*, ed. L. A. Selby-Bigge, Oxford: Clarendon Press.

Jackson, Frank, 1977, 'Statements about Universals', *Mind*, 86, 427–9.

James, William, 1943 [1912], *Radical Empiricism and A Pluralistic Universe*, New York: Longmans, Green and Co.

Johnson, W. E., 1964 [1921, 1924], *Logic: Part 1, 3*, New York: Dover Publications.

Kant, Immanuel, 1950 [1787], *Critique of Pure Reason*, trans. Norman Kemp Smith, London: Macmillan.

Kitcher, Philip, 1981, 'Explanatory Unification', *Philosophy of Science*, 48, 507–31.

Kripke, Saul, 1979, 'Identity Through Time', presented at the Conference of The American Philosophical Association, Eastern Division, and elsewhere.

Küng, Guido, 1967, *Ontology and the Logistic Analysis of Language*, trans. E. C. Mays, Dordrecht: Reidel.

Leibniz, G. W., 1953 [1685–6], *Discourse on Metaphysics*, trans. Peter G. Lucas and Leslie Grint, Manchester: The University Press.

Leonard, Henry S. and Goodman, Nelson, 1940, 'The Calculus of Individuals and its uses', *Journal of Symbolic Logic*, 5, 45–55.

Leslie, John, 1989, *Universes*, London and New York: Routledge.

Lewis, David, 1983a, 'Survival and Identity', in *Philosophical Papers*, Vol. 1, by David Lewis, New York: Oxford University Press, 55–77.

1983b, 'New Work for a Theory of Universals', *Australasian Journal of Philosophy*, 61, 343–77.

1986a, 'Against. Structural Universals', *Australasian Journal of Philosophy*, 62, 25–46.

1986b, *On the Plurality of Worlds*, Oxford: Blackwell.

1986c, *Philosophical Papers*, Vol.II, Oxford: Blackwell.

1986d, 'A Comment on Armstrong and Forrest', *Australasian Journal of Philosophy*, 64, 92–3.

1991, *Parts of Classes*, Oxford: Blackwell.

1993, 'Many, but Almost One', in *Ontology, Causality and Mind*, ed. John Bacon, Keith Campbell and Lloyd Reinhardt, Cambridge: Cambridge University Press.

Linde, Andrei, 1994, 'The Self-Reproducing Inflationary Universe', *Scientific American*, 271 No.5, 32–9.

Locke, John, 1975, *Essay concerning Human Understanding*, ed. Peter Nidditch, Oxford: Oxford University Press.

Mackie, J. L., 1962, 'Counterfactuals and Causal Laws', in *Analytical Philosophy: First Series*, ed. R. J. Butler, Oxford: Basil Blackwell.

1978, 'Dispositions, Grounds, and Causes', in *Dispositions*, ed. Raimo Tuomela, Dordrecht: D. Reidel. Also published in *Synthese*, 34, 361–70, 1977.

Martin, C. B., 1980, 'Substance Substantiated', *Australasian Journal of Philosophy*, 58, 3–10.

1984, 'Anti-Realism and the World's Undoing', *Pacific Philosophical Quarterly*, 65, 3–20.

1993, 'Power for Realists', in *Ontology, Causality and Mind*, ed. John Bacon, Keith Campbell, and Lloyd Reinhardt, Cambridge: Cambridge University Press.

1994, 'Dispositions and Conditionals', *Philosophical Quarterly*, 44, 1–8.

Martin, C. B. and Pfeifer, K., 1986, 'Intentionality and the Non-psychological', *Philosophy and Phenomenological Research*, 46, 531–54.

Mellor, D. H., 1974, 'In Defence of Dispositions', *Philosophical Review*, 83, 157–81. Reprinted in *Matters of Metaphysics*, by D. H. Mellor, Cambridge: Cambridge University Press, ch. 6.

Menzies, Peter, 1993, 'Laws of Nature, Modality and Humean Supervenience', in *Ontology, Causality and Mind*, ed. John Bacon, Keith Campbell and Lloyd Reinhardt, Cambridge: Cambridge University Press.

Michell, Joel, 1993, 'Numbers, Ratios and Structural Relations', *Australasian Journal of Philosophy*, 71, 325–32.

1994, 'Numbers as Quantitative Relations and the Traditional Theory of Measurement', *British Journal for the Philosophy of Science*, 45, 389–406.

Michotte, A., 1963 [1946], *The Perception of Causality*, trans. T. R. and Elaine Miles, London: Methuen.

Newman, Andrew, 1992, *The Physical Basis of Predication*, Cambridge: Cambridge University Press.

Newton, Isaac, 1769, *Universal Arithmetic*.

Oddie, Graham, 1982, 'Armstrong on the Eleatic Principle and Abstract Entities', *Philosophical Studies*, 41, 285–95.

Oliver, Alex, 1992, 'The Metaphysics of Singletons', *Mind* , 101, 129–40.

Olson, Kenneth R., 1987, *An Essay on Facts*, Stanford: CSLI.

Pap, Arthur, 1959, 'Nominalism, Empiricism and Universals: 1', *Philosophical Quarterly*, 9, 330–40.

Pargetter, Robert, and Prior, Elizabeth, 1982, 'The Dispositional and the Categorical', *Pacific Philosophical Quarterly*, 63, 366–70.

Place, U. T., 1988, 'Thirty Years On – Is Consciousness still a Brain-process?', *Australasian Journal of Philosophy*, 66, 208–19.

Plato, 1975, *Phaedo*, trans. David Gallop, Oxford: Clarendon Press.

Prior, Elizabeth, 1985, *Dispositions*, Aberdeen: Aberdeen University Press.

Prior, Elizabeth, Pargetter, Robert and Jackson, Frank, 1982, 'Three Theses about Dispositions', *American Philosophical Quarterly*, 19, 251–7.

Quine, Willard V. O., 1961 [1953], *From a Logical Point of View*, New York: Harper and Row.

Reichenbach, Hans, 1956, *The Direction of Time*, Berkeley: University of California Press.

Robinson, Denis, 1989, 'Matter, Motion and Humean Supervenience', *Australasian Journal of Philosophy*, 67, 394–409.

Rosen, Gideon, 1990, 'Modal Fictionalism', *Mind*, 99, 327–54.

1993, 'A Problem for Fictionalism about Possible Worlds', *Analysis*, 53, 71–81.

1995, 'Armstrong on Classes as States of Affairs', *Australasian Journal of Philosophy*, 73, 613–25.

Russell, Bertrand, 1910–11, 'Knowledge by Acquaintance and Knowledge by Description', *Proceedings of the Aristotelian Society*, Vol. 11, 108–28. Reprinted in *Mysticism and Logic*, London: Allen and Unwin, 1917.

1918, *The Philosophy of Logical Atomism*, reprinted in *Russell's Logical Atomism*, ed. David Pears, London: Fontana/Collins, 1972.

1926 [1914], *Our Knowledge of the External World*, London: Allen and Unwin.

1937 [1903], *The Principles of Mathematics*, London: George Allen and Unwin.

1948, *Human Knowledge: Its Scope and Limits*, London: George Allen and Unwin.

Russell, Bertrand and Whitehead, Alfred N., 1962 [1910], *Principia Mathematica*, Cambridge: Cambridge University Press.

Seargent, David A. J., 1985, *Plurality and Continuity*, Dordrecht: Martinus Nijhoff Publishers.

Shalkowski, Scott, 1994, 'The Ontological Ground of Alethic Modality', *Philosophical Review*, 103, 669–88.

Shoemaker, Sydney, 1979, 'Identity, Properties, and Causality', *Midwest Studies in Philosophy*, 4, 321–42, reprinted with in *Identity, Cause, and Mind*, by Sydney Shoemaker, Cambridge: Cambridge University Press, 234–60 (1984).

1980, 'Causality and Properties', in *Time and Cause*, ed. Peter van Inwagen, Dordrecht: D. Reidel, reprinted in *Identity, Cause, and Mind*, by Sydney Shoemaker, Cambridge: Cambridge University Press, 206–33 (1984).

1983, 'Properties, Causation, and Projectibility', in *Aspects of Inductive Logic*, ed. L. J. Cohen and Mary Hesse, Oxford: Oxford University Press, 291–312.

Simons, Peter, 1982, 'Against the Aggregate Theory of Number', *Journal of Philosophy*, 79, 163–7.

1987, *Parts: A Study in Ontology*, Oxford: Clarendon Press.

Skyrms, Brian, 1981, 'Tractarian Nominalism', *Philosophical Studies*, 40, 199–206; reprinted as an Appendix in *A Combinatorial Theory of Possibility*, by D. M. Armstrong, Cambridge: Cambridge University Press, 1989.

Smart, J. J. C., 1963, *Philosophy and Scientific Realism*, London: Routledge and Kegan Paul.

Sober, Elliot, 1982, 'Why Logically Equivalent Properties may pick out Different Properties', *American Philosophical Quarterly*, 19, 183–9.

Sorensen, Roy A., 1992, 'Thought Experiments and the Epistemology of Laws', *Canadian Journal of Philosophy*, 22, 15–44.

Stout, G. F., 1921, 'The Nature of Universals and Propositions', Oxford University Press (British Academy Lecture), reprinted in Stout, G. F., *Studies in Philosophy and Psychology*, London: Macmillan, 1930.

Strawson, P. F., 1950, 'Truth', *Proceedings of the Aristotelian Society*, Supp. vol. 24, 129–56.

1959, *Individuals*, London: Methuen & Co.

Swinburne, Richard, 1983, 'Reply to Shoemaker', in *Aspects of Inductive Logic*, ed. L. J. Cohen and Mary Hesse, Oxford: Oxford University Press, 313–20.

Swoyer, Chris, 1982, 'The Nature of Natural Laws', *Australasian Journal of Philosophy*, 60, 203–23.

Tooley, Michael, 1977, 'The Nature of Laws', *Canadian Journal of Philosophy*, 7, 667–98.

1987, *Causation: A Realist Approach*, Oxford: Clarendon Press.

1988, 'In Defense of the Existence of States of Motion', *Philosophical Topics*, 16, 225–54.

Tweedale, Martin M., 1984, 'Armstrong on Determinable and Substantival Universals', in *Profiles*: Vol.4, *D.M.Armstrong*, ed. Radu J. Bogdan, Dordrecht: D. Reidel, 171–89.

Van Fraassen, Bas C., 1987, 'Armstrong on Laws and Probabilities', *Australasian Journal of Philosophy*, 65, 243–60.

1989, *Laws and Symmetry*, Oxford: Clarendon Press.

1993, 'Armstrong, Cartwright, and Earman on *Laws and Symmetry*', *Philosophy and Phenomenological Research*, 53, 421–2.

Van Inwagen, Peter, 1990, 'Four-Dimensional Objects', *Noûs*, 24, 245–55.

Weinberg, Julius R., 1965, *Abstraction, Relation, and Induction*, Madison & Milwaukee: University of Wisconsin Press.

Weinberg, Steven, 1993, *Dreams of a Final Theory*, New York: Vintage Books.

Williams, Donald C., 1953, 'The Elements of Being', *Review of Metaphysics*, 7, 3–18 & 171–92, reprinted in *Principles of Empirical Realism*, Springfield Illinois: Charles C Thomas, 1966.

1963, 'Necessary Facts', *Review of Metaphysics*, 16, 601–26.

Wittgenstein, Ludwig, 1961 [1921], *Tractatus Logico-Philosophicus*, trans. D. F. Pears & B. F. McGuinness, London: Routledge and Kegan Paul.

1953, *Philosophical Investigations*, trans. G. E. M. Anscombe, Oxford: Basil Blackwell.

Index

Index